Ideale Stadt – Reale Projekte
Ideal City – Real Projects
Architekten von Gerkan, Marg
und Partner in China

Impressum / Imprint

Diese Publikation erscheint anlässlich der Ausstellung /
This catalogue is published in conjunction with the exhibition
Ideale Stadt – Reale Projekte
von Gerkan, Marg und Partner in China
Architekturmuseum der Technischen Universität München
in der Pinakothek der Moderne
30. Juni – 2. Oktober 2005

Ausstellung / Exhibition

Projektleitung / Projectmanagement: Mechthild Kaufmann, Bernd Pastuschka, Michael Kuhn

Ausstellungsgestaltung / Exhibition Design:
Bernd Pastuschka
Mitarbeit: Heidi Knaut, Michael Kuhn

Grafik / Graphic Design: Birgit Meyer, Heidi Knaut

Reproduktion / Reproduction: Beatrix Hansen

Wir danken allen, die zum Gelingen der Ausstellung beigetragen haben, insbesondere den Sponsoren.
We thank all those who have contributed to the success of this project, especially the sponsors.

Katalog / Catalogue

Herausgeber / Editor: Winfried Nerdinger

Redaktion / Editing: Bettina Ahrens, Bernd Pastuschka

Lektorat / Copyediting: Ingrid Nina Bell

Übersetzungen / Translations: Bianca Murphy, Martin Murphy, Annette Wiethüchter,

Grafische Gestaltung / Graphic Design: Birgit Meyer

Satz / Typesetting: Birgit Meyer

Schrift / Typeface: Trade Gothic Condensed

Reproduktion / Reproduction: Beatrix Hansen

Papier / Paper: LuxoSamtoffset, 150 g/m²

Buchbinderei / Binding: Conzella Verlagsbuchbinderei, Urban Meister GmbH, Aschheim-Dornach bei München

Gesamtherstellung / Printed by: Dr. Cantz'sche Druckerei, Ostfildern-Ruit

© 2005 Architekturmuseum der Technischen Universität München in der Pinakothek der Moderne, Hatje Cantz Verlag, Ostfildern-Ruit, und Autoren / and authors
Das Copyright für die Texte liegt bei den Autoren.
Das Copyright für die Abbildungen liegt bei den Fotografen bzw. bei den Bildrechteinhabern.

© 2005 für die abgebildeten Arbeiten / for the reproduced works: von Gerkan, Marg und Partner

Erschienen im / Published by
Hatje Cantz Verlag
Senefelderstraße 12
73760 Ostfildern-Ruit
Deutschland / Germany
Tel. +49 711 4405-0
Fax +49 711 4405-220
www.hatjecantz.com

Hatje Cantz books are available internationally at selected bookstores and from the following distribution partners:

USA/North America – D.A.P., Distributed Art Publishers, New York, www.artbook.com
UK – Art Books International, London, sales@art-bks.com
Australia – Towerbooks, French Forest (Sydney), towerbks@zipworld.com.au
France – Interart, Paris, commercial@interart.fr
Belgium – Exhibitions International, Leuven, www.exhibitionsinternational.be
Switzerland – Scheidegger, Affoltern am Albis, scheidegger@ava.ch

For Asia, Japan, South America, and Africa, as well as for general questions, please contact Hatje Cantz directly at sales@hatjecantz.de, or visit our homepage www.hatjecantz.com for further information.

Buchhandelsausgabe / Trade edition: Pappband/Hardcover, ISBN 3-7757-1667-X
Museumsausgabe / Museum edition: Broschur/Softcover
Printed in Germany

Umschlagabbildung / Cover illustration:
Skizze / Sketch Lingang New City, Meinhard von Gerkan

Frontispiz / Frontispiece:
Skizze / Sketch Lingang New City, Meinhard von Gerkan

Ideale Stadt – Reale Projekte

Ideal City – Real Projects

Architekten von Gerkan, Marg

und Partner in China

Hatje Cantz

Inhalt Content

6   Winfried Nerdinger, Vorwort
    Winfried Nerdinger, Foreword

9   Meinhard von Gerkan im Gespräch mit Xu Xiaofei von der Tsinghua Universität Peking
    Meinhard von Gerkan in Conversation with Xu Xiaofei of Tsinghua University Beijing

14 Zheng Shiling, Stadt und Architektur in China im Wandel zwischen gestern und heute
    Zheng Shiling, Chinese City and Architecture in Transformation between Yesterday and Tomorrow

22 Bernd Pastuschka, Die europäische Stadt – Die Idealstadt im Spiegel der Zeit
    Bernd Pastuschka, The European City – The Ideal City as Reflected through the Ages

39 Meinhard von Gerkan, Lingang New City – Eine Großstadt im Chinesischen Meer
    Meinhard von Gerkan, Lingang New City – A Metropolis in the East China Sea

114 Stadtbausteine
    Urban Modules

178 Anhang
    Appendix

    Chinakarte
    Map of China

    Verzeichnis der chinesischen Projekte, 1998–2005
    Index of Chinese Projects, 1998–2005

Vernunft als architektonische Tugend - zur Arbeit von gmp

China ist derzeit die größte Baustelle der Welt, und im Zeitalter der Globalisierung drängen sich dort die international berühmtesten Architekten, um Aufträge zu erhalten, die nur mit Superlativen wiedergegeben werden können: die größte Bibliothek, der höchste Wolkenkratzer oder die aufwändigsten Olympiabauten aller Zeiten sollen entstehen. Von Gerkan, Marg und Partner, die schon in Deutschland in den vergangenen 40 Jahren mehr Wettbewerbe als jedes andere Architekturbüro gewonnen haben, sind mit 17 ersten Preisen und derzeit über 100 Entwürfen auch in China erfolgreicher als alle Konkurrenten aus Europa. Bisheriger Höhepunkt ist sicher der Auftrag zum Bau der neuen Stadt Lingang, dem geplanten Business Center für Shanghai für ursprünglich 300.000, inzwischen bereits 800.000 Einwohner. Man mag über Wettbewerbserfolge im Einzelnen diskutieren, die schier unglaubliche Zahl von 170 ersten Preisen, die gmp bis heute vorweisen können, ist als Gesamtleistung zweifelsfrei ein Ausweis architektonischer Qualität, insbesondere wenn man erkennt, daß diese Erfolge auf einer Konstanz der architektonischen Haltung basieren und gerade nicht aus dem Kreieren von Moden oder dem Nachlaufen von Trends resultieren.

Meinhard von Gerkan hat das Glaubensbekenntnis, beziehungsweise die Philosophie von gmp als dialogisches Entwerfen oder als Bauen im Dialog bezeichnet: jeder Entwurf entsteht aus einem Dialog des Architekten mit dem Ort, der Nutzung, dem Bauherrn sowie mit den konstruktiven, ökonomischen, rechtlichen und technischen Bedingungen. Die Metapher des Dialogs ist weitreichend tragfähig, sie führt buchstäblich ins Zentrum der Architektur von gmp. Im Dialog muss das Gegenüber als Partner gleichwertig behandelt werden, es geht um einen gemeinsamen Weg, den man durch Sprechen klären will, dazu muss man den anderen ernst nehmen, muss zuhören, Argumente aufnehmen, abwägen und weiterführen. Martin Buber hat deshalb das dialogische Gespräch sogar als das Element bezeichnet, das den Menschen erst zum Menschen macht. Dialog funktioniert nur rational und im Wechsel, wer sich irrational ausdrückt, den anderen übertönt, dogmatische Positionen vertritt oder monologisiert, zerschneidet das Verbindende zwischen Menschen. All das lässt sich direkt auch auf Architektur übertragen. Insbesondere wer sich nicht auf die Charakteristika und Determinanten der jeweiligen Bauaufgabe einlässt, der monologisiert, und reproduziert nur sich selbst. Meinhard von Gerkan bezeichnet die Produkte vieler Kollegen, die ihre monologische Architektur als Markenzeichen verkaufen, mit erfrischender Deutlichkeit als „Designer-Unikate", „angeberische Varietéshow", „Inszenierung von gesellschaftlichen Verwerfungen als designtes

Common Sense as an Architectural Virtue: On the Work of gmp

At present, China is the largest building site worldwide. In the age of globalization, the most famous international architects jostle to win contracts there that can only be described in superlatives. The largest library ever, the tallest skyscraper or the most elaborate and expensive Olympic structures of all times – all these are to be built in China. Von Gerkan, Marg and Partners, who in the past forty years have won more competitions than any other architectural office, are currently also more successful in China than all their European competitors, having won seventeen competitions and having made over one hundred designs there. Certainly the most important so far is the commission to build the new city of Lingang, i.e. the new business district of Shanghai initially planned for a population of 300,000, now augmented to 800,000. Though individual competition wins may be open to debate, the sheer incredible total number of one hundred and seventy first prizes in gmp's portfolio no doubt represents proof of architectural quality, especially when one realizes that these successes are the result of a consistent architectural stance, and not of following fashions and trying to keep up with changing trends.

Meinhard von Gerkan defines gmp's credo or philosophy as dialogical design or building in dialogue. This means every design emerges from the dialogue of the architect with the respective place, use (function) and client as well as structural, economic, legal and technical conditions. The dialogue metaphor carries far, literally into the core of gmp's architecture. In a dialogue, each partner must treat the other as an equal; the aim being to find a common way forward by talking to each other. For this each has to take the other seriously, listen and take in, weigh up and expand each other's arguments. Martin Buber even identified dialogue as the one thing that makes man human. Dialogue only functions if it is conducted rationally and is a real exchange. Expressing irrational views, shouting the other down, taking a dogmatic stand, or monopolizing the conversation will sever the common human bond between the partners. All this is directly applicable to architecture, too. In particular a person who does not enter into the features and determinants of the respective commission and only soliloquizes, will only reproduce himself. With refreshing directness Meinhard von Gerkan uses the terms "designer one-offs" and "bragging variety shows" for the products of many of his colleagues,

„Umweltchaos" oder „konstruktiven Manierismus". Die Architektur von gmp ist das genaue Gegenteil, sie ist dialogisch rational, von der Vernunft geprägt und entsteht aus dem Abwägen zwischen Erfindung, Rahmenbedingungen und Zielsetzung. Da diese Elemente mit jeder Aufgabe wechseln, ändert sich auch der architektonische Ausdruck, der durch seinen dialogischen Charakter jedoch wieder spezifisch und unverwechselbar wird.

Wie können nun Architekten über Kontinente hinweg in einen Dialog mit einer anderen Kultur treten? Was wir heute als Globalisierung der Architektur bezeichnen, ist keineswegs so ungewöhnlich oder neuartig, sondern hat viele historische Vorläufer. Ein länderübergreifender Architekturtransfer findet sich von der Verbreitung der Gotik im Mittelalter durch französische Baumeister und wandernde Bauhütten bis zu den Barockbauten, die italienische Baumeister von Madrid über München bis St. Petersburg errichteten. Hier wurde jedoch durchweg eine neue Architektursprache den jeweiligen Auftraggebern angepasst, ein Dialog mit den regionalen Bautraditionen fand ebenso selten statt, wie bei den kolonialen Verpflanzungen europäischer Architektur im 18. und 19. Jahrhundert oder bei der Übernahme der Moderne im 20. Jahrhundert durch traditionelle Gesellschaften.

Die verordnete Übernahme moderner Technik, Architektur und Kultur, beispielsweise in der Türkei nach dem Ersten Weltkrieg, ist ein warnendes Beispiel dafür, wie der radikale Bruch zwischen traditioneller Lebensweise und moderner Zivilisation gesellschaftliche Probleme verstärken kann. Joachim Ritter hat in diesem Zusammenhang bereits 1955 von der notwendigen „Versöhnung der Herkunft mit der durch die moderne Zivilisation bestimmten Zukunft" gesprochen. Ohne eine derartige Versöhnung geraten die betroffenen Menschen zwischen zwei Ordnungen, die ohne Beziehung miteinander sind, und dann können irrationale oder fundamentalistische Gegenbewegungen zur Moderne Fuß fassen. Diese politische Aufgabe kann allerdings nicht mit Architektur gelöst werden, der Architekt kann bestenfalls mitwirken, „den Wolf zu zähmen", wie Meinhard von Gerkan einmal diese Aufgabe bezeichnete.

Beim derzeitigen Bauboom in China findet ein derartiger Maßstabs- und Zeitsprung statt, daß zumeist überhaupt keine Verbindung zur traditionellen Architektur mehr gefunden werden kann. Die Dekoration moderner Bauten mit chinesischen Motiven führt nur zu lächerlichen Karikaturen. Gmp versucht den Dialog auf einer strukturellen Ebene. Gemäß dem Leitspruch des Büros, „tradierte Einfachheit" zu gestalten, werden traditionelle bewährte Elemente, wie die Struktur des chinesischen Hofhauses, aufgenommen und beispielsweise in die Anordnung der Wohnquartiere von Lingang transformiert. Diese neu geschaffene Stadt selbst basiert auf geometrischen Prinzipien, die seit der Antike Idealstädten in vielen

who sell their "monologue architecture" as branded designs, or describes these as the "staging of social faults as designed environmental chaos" or "constructive mannerism". The architecture of gmp is the exact opposite. It is dialogically rational, informed by common sense and the result of weighing up invention, framework conditions and purpose. As these parameters change with every project, so does architectural expression which, however, will again be specific and inimitable due to its dialogical nature.

How then can architects enter into dialogue across continents with another culture? What is termed the globalization of architecture today is by no means unusual or new, but has many historic precedents. Transnational transfers of architecture took place as early as in medieval times when French master builders and itinerant stonemasons' lodges spread the Gothic style, and later when Italian architects erected baroque buildings from Madrid via Munich to St Petersburg. In these cases, a novel architectural language was adapted to every commission, with dialogue with regional building traditions being a rare occurrence, just like it was in the transfer of European architecture to the colonial territories of the 18th and 19th centuries, or in the adoption of 20th-century Modernism by traditionalist societies.

The imposed adoption of modern technology, architecture and culture – for example in Turkey after World War II – is a warning example of how an all-too radical change from traditional to modern ways of life can aggravate a society's problems. In this context, Joachim Ritter, as early as 1955 talked of the necessary "reconciliation of the origin with the future determined by modern civilization". Without such reconciliation, the people concerned will be caught between two different, unconnected, social orders so that irrational or fundamentalist counter-movements of Modernism can take hold. Yet this political problem cannot be solved with architecture. At best, architects may help "to tame the wolf", as Meinhard von Gerkan once described the task of reconciling history and future.

In the current construction boom in China, there is such a leap of time and scale that in most cases it is impossible to find any link with traditional architecture. The decoration of modern buildings with Chinese motifs only produces ridiculous caricatures. Gmp tries dialogue at a structural level instead. According to the motto of the office to create "handed-down simplicity", gmp architects use traditional structural elements such as that of the old Chinese patio house and adapt them to the arrangement of the residential quarters of Lingang, for

Kulturen zugrunde lagen, allerdings mit einem entscheidenden Unterschied: die Stadtmitte wird nicht mit einem Machtzeichen besetzt, sondern von der Natur geformt. Eine ingeniöse Lösung, die ökologische, ökonomische und humane Elemente verknüpft und hoffentlich neue Perspektiven des Bauens in China eröffnet.

Winfried Nerdinger
Architekturmuseum der TU München

example. This new city was laid out following the same geometric principles that since antiquity have formed the basis of ideal cities in many cultures – albeit with a decisive difference. The city centre is not occupied by a sign of power, but by nature. An ingenious solution which combines ecological, economic and humane elements and will hopefully open up new prospects for building in China.

Winfried Nerdinger
Architectural Museum of Munich Technical University

Meinhard von Gerkan im Gespräch mit Xu Xiaofei von der Tsinghua Universität Peking

Vor dem Hintergrund der wachsenden Bedeutung der Philosophie und Architektur von gmp in China hat der Verlag der Universität in Tsinghua, vertreten durch Xu Xiaofei, die Position Meinhard von Gerkans hinterfragt.

Wie ist Ihre Meinung zur heutigen Architektur chinesischer Architekten?
Zwischen den vielen neuen Bauten, die in den letzten Jahren in China entstanden sind, vermag ich kaum Unterschiede zwischen denen chinesischer Architekten und solchen von ausländischen Architekten festzustellen. Ihnen allen ist offenkundig eines gemeinsam: amerikanische Vorbilder nachzuahmen, Materialien zu verwenden, die High-Tech und Fortschritt signalisieren und dieses gleichwohl mit vermeintlich traditionellen chinesischen Elementen zu dekorieren.
Ich denke, dass diese Architektur ebenfalls aus der Wechselwirkung zwischen dem Bewusstsein der Bevölkerung, die sich einerseits traditionelle Elemente wünscht, auf der anderen Seite den Fortschritt der Vereinigten Staaten trotz aller kritischen Distanz hoch schätzt, in ihren Städten manifestiert sehen möchte und den Architekten, die sich im Interesse, diese Wünsche zu erfüllen, derjenigen Mittel bedienen, die eine Melange aus Fortschritt, Traditionalismus und Gefälligkeit zu Tage fördern.

Was ist das größte Problem der städtebaulichen Entwicklung in chinesischen Städten? Insbesondere in Städten wie Peking und Shanghai, in denen Sie Projekte haben?
Für mich ist in der städtebaulichen Entwicklung fast aller chinesischen Städte keine hierarchisch strukturelle Strategie erkennbar.
Nach meiner Meinung werden Entscheidungen zu sehr fraktioniert, also auf einzelne Projekte hin getroffen unter Vernachlässigung des übergeordneten städtebaulichen Zusammenhangs. Auf diese Weise geht auch viel von der spezifischen Identität einzelner chinesischer Städte verloren.

Gibt es einen Unterschied im Entwurfsprozess oder der Organisation zwischen gmp und anderen Architekturbüros,

Meinhard von Gerkan in Conversation with Xu Xiaofei of Tsinghua University Beijing

Against the background of the growing significance of gmp's philosophy and architecture in China, the publishers of Tsinghua University, represented by Xu Xiaofei, have questioned Meinhard von Gerkan's position.

What is your opinion of modern-day Chinese architecture?
I can hardly determine the differences between the many new buildings being designed by Chinese architects and those by foreign architects that have been realized over the last few years in China. Obviously they have one common denominator: to copy American models, use materials that convey high-tech and progress and nevertheless decorate them with seemingly traditional Chinese elements.
I believe that this architecture is influenced by the interaction of the people's consciousness that still wants to maintain traditional elements, but at the same time would like to emulate the progress of the United States of America in their cities, which is despite all critical detachment highly valued, and the architects, who use those means in their intention to fulfil this wish generating a mix of progress, traditionalism and pleasant accessories.

What is the major problem of town planning developments in Chinese cities, especially in cities such as Beijing and Shanghai, where you are also involved in some projects?
I cannot identify a hierarchical structural strategy in the town planning development of any Chinese city. According to my opinion decisions are extensively fragmented, that means they are made with regard to single projects whilst neglecting the super-ordinate town planning context.
In doing so, much of the specific identity of individual Chinese cities is being lost.

Are there differences in the design process or the organization of gmp and other architectural practices, especially Chinese practices? If so, which are the most significant differences?
As I do not know the design process in Chinese practices, I cannot make a direct comparison with our work-

insbesondere chinesischen Büros? Wenn ja, wo liegt der signifikante Unterschied?
Da ich den Entwurfsprozess in chinesischen Büros nicht kenne, kann ich einen direkten Vergleich mit unserer Arbeitsweise nicht anstellen. Signifikant für unsere Arbeitsweise ist jedoch die sehr hierarchische, konzeptionelle Vorgehensweise: Zunächst nur aus der Hand oder dem Kopf des Entwerfers selbst trotz der mehr als 300 Mitarbeiter; Fragen zu stellen und eine Konzeption zu erdenken und erst basierend hierauf die Planung im Detail voranzubringen. Bei vielen großen Büros, speziell in den USA, habe ich beobachtet, dass die Arbeitsweise sehr arbeitsteilig ist, dass einzelne Entwurfselemente gewissermaßen zusammengefügt werden und nicht die Konzeption oben ansteht, sondern die bereits fertigen Detailüberlegungen, die aus der Schublade geholt und zu einem Gesamtwerk zusammengenäht werden.

Was ist die größte Schwierigkeit für Ihr Büro in China?
Das „Gambé"-Zeremoniell bei jedem Abendessen, das unsere Trinkfestigkeit als Europäer testen will.

Unterschiedliche kulturelle Traditionen und Hintergründe können unterschiedlichen Lebensstile und Anforderungen an städtische Strukturen und Lebensräume zur Folge haben. Gibt es zwischen Europa und China Unterschiede in der Stadtplanung, dem Städtebau und der Architektur? Welches sind diese Unterschiede?
Traditionelle Unterschiede zwischen den Lebensstilen und Anforderungen an städtische Strukturen und Lebensräume in Europa und China sind sehr groß. Mittlerweile nähert sich jedoch geradezu in einem dynamischen Galopp die Entwicklung Chinas an die strukturellen Merkmale amerikanischer Städte mit der dominanten Bedeutung des Autoverkehrs. In den meisten europäischen Städten ist der traditionelle Charakter und das Typische der Stadt bis heute erhalten geblieben.
Städte wie Paris, London, Berlin oder Mailand kann man bereits mit der Nase identifizieren. Mit geschlossenen Augen genügt der Duft, das Atmosphärische der jeweiligen Stadt, um sie als solche zu erkennen. Dies gilt für viele Quartiere, für Stadträume, nicht nur für Landmarken und für dominante touristische Gebäude.
Auf diese Weise ist die Identität im Städtebau in Europa weitgehend erhalten geblieben. In China hingegen wird durch die Modernisierung nahezu alles, was traditionell bestimmend war, von wenigen wichtigen Bauten und

ing method. The significant characteristic of our method is the strictly hierarchical, conceptional procedure: Development of the initial concept by hand or thoughts of the designer himself despite our more than 300 employees; asking of questions and development of a concept and subsequently the generation of a detailed planning on that basis. In many large practices, especially in the USA, I have observed that the working method is characterized by a strong division of tasks, with single design elements being brought together and priority being given to existing detailed considerations "off the shelf" that are assembled to form an overall solution, instead of the prevalence of an overall concept.

Please define the main difficulty your practice is confronted with in China?
The "Gambé" ceremony during every dinner that tries to test our ability as Europeans to hold our drink.

Different cultural traditions and backgrounds can result in varying lifestyles and demands in urban structures and living spaces. Are there any differences between Europe and China regarding town planning and architecture? Could you describe these differences?
Traditional differences between the lifestyles and requirements in urban structures and living environments in Europe and China are considerable. In the meantime China's development approaches in a dynamic gallop the structural characteristics of American cities with the dominant relevance of motor traffic. In most European cities the traditional character and typical features have been maintained up to the present day. Cities such as Paris, London, Berlin or Milan can be identified by nose. When closing the eyes, the odour, the atmosphere of the respective city alone is sufficient to identify the city. This applies to many districts and urban scopes, not only to landmarks and prominent tourist buildings.
This helped to maintain the identity of town planning in Europe to a great extent. Whereas in China the modernization leads to the destruction and replacement of almost everything with a traditional character, with the exception of a few significant buildings and memorials, while roads take on enormously wide dimensions. This results in a comprehensive change of scale, generating identical characteristics in almost all cities. Indeed Beijing's ring structure with the low centre of the Forbidden City can still be perceived as a structural char-

Denkmälern abgesehen, zerstört und durch Neubauten ersetzt, wobei die Straßen gewaltig breite Dimensionen annehmen. Auf diese Weise entsteht eine völlige Maßstabsveränderung, die nahezu allen Städten gleiche Merkmale beschert. Zwar kann man noch heute die Ringstruktur von Peking mit dem niedrigen Zentrum der verbotenen Stadt als strukturelles Merkmal erkennen, noch tritt die Dominanz der vielen Hochstraßen in Guangzhou hervor oder die Dualität vom Bund und Pudong entlang des Flusses.
Sowie man jedoch die prägnanten zentralen Orte der Städte verlässt, vermischt sich das Bild zu einem diffusen Einerlei, ohne Identität und Charakteristik.
Lediglich die Klimaunterschiede machen sich zwischen Nord und Süd noch in der Erscheinung der Architektur bemerkbar.

Unter chinesischen Architekten gibt es häufig Diskussionen, wie mit der architektonischen Tradition bei zeitgenössischer Architektur umgegangen werden sollte. Ist dies in Europa auch so? Welche Rolle spielt für Sie traditionelle Architektur, wenn Sie Gebäude mit völlig neuen Funktionen entwerfen? Haben Sie solche Probleme auch in China?
Die Diskussion im Hinblick auf traditionelle Architektur und historische Bauweise ist in Europa mindestens so ausgeprägt, jedoch mit einem wesentlichen Unterschied: Die historischen Bauten, die in Europa teilweise als Repliken wieder hergestellt werden – zum Beispiel das Berliner Schloss mit Barocker Fassade und neuer Bauform im Inneren – haben nahezu allesamt in

Oben: Das Chinesische Nationalmuseum auf dem Platz des Himmlischen Friedens in Peking.
Top: The National Museum of China on the Tian Men Sqare in Beijing.
Unten: Die Deutsche Schule in Peking.
Bottom: The German School in Beijing.

acteristic, the dominance of the numerous elevated roads in Guangzhou is still prominent as well as Shanghai's duality of the boulevard "Bund" and Pudong along the river.
But as soon as the succinct central locations of the cities are left behind, the appearance blends into a diffuse monotony lacking any identity and characteristic.
Solely the climatic differences between the north and south are perceptible in the architectural appearance.

Discussions frequently arise amongst Chinese architects on how traditional architecture should be considered in modern architecture. Is this also the case in Europe? What role do you ascribe to traditional architecture for the design of buildings with completely new functions? Do you encounter similar problems in China?
The discussion with regard to traditional architecture and historic building methods in Europe is at least equally pronounced, but with one essential difference: Those historic buildings in Europe that are restored as replicas – for example the Berlin Castle with its Baroque façade and new constructional form in the interior – often have a form, regarding their scale, number of floors and structural organization that allows for the integration of modern uses.
In China, on the contrary, buildings with a floor area of 50,000, 100,000, 150,000 or even 250,000 m² are constructed as one overall building. This immense jump in scale has nothing in common with China's traditional small-scale architecture, so that traditional attributes that are decoratively attached to the façade or motifs painted in polished glass façades rather become a caricature. There are however traditional town planning

Größe, Anzahl der Geschosse und struktureller Ordnung eine Form, die es erlaubt, dass heutige Nutzungsanforderungen darin untergebracht werden können.

In China hingegen werden Bauten mit 50.000, 100.000, 150.000 oder gar 250.000 m² als ein Gesamtgebäude erstellt. Dieser immense Maßstabssprung hat mit der traditionellen kleinmaßstäblichen Architektur Chinas überhaupt nichts gemeinsames, weshalb traditionelle Attribute, die an der Fassade dekorativ angebracht werden oder Motive, die in Spiegelglasfassaden nachgezeichnet werden, eher zu einer Karikatur geraten. Es gibt aber sehr wohl traditionelle Elemente des Städtebaus, die in ihrer Transformation Eingang in unsere Entwürfe finden. So zum Beispiel das Hofhaus, das bei unseren städtebaulichen Entwürfen zwar mehrgeschossig in Erschei-nung tritt, aber dem gleichen Prinzip von Intimität, Geborgenheit und Abgeschiedenheit des Wohnlebens von der lauten Umwelt zum Ziel hat.

Hier steht uns eine andere Tradition des chinesischen Wohnungsbaus entgegen, nämlich, dass offenkundig aufgrund einer heiligen Regel alle Wohnbauten nach Norden und Süden orientiert sein müssen und dann nur Zeilenbauten entstehen. Das verhindert jede urbane Struktur, die von Straßen- und Platzräumen lebt.

Was sind die wichtigen Aufgaben für die städtische und architektonische Entwicklung in China zum Beginn des 21. Jahrhunderts?

China sollte sich aufgrund seiner Historie und seines dynamischen Wachstums mit dem Sprung in die Neuzeit zu einer eigenständigen Kultur bekennen, die nicht kopiert, keine Klischees benutzt, nicht den Quantensprung in den Dimensionen leugnet oder verbrämt.

Die städtebaulichen Strukturentscheidungen sollten streng nach ausschließlich konzeptionellen Kriterien erfolgen und ökonomische Einzelinteressen sich in eine klare Hierarchie einordnen.

Die heute überwiegend bevorzugte Architektur, die mit

elements that find their way into our designs in their transformation. One example is the courtyard house, that however appears as a multi-storeyed building in our town planning designs, but simultaneously aims for the same principles of intimacy, security and seclusion of residential living from the noisy environment.

Here we are confronted with another tradition of the Chinese housing construction, namely that apparently according to a sacred rule all residential buildings must be orientated towards the north and the south resulting in terraced housing alone, preventing any urban structure, which benefits from street and square scapes.

Which are the most important tasks for the urban and architectural development in China at the beginning of the 21st century?

Based on its history and dynamic growth, China should utilize the leap into modern times to prove itself as an independent culture, one that does not copy, use stereotypes, deny or conceal this quantum jump of dimensions.

Structural town planning decisions should be made strictly according to exclusively conceptional criteria, and individual economic interests should be integrated into a clear hierarchy.

The presently preferred architecture, the one operating with pseudo-historic garnishing and decorative, ostensible Chinese accessories, is only suited for a generation of facelessness. A courageous modern architecture alone is able to leave its prominent mark.

A 60-storeyed high-rise building cannot be disguised as a doll's house. However, a new expression can be developed, that gains a characteristic quality from the building's utilization, its scale and structure.

pseudohistorisierenden Verbrämungen und dekorativen, vordergründig chinesischen Zutaten operiert, ist nur geeignet, Gesichtslosigkeit zu erzeugen. Nur eine mutige zeitgemäße Architektur kann markante Spuren hinterlassen.

Man kann ein 60-geschossiges Hochhaus nicht zur Puppenstube verkleiden. Man kann dafür aber einen neuen Ausdruck finden, der aus der Nutzung des Gebäudes, seiner Größe, seiner Konstruktion charaktervolle Qualität gewinnt.

Chinesische Architekten und Regierungsmitglieder möchten eine „Architektur mit chinesischen Charakteristika" schaffen. Denken Sie, dass es vor dem Hintergrund der Globalisierung notwendig oder möglich ist, ein solches Ziel zu erreichen? Wie sieht für Sie „Architektur mit chinesischen Charakteristika" aus?

In einem deutschen Märchen, *Rotkäppchen und der Wolf*, verkleidet sich der Wolf als harmlose Großmutter, um das kleine Mädchen einzufangen und zu fressen.

Für viele Menschen, nicht nur in China, ist die heutige Architektur wie der Wolf. Der Versuch, sie als Großmutter freundlich und niedlich zu machen, ist gescheitert und misslingt immer aufs Neue.

Den Wolf zu zähmen und aus seinen Eigenschaften einen positiven Charakterausdruck zu gewinnen, ist die Aufgabe.

Linke Seite: Guangzhou Development Central Building, China.
Left page: Guangzhou Development Central Building, China.
Rechte Seite: Stadttor.
Right page: Citygate.

Chinese architects and members of government would like to create an "architecture bearing Chinese characteristics". Do you consider it necessary or possible to achieve such an aim in view of globalization? How would you describe "architecture with Chinese characteristics"?

In the German fairytale *Little Red Riding Hood and the Wolf*, the wolf dresses up as the harmless grandmother, in order to catch and eat the little girl.

Many people, not only in China, perceive modern architecture as the wolf. The attempt to make it appear like the friendly and adorable granny has failed and fails repeatedly.

The given task is to tame the wolf and change his character into a positive one.

Stadt und Architektur in China im Wandel zwischen gestern und heute
Zheng Shiling

Die Identität der chinesischen Stadt und Architektur

Die traditionelle chinesische Kultur hat herausragende städtische Strukturen und großartige Architekturen von Weltrang geschaffen. Drei wesentliche Faktoren haben die Entwicklung der chinesischen Stadt und Architektur beeinflusst: die Globalisierung, die postmoderne Bewegung und der ökonomische Aufschwung.

Die beherrschende „Globalisierung" ist Teil des Diskurses, der auf dem westlichen Wertesystem basiert. Dies drückt sich in der Internationalisierung der Baukultur und der Angleichung urbaner Räume aus. Egal ob Peking, Shanghai, Chongquing, Hongkong oder Taipeh, der größte Teil dieser Städte hat bereits seine Identität verloren. Als ein Teil der Verwestlichung erreichte die Globalisierung China im Laufe der Modernisierung seit den späten 70er und frühen 80er Jahren des 20. Jahrhunderts. Die so genannten vier Aspekte der Modernisierung sind: die Modernisierung der Industrie, der Landwirtschaft, der Wissenschaft und Technologie und der Landesverteidigung. Dies setzte das Verlangen voraus, die materielle westliche Welt zu kopieren.

Aufgrund der Politik der Öffnung des Staates seit Beginn der 80er Jahre wurde die westliche Kultur erneut in China eingeführt, allerdings in ständig wachsendem Maßstab und mit rasender Geschwindigkeit. Die Politik der Öffnung hat für ganz China einen weiten Sprung nach vorn gebracht, Stadt und Architektur stehen vor einer radikalen Umwandlung. Auf der einen Seite wollen die Chinesen die internationale Geschwindigkeit aufholen, um Wohlstand nach China zu bringen, auf der anderen Seite sind die Vorbereitungen weder im ideologischen noch im institutionellen System abgeschlossen. Von postmoderner Kultur beeinflusste Kommerzialisierung verbunden mit marktorientierter Wirtschaft hat zu einer Art Missverständnis von Modernisierung und Urbanisierung geführt, was sich nun in einer unvernünftigen Stadtentwicklung widerspiegelt.

Unter dem Einfluss der globalen Kultur haben viele chinesische Städte ihre Identität verloren, und alle sehen gleich aus. Es gibt sogar Bestrebungen, Peking als Welt-Architekturmesse zu gestalten. Dies zeigt, dass das heutige chinesische Stadtplanungssystem noch nicht auf eine sinnvolle und langfristige Entwicklung vorbereitet ist. Einer der Gründe hierfür ist, dass Wolkenkratzer als ein Symbol der modernen, internationalen Metropole angesehen und zu

Chinese City and Architecture in Transformation between Yesterday and Tomorrow
Zheng Shiling

The Identity of the Chinese City and Architecture

Traditional Chinese culture has created outstanding urban structures and magnificent architecture of international significance. In this period, there are three main factors which have influenced the development of the Chinese city and the Chinese architecture: the globalisation, the post-modern movement, and the economical boom.

The dominant "globalisation" is a domain of the discourse based on the Western sense of value, which is expressed in the internationalisation of the architectural culture and the assimilation of urban space. No matter if it is Beijing, Shanghai, Chongqing, or Hong Kong, Taipei, most of these cities have already lost their identity. As a part of Westernisation, globalisation came into China in the course of modernisation since the late 1970s and the early 1980s. The so-called Four Aspects of Modernisation are the modernisation of the industry, agriculture, science and technology, the national defence. It implied a demand to copy the Western material world.

Due to of the opening policy of the state since the early 1980s, Western culture has been introduced into China again, but on an ever-growing scale and with rapid speed. The opening policy has brought a rapid leap forward everywhere in China, and the Chinese city and architecture are facing a radical transformation. On the one hand, the Chinese would like to catch up with the international pace to bring China prosperity. On the other hand, the preparations in both the ideological system and the institutional system are not finished. Commercialisation influenced by post-modern culture has together with the market oriented economy led to a somehow misunderstanding of modernisation and urbanisation, which has brought irrationality into the urban development.

Under the impact of global culture, many Chinese cities have lost their identity, all cities look alike. There is even an intention to construct Beijing as a fair of world architecture, that reveals that today's Chinese urban planning system is not yet prepared for rational and long-term development. The reason is that skyscrapers

viele chinesische Städte als solche gestaltet wurden. In diesem Fall dienten Manhattan in New York City, Ginza in Tokio und die Central Area in Hongkong als Paradigmen für die moderne Stadt. Heute gibt es über 4.500 Hochhäuser in Shanghai, dessen Skyline dadurch in Unordnung geraten ist. Über diesen großen Dimensionen wird der Denkmalschutz vernachlässigt. Hier zeigt sich, dass nach einem schnellen Wechsel gestrebt wird, ohne festgelegte Ziele zu haben.

Die Globalisierung hat das Bewusstsein für die Themen der chinesischen Architektur und Kultur geschwächt und die Angleichung stadträumlicher Formen verursacht. Einerseits wandert China in den Mittelpunkt der Weltwirtschaft, andererseits stehen chinesische Architektur und chinesische Architekten am Rande der weltweiten Stadtplanung und Architektur. Eine zeitgenössische Architekturtheorie zu formen, Architektur, die einer kritischen Auseinandersetzung standhält, zu schaffen und die chinesische Architektur in der zeitgenössischen Weltarchitektur zu positionieren wird eine ebenso schwierige wie dringende Aufgabe sein.

Der größte Einfluss der Globalisierung auf chinesische Stadtflächen zeigt sich in der rasanten Urbanisierung, der Beteiligung internationaler Architekten und Stadtplaner an chinesischer Architektur und Stadtplanung und in den großen Auswirkungen des internationalen Stils auf die Baukultur. Im Verlauf der Urbanisierung haben viele kleine und mittlere Städte allmählich ihre Identität verloren. Die städtischen Räume und Architekturen haben in jeder Stadt an Ähnlichkeit gewonnen und dadurch an Charakter verloren.

Die historischen Sehenswürdigkeiten chinesischer Städte sind schnell verschwunden und im Ozean der Hochhäuser versunken. Veränderung und Neubau wurden zur pragmatischen Zielsetzung. Unter dem Druck, die Profite in die Höhe zu treiben, konnten die chinesischen Städte die neuen Entwicklungen kaum kontrollieren. In den letzten 20 Jahren wur-

Oben: Die Transformation der Pekinger Altstadt.
Top: Old Beijing City in transformation.
Unten: Die Skyline von Shanghai.
Bottom: The skyline of Shanghai.

have been considered a symbol of the modern international metropolis, and too many Chinese cities have been constructed as international metropolis. In this case, Manhattan of New York City, Ginza of Tokyo, Central Area of Hong Kong have been taken as paradigms of the modern city. Today there are over 4,500 high-rise buildings in Shanghai and the skyline is out of order. The large-scale construction neglects the preservation of historical buildings and historical urban space. This reflects the circumstance that it is sought for a rapid change, but without ultimate ideals.

The discourse of globalisation has weakened the subject consciousness of Chinese architecture and culture and has caused the assimilation of urban space shapes. On the one hand China is marching into the centre of world economy, but on the other hand, Chinese architecture and Chinese architects play a marginal role in world urban planning and architecture. To develop a contemporary architectural theory, to design architecture with a critical meaning and to establish a position for Chinese architecture in the history of contemporary world architecture are very difficult but urgent missions.

The main influence of globalisation on Chinese urban space and architecture is the rapid urbanisation, the participation of international architects and urban planners in Chinese urban planning and architectural design, and the great impact of international style upon architectural culture. During the course of urbanisation, many small and medium cities have gradually lost their identity. The urban space and urban architecture in every city has become increasingly similar and lost its character.

The historical landmarks of Chinese cities have quickly disappeared and sunken into the ocean of high-rise buildings. To change and construct something new has become the pragmatic objective. Under the pressure of profit driving, Chinese cities could hardly control the new developments. In the last 20 years, with the market-oriented economy and the commercialisation of the cities, a lot of historical buildings with qualified crafts-

den durch die Marktwirtschaft und die Kommerzialisierung der Städte viele historische Gebäude mit qualifizierter Handwerkskunst durch plump konstruierte Baumassen ersetzt. Seit Mitte der 80er Jahre hat sich ein so genannter Pseudo-Neoklassizismus in chinesischen Städten verbreitet. Die chinesische Architektur ist bedroht durch die Kopie des oberflächlichen Disneyland- und Cartoon-Stils.

Um die Identität sowohl von Kultur als auch von städtischen Räumen zu erhalten, ist es wichtig, die internationalen Erfahrungen zu studieren und so einen angemessenen Weg der Erhaltung zu finden. In diesem Fall ist eine rationale Urbanisierung notwendig, um einen klaren Kopf für eine vernünftige und schnelle Entwicklung zu behalten. Nach einer langen Zeit der Isolation von der übrigen Welt müssen chinesische Stadtplaner und Architekten mit ihren internationalen Kollegen zusammenarbeiten, um ein städtisches Umfeld mit menschlichem Maßstab und Identität aufzubauen.

Mit der rasanten Entwicklung der chinesischen Wirtschaft und Sozialordnung nach der Anerkennung durch die Welthandelsorganisation sind die meisten chinesischen Städte einer völligen Neuorganisation in der Industrie-, Wirtschafts- und Stadtstruktur unterworfen. Die Einflüsse der Globalisierung bewirken, dass die bestehenden chinesischen Systeme der Stadtplanung und Planungsverwaltung, der Architektur und der Bauverwaltung etc. internationalen Vorbildern folgen werden. Der Zustand der „Stadtplanung ohne Planung" wird sich ändern.

Internationale Architekten in China

Unter dem Einfluss der wirtschaftlichen, wissenschaftlichen und technologischen Globalisierung wird die Urbanisierung in China generell beschleunigt werden. Es haben sich einige exportorientierte Wirtschaftszentren, wie z.B. Shanghai, Hongkong und andere, gebildet. Am Bohai Golfring, im Jangtse-Delta und im Pearl River Delta werden große Stadtgebiete mit einer hohen Dichte entstehen. Die rasche Entwicklung der Urbanisierung hat einige Probleme für Städtebau und Stadtplanung mit sich gebracht, die sich nur mit Hilfe von systematischen Reformen und sinnvollen Verwaltungsmechanismen lösen lassen. Die Globalisierung erzeugt im großen Maßstab Auswirkungen auf das Bevölkerungswachstum und den Verbrauch von Land. Während der letzten zehn Jahre wurden sehr viele internationale Wettbewerbe und Studien in den Bereichen Stadtplanung und Architektur ausgelobt. Mit den Olympischen Spielen 2008 in Peking und der Expo 2010 in Shanghai wird es noch mehr Planungs- und Bau-

manship have been replaced by crudely constructed masses. Since the middle of the 1980s, a so-called pseudo-neo-classicism popularly diffused in Chinese cities. Chinese architecture is threatened by the copies of superficial Disneyland and cartoon style.

To preserve the identity both in culture and urban space, the key point is to study the international experiences and to find an appropriate way of preservation. In this case the spirit of rationality for urbanisation is necessary in order to have a clear mind for a rational rapid development. After a long-term isolation from the international world, Chinese urban planners and architects must work together with their international colleagues to build up an urban environment with human scale and identity.

With the rapid development in Chinese economical construction and social affairs, after being accepted by the World Trade Organisation, most Chinese cities are undergoing an entire readjustment in the industrial, economical and urban structure. The influences of globalisation signify that the existing Chinese system of urban planning and planning administration, the architectural design system, the construction administrative system and others will follow the international models. The situation of "urban planning without planning" will be altered.

International Architects in China

Under the influence of economical globalisation and scientific and technological globalisation, urbanisation in China will be generally accelerated. Some export-oriented economical centres like Shanghai, Hong Kong and others are developed. The Bohai Gulf Ring, the Yangtse Delta Area, the Pearl Delta Area will form large city groups with high density. The rapid development of urbanisation has presented some problems for urban planning and urban construction, which will only be solved by a systematic reform and rational administrative mechanisms. Globalisation is generating more impact on population growth and consumption of land resource on a large scale. Chinese practice in urban planning has presented many experiences and experiments to the world's urban planning. For the last ten years, there have been so many competitions and scheme collections held in China for urban planning, urban design and architectural design. With the Olympic Games 2008 in Beijing and the EXPO 2010 in Shanghai, there will be more urban planning and construction activities in China.

aktivitäten in China geben, für deren Einfluss und Umfang es in den letzten 100 Jahren keinen Vergleich gibt. Die Auswirkungen der Globalisierung hat es bereits in der Geschichte der chinesischen Architektur, Stadtplanung und -gestaltung gegeben. Im frühen 18. Jahrhundert waren westliche Architekten sehr aktiv in China. Die Einflüsse der Globalisierung werden beim Aufeinandertreffen der internationalen und der traditionellen chinesischen Baukultur deutlich, gefördert durch neues Denken und moderne Wissenschaft und Technologie. In China gab es bereits eine sowjetische Globalisierung in den 50er Jahren in Form der Industrialisierung. Der schwarze Qualm, der aus den Schornsteinwäldern aufstieg, war das Symbol des neuen China. Um die globale Industrialisierung realisieren zu können, wurden viele Waldressourcen niedergebrannt.

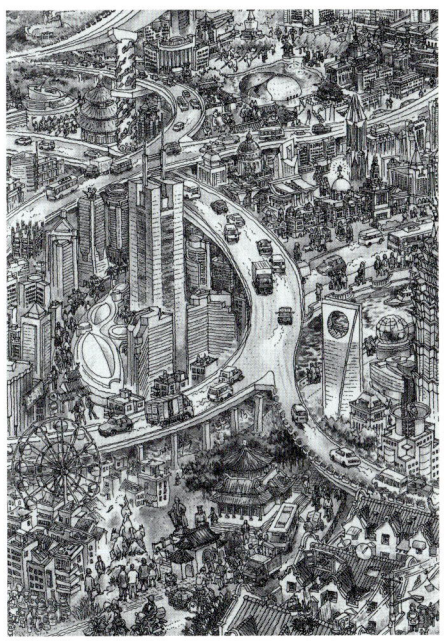

Seit den frühen 80er Jahren kamen Architekten aus dem Westen, Hongkong, und Taiwan zurück auf das chinesische Festland, um Karriere zu machen. Das Fragrant Hill Hotel (1980–1982) von I.M. Pei, das Great Wall Hotel (1980–1984) von Becket International, das Jianguo Hotel (1980–1982) von Clement Chen and Associates aus San Francisco, das Jinling Hotel Nanjing (1980–1983) von Palmer and Turner, Hongkong, und das Shanghai Huating Sheraton Hotel (1982–1986) von Wong & Tung International sind Beispiele hierfür. Nach einer langen Zeit der Abgrenzung von der Außenwelt entdeckten die chinesischen Architekten die Arbeit ihrer zeitgenössischen internationalen Kollegen. Es gab jedoch einen großen Kontrast zwischen den Ideologien und dem architektonischen Denken der chinesischen

Oben: Drei chinesische Städte.
Top: Three Chinese cities.
Unten: Das Fragrant Hill Hotel.
Bottom: The Fragrant Hill Hotel.

Their influences and scale in the world are unmatched in the last 100 years.
The influence of globalisation already existed in Chinese urban planning, urban design and architecture. Early in the 18th century, Western architects had been very active in China. The impact of globalisation is expressed in the clash of international architectural culture with traditional culture under the promotion of new thinking and modern science and technology. In China there was a former Soviet globalisation in the 1950s, i.e. the industrialisation. That black smoke that surged from a forest of chimneys was the symbol of the new China. For the realisation of global industrialisation, a lot of forest resources were burned down.

Since the early 1980s, Western, Hong Kong and Taiwan architects came to the mainland again for their career. The Fragrant Hill Hotel (1980–1982) designed by I.M.Pei, the Great Wall Hotel (1980–1984) designed by Becket International, the Jianguo Hotel (1980–1982) designed by Clement Chen and Associates from San Francisco, the Jinling Hotel, Nanjing (1980–1983) designed by Palmer and Turner, Hong Kong, Shanghai Huating Sheraton Hotel (1982–1986) designed by Wong & Tung International are examples. At the same time, Chinese architects recognized the contemporary international architects after a very long period of segregation from the outside world. On the one hand, there was a sharp contrast between Chinese architects and international architects in ideology and architectural thinking. On the other hand, there was also a clash between two different ideologies.

Since the beginning of the 1980s, international architects have been very active in China in contributing to architectural design, urban planning, urban design and consulting works. Today, there are architects and urban planners from the U.S., France, Canada, Japan, Germany, U.K., Italy, Spain, Korea, Australia, Austria, Russia, Holland, Singapore, Sweden, Switzerland and other countries working in China on urban planning, urban design and architectural design.

und der internationalen Architekten, denn es trafen zwei grundsätzlich verschiedene Ideologien aufeinander.
Seit Beginn der 1980er Jahre sind internationale Architekten sehr aktiv in China, sie leisten sowohl Beiträge zu Architektur, Stadtplanung und Stadtgestaltung als auch beratende Tätigkeiten. Heute arbeiten Architekten und Stadtplaner aus den USA, Frankreich, Kanada, Japan, Deutschland, Großbritannien, Italien, Spanien, Korea, Australien, Österreich, Russland, Holland, Singapur, Schweden, der Schweiz und anderen Ländern in China.
Seit den 90er Jahren gab es vier Ereignisse von besonderer Bedeutung: zunächst das internationale Gutachten für die Stadtplanung des Central Business Districts in Lu-Jia-Zui, Pudong, Shanghai, im Jahr 1992, als zweites das Jinmao Tower Projekt, als drittes das Nationaltheater in Peking und zuletzt den internationalen Wettbewerb für neue Städte in Shanghai.
Für den Central Business District in Lu-Jia-Zui haben Richard Rogers aus Großbritannien, Dominique Perrault aus Frankreich, Massimiliano Fuksas aus Italien und Toyo Ito aus Japan neue Ideen für eine asiatische Kompaktstadt erarbeitet. Durch den Wettbewerb wurden die westlichen Planungsmethoden eingeführt und somit die Isolation der chinesischen Stadtplanung von der westlichen Welt beendet. Dieses Ereignis hat ein breiteres Spektrum für eine internationale Mitwirkung geöffnet. Der endgültige Masterplan kennzeichnet den Konflikt zwischen der chinesisch-pragmatischen und der westlich-utopischen Stadt.
Der Wettbewerb für den Jinmao Tower hat einen Streit über Globalisierung und sinnvolle Regionalisierung ausge-

löst. Der Streit konzentrierte sich hauptsächlich auf die Form des Turms und die Frage, ob er hochmodern oder in traditionell-chinesischer Art sein sollte. Hier wird deutlich, dass Kultur nicht global sein kann, obwohl sie universal ist. Vor allem im kulturellen Bereich existieren Lokalisierung und Globalisierung nebeneinander. Der Jinmao Tower wurde zum

Oben: Das Zentrum von Pudong.
Top: The Pudong CBD area.
Unten: Das Zentrum von Pudong in der Entstehung.
Bottom: The Pudong CBD area in development.

**Since the 1990s, there have been four events that have a special significance. The first one is the 1992 Inter-national Survey on the Urban Design of the Central Business District in Lu-Jia-Zui, Pudong, Shanghai, the second one is the Jinmao Tower project, the third one is the Beijing National Theatre, the latest one is the International Competition for new cities in Shanghai.
For the Lu-Jia-Zui CBD projects, Richard Rogers from the U.K., Dominique Perrault from France, Massimiliano Fuksas from Italy and Toyo Ito from Japan worked out new ideas for an Asian compact city. The competition**

**introduced the Western planning policy and broke the isolation of Chinese urban planning from the Western world. This event made possible a wider range of international participation. The final master plan characterises the clash between the Chinese pragmatic city and the Western utopian city.
The competition for the Jinmao Tower opened an argument on globalisation and rational regionalisation. The argument mainly concentrated on the form, whether the tower should be highly modern or in a traditional Chinese shape. This shows that culture cannot be global even though it is universal. Especially, in the realm related to culture, localisation coexists with globalisation. Jinmao Tower became the best project of SOM in the last ten years, afterwards, SOM designed the Industrial & Commercial Bank of China Headquarters in Beijing. The deep understanding of Chinese culture made SOM successful in Shanghai with the Waterfront Redevelopment Urban Design in 2000 and Shanghai Xin-Tian-Di Project in 2001.
The Beijing National Theatre opened a national argument. For the first time, Beijing introduced a modern idea of urban redevelopment and broke with Chinese neo-classicism. This argument is not a simple discussion about the architectural form for such an old historical capital. But it has generated a new period for the transformation into avant-garde and star architects. The significant argument about the National Theatre since 1999 has also touched the issue related to culture and urban context. It does not relate to the**

besten Projekt der letzten zehn Jahre von SOM. Danach entwarf SOM die Zentrale der Industrial & Commercial Bank of China in Peking. Das tiefe Verständnis der chinesischen Kultur bescherte SOM die Erfolge des städtebaulichen Entwurfs für das Shanghai Waterfront Redevelopment im Jahr 2000 und des Shanghai Xin-Tian-Di Projekts im darauffolgenden Jahr.

Das Nationaltheater in Peking löste einen nationalen Streit aus. Zum ersten Mal brach Peking mit dem chinesischen Neo-Klassizismus und führte moderne Vorstellungen der städtischen Sanierung ein. Dieser Streit ist nicht nur eine einfache Diskussion über architektonische Gestaltung für die alte, historische Hauptstadt, sondern hat außerdem eine neue Zeit des Wandels hin zu Avantgarde und Stararchitekten mit sich gebracht. Diese seit 1999 andauernde Diskussion berührt außerdem die Themen Kultur und städtebauliches Umfeld. Sie steht jedoch nicht im Zusammenhang mit der konkreten Frage, ob ausländische Architekten für Projekte dieser Art verantwortlich sein sollten oder nicht. Der springende Punkt ist die Frage, wie außergewöhnliche chinesische Architektur geschaffen werden kann und wie sich der neue internationale Stil und die pluralistische Baukultur auf lokale Bauvorhaben unter der Wirkung der Globalisierung auswirken werden.

Im Jahr 2001 haben drei Satellitenstädte und sechs Vororte Shanghais Architekten und Stadtplaner aus den USA, Großbritannien, Deutschland, Italien, Frankreich, Australien, Schweden, Spanien, Holland, Japan und China dazu aufgerufen, ihre Konzepte vorzulegen. Alle Planungen mussten sich mit den ausgedehnten Landflächen auseinander setzen. Das Maß der Ausdehnung und Erschließung ist unglaublich. Einige Konzepte zeigten gute Ideen, einige griffen Gedanken aus der Architekturgeschichte auf, wie z.B. Ebenezer Howards Gartenstadt, Arturo Sorias Ciudad Lineal, Le Corbusiers Plan Voisin u.a., und passten sie der

Oben: Der Hauptsitz der Industrial & Commercial Bank of China in Peking, 2001.
Top: The Industrial & Commercial Bank of China Headquarters in Beijing, 2001.
Unten: Das Xian-Tian-Di Projekt.
Bottom: The Xian-Tian-Di project.

concrete question whether foreign architects should be responsible for such kind of projects or not. The key point is how to create outstanding Chinese architecture, and how will the new international style and plural architectural culture affect the related localisation under the impact of globalisation.

In 2001, three satellite cities and six suburb towns of Shanghai invited architects and urban planners from the U.S., U.K., Germany, Italy, France, Australia, Sweden, Spain, Holland, Japan and China to present their conceptual plans. All of those plans had to deal with a vast land area. The scale of expansion and development is

really incredible. Some plans have revealed promising ideas, some have picked up ideas of architecture history and adapted them to the contemporary situation, such as Ebenezer Howard's Garden City, Arturo Soria's Ciudad Lineal, and Le Corbusier's Plan Voisin and others. Some have presented the concept of a utopian and idealistic city. Among those satellite cities, three are of international significance. These are Zhu-Jia-Jiao Town, Pujiang Town and Luchao Harbour City. Zhu-Jia-Jiao Town has a history of more than 1,700 years. The scheme is presented by Mr. C.Y. Lee from Taipei. His idea is to preserve the water town's traditional identity and regenerate it with new activities and vigour using a thoughtful arrangement of circulation. Pujiang Town scheme is presented by the Italian architect Vittorio Gregotti with a rational master plan for a 20 km² new town.

Luchao Harbour City is presented by the Architect Meinhard von Gerkan. The idea of the German architects von Gerkan, Marg und Partner is to create an idealistic city of the 21st century.

With these three city plans, a rational urban planning era to meet the requirements of modern society is created, which has adapted the appropriate situation. gmp's master plan for Luchao Harbour City is an intelligent and rational combination of water, city and industry with impressive urban shape and space. The logic of a concentric urban structure has condensed the Chinese philosophy of the city. This is the result of a series

heutigen Situation an. Andere präsentierten das Konzept einer utopischen und idealistischen Stadt.

Von diesen Satellitenstädten sind drei von internationaler Bedeutung: Zhu-Jia-Jiao Town, Pujiang Town und Luchao Harbour City. Zhu-Jia-Jiao Town blickt auf eine Geschichte von mehr als 1.700 Jahren zurück. Der Entwurf von C.Y. Lee aus Taipeh erhält die traditionelle Identität der Wasserstadt und regeneriert sie mithilfe neuer Aktivitäten und neuer Vitalität in wohlüberlegten Arrangements. Der Entwurf für Pujiang Town, ein rationaler Masterplan für eine 20 km² große Stadt, stammt von dem italienischen Architekten Vittorio Gregotti.

Luchao Harbour City wird von dem Architekten Meinhard von Gerkan vorgestellt. Die Idee des deutschen Architekturbüros von Gerkan, Marg und Partner ist, eine idealistische Stadt des 21. Jahrhunderts zu schaffen.

Mit diesen drei Stadtentwürfen wird eine Stadtplanungsära der Vernunft eingeläutet, die den Erfordernissen einer modernen Gesellschaft gerecht wird und sich der entsprechenden Situation anpasst.

Der Masterplan für Luchao Harbour City von gmp ist eine intelligente und sinnvolle Kombination von Wasser, Stadt und Industrie in einer beeindruckenden städtebaulichen Form. Die Logik einer konzentrischen Stadtstruktur fasst die chinesische Philosophie der Stadt zusammen. Sie ist das Ergebnis einer Reihe von Untersuchungen, die gmp bei chinesischen Projekten gemacht hat, und markiert den Höhepunkt des neueren Städtebaus in China. gmp hat die Logik der städtischen Struktur bei dem Masterplan für den Telecom Information Park, Shanghai 2003, noch einmal verstärkt. In diesen Projekten zeigt sich deutlich ein rationales städtebauliches Konzept.

Die Planungen für die Satellitenstädte Shanghais kündigen einen neuen Trend an, und die weitgehende Beteiligung ausländischer Architekten und Stadtplaner geht nun vom Planen einzelner Häuser über städtebauliche Entwürfe und Stadtplanung sogar bis hin zu Denkmalschutzkonzepten für die historischen chinesischen Bauwerke und Städte. Neben den bereits genannten Architekten haben Kisho Kurokawa aus Japan, Terry Farrell & Partners aus Großbritannien, Architecture Studio aus Frankreich, SOM, RTKL und Philip Johnson aus den USA, Philip Cox aus Australien, Albert Speer & Partner aus Deutschland und andere, ebenfalls wichtige Masterpläne für chinesische Städte vorgelegt.

Seit dem 20. Jahrhundert haben sich chinesische Architekten und Gelehrte, Generation für Generation, dem Aufbau einer chinesischen Architekturrichtung gewidmet und den Lebensgeist der chinesischen Architektur im Bereich der architektonischen Lehre und Gestaltung erforscht.

of investigations by gmp on the projects in China. It represents the peak of urban planning for new Chinese cities. gmp has strengthened the logic of urban fabric in the master plan of the Telecom Information Park, Shanghai, in 2003. Those projects clearly present a rational idea for urban planning.

The Shanghai satellite city planning announced a new trend so that the profound involvement of foreign architects and urban planners has extended from single building design to urban design and urban planning, and even to the preservation plan for historical Chinese cities and buildings. Apart from the architects mentioned above, Kisho Kurokawa from Japan, Terry Farrell & Partners from the U.K., Architecture Studio from France, SOM, RTKL and Philip Johnson from the U.S.A., Philip Cox from Australia, Albert Speer & Partner from Germany and others also presented significant master plans for Chinese cities.

Since the 20th century, Chinese scholars and architects, generation after generation, have devoted themselves to establishing a Chinese architecture discourse and to exploring the life spirit of Chinese architecture in the field of architectural education and architectural design. We are still in the course of finding a way for the development of the Chinese city and architecture.

In China, it is said that a six-year-old child will first do something, then think about it; an old person of 60 years will first think about something, then do it. Chinese urban planning and architecture are still in the process of growth. Although there are outstanding Chinese architects and planners and they have experienced a period of the most rapid development ever in Chinese history, such a vast development on other continents and countries may take 100 or even 200 years.

The young generation of architects and planners has matured rapidly while being directly engaged in real practice. Their teachers and the older generation were not able to experience that. On the other hand, the architects and planners are too busy to study and think about architectural theory. The sense of criticism and the sense of value in architectural design and planning are still to be cultivated both for architects and non-professional people. The architectural and urban theory is not yet systematically studied and most professionals only have a superficial knowledge of it.

Since 1997, the registered architects' system has been established in China, but the architects are still constrained by the sense of traditional hierarchy. Their social status is still very low, not only for the economic

Wir sind heute noch immer dabei, einen Weg zur Entwicklung der chinesischen Stadt und ihrer Architektur zu finden.

In China sagt man, ein sechsjähriges Kind wird zuerst etwas tun und dann darüber nachdenken, ein älterer Mann von 60 Jahren wird erst nachdenken und dann handeln. Die chinesische Architektur und der Städtebau befinden sich noch im Wachstum. Obwohl es herausragende chinesische Architekten und Planer gibt und sie eine Phase der rasanten Entwicklung in der chinesischen Geschichte erfahren haben, würde eine solch schnelle Entwicklung in anderen Kontinenten und Ländern hundert oder sogar zweihundert Jahre dauern.

Die junge Generation der Architekten und Planer ist schnell gereift, während sie direkt in die Praxis eingebunden war. Diese Erfahrung konnten ihre Lehrer und die ältere Generation nicht machen. Auf der anderen Seite sind die Architekten und Planer heute zu beschäftigt, um zu forschen und sich mit Architekturtheorie auseinander zu setzen. Der Sinn für Kritik und Werte im architektonischen Gestalten und Planen muss sowohl für die Architekten als auch die Laien erst noch kultiviert werden. Die Theorie der Architektur und des Städtebaus wird noch nicht systematisch untersucht und die meisten Architekten haben davon nur ein oberflächliches Wissen.

Seit 1997 hat sich das System der registrierten Architekten in China durchgesetzt. Dennoch leiden die Architekten immer noch unter der traditionellen Hierarchie. Ihr sozialer Status ist sehr niedrig, nicht nur was ihre ökonomische Situation betrifft, sondern sie sind auch sehr weit von der führenden gesellschaftlichen Klasse entfernt. Die Verantwortung der Architekten ist stark begrenzt, und die Bezahlung der Projekte nur gering. Die Regierung befürwortet die Globalisierung, ohne zu bedenken, dass professionelles Wissen die treibende Kraft für die zukünftige Entwicklung einer Stadt ist. Sie vertrauen lieber ausländischen Architekten als chinesischen. So gesehen befinden sich die künftige chinesische Architektur und Stadtplanung noch auf dem Weg zu einer vernünftigeren sozialen Umgebung.

Wie bereits erläutert, entsteht die Architekturgeschichte in der Zusammenarbeit der internationalen Architekten mit ihren chinesischen Kollegen. Wenn internationale Architekten in China arbeiten und eine Architektur von Weltrang schaffen möchten, müssen sie die chinesische Kultur anerkennen und detaillierte Kenntnis von ihr, ihren Wurzeln und ihren räumlichen Bezügen haben.

position but they are also far from being the leading class of social life. The responsibility of the architects is strongly limited and the payment is very low. The government officials are fond of the globalisation without knowing that professional knowledge is the power for the future development of a city. They believe in the foreign architects' participation much more than in Chinese architects. In this sense, the future Chinese architecture and urban planning are still on a course towards a more rational social environment.

As we have discussed, the international architects are creating architectural history together with their Chinese colleagues. If international architects want to work in China creating architecture with a critical significance for the world architectural history, they have to acknowledge and to have an intimate knowledge of Chinese culture, its roots and its spatial relationship.

Bibliography

Alan Balfour, Zheng Shiling. World Cities Shanghai. Wiley-Academy. London. 2002

Erlebnisräume – Spaces, Design + Construction. gmp – Architekten von Gerkan, Marg und Partner. awf-verlag. Heidelberg. 2002

Ten Years: Ten Cities: The Work of Terry Farrell & Partners 1991-2001. Laurence King Publishing Ltd. London. 2002

Pamela Yatsko. New Shanghai: The Rocky Rebirth of China's Legendary City. John Wiley & Sons. Inc. Singapore. 2001

Zhou Denon. A History of Modern Chinese Architecture. Tianjin Science and Technology Press. Tianjin. 2001

Kenneth Powell. City Transformed: Urban Architecture at the Beginning of the 21st Century. Laurence King Publishing Ltd. London. 2000

Liu Erming, Yi Feng. International Architects in China, Selected Works since 1980

China Planning Press. Encyclopaedia of China Publishing House. Beijing. 1999

Richard Rogers. Cities for a Small Planet. Faber and Faber. London. 1997

Die europäische Stadt

"Die Geschichte der Urbanisierung ist alt. Seit über 7000 Jahren gibt es Städte. Die mitteleuropäische Stadt existiert gerade mal 1000 Jahre, ..."
Hochglanzprospekte legen uns Städte als lohnende Reiseziele nahe. Ob Siena, Prag, Lübeck oder Quedlinburg – sie werden uns näher gebracht, als eine Ansammlung von Events und Vielfalt kulinarischer Genüsse. Malerische Altstädte mit illuminierten historischen Fassaden, einem Springbrunnen und möglichst einem Königshaus, dessen Herrscher ihre Stadt geliebt haben.

Könnte man eine Zeitreise zu den Städten der Vergangenheit machen, so würde man sich an Orten befinden, die durch Enge gekennzeichnet sind, bedingt durch den Schutz der Stadtmauern. Menschenfülle in den Gassen, hygienische Verhältnisse, die Herde für Pest, Cholera und Typhus boten. Mittelalterliche und frühkapitalistische Zustände, wie sie auch im einundzwanzigsten Jahrhundert noch in außereuropäischen Ländern zu finden sind. Heute genießen wir das Schlendern in Gassen oder auf großzügigen Boulevards, vorbei an restaurierten erhabenen Fassaden, pittoresken schiefen Giebeln. Wir versuchen Blicke in Gärten und Eingangsportale zu erhaschen, freuen uns, wenn sich Gassen und Straßen zu Plätzen öffnen, und genießen nach den engen, schattigen Gassen die offenen, hellen und sonnigen Plätze. Ohne Mühe schauen wir die drei bis vier Stockwerke hoch zum Himmel, um in der Ferne die Silhouette eines Kirchturms zu

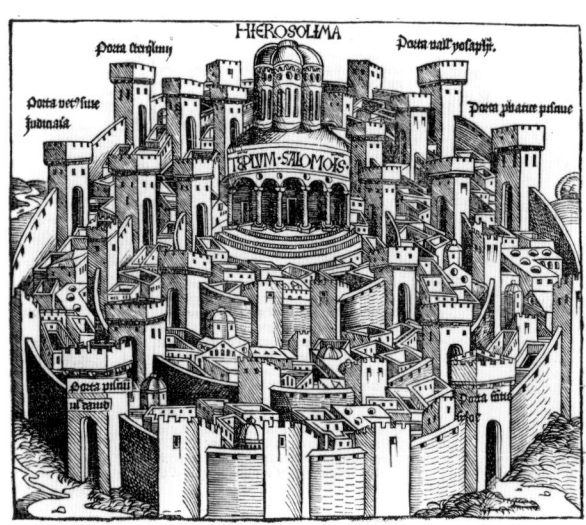

01

The European City

"The history of urbanization is ages old. There have been cities for over seven thousand years, but the central European city has only existed for about 1,000 years, ..."
High-gloss travel brochures recommend cities as places worth seeing. From Siena and Prague to Lübeck or Quedlinburg, they are presented to us as agglomerations of events and a great variety of culinary delights. Picturesque city centres full of flood-lit historic buildings, fountains and, preferably, a royal palace whose owners – past rulers – had loved their city.

If it were possible to make a time journey to cities of the past, one would find oneself in places providing a sense of being cramped for space within the city walls. One would find overcrowded streets and sanitary conditions as hotbeds of the plague, cholera and typhoid fever – medieval, early capitalist conditions as we find them outside Europe in this, the 21st century. Today we enjoy strolling along alleyways or wide boulevards, past impressive restored façades and picturesquely leaning gabled houses. We try to get a glimpse of back gardens and entrance portals and feel elated when alleys and streets release us onto wide open squares where, after the narrow shaded passages, we enjoy the bright sun on the plaza. Without having to strain our necks, we look over and beyond three or four-storey buildings up to the sky and may see the silhouette of a far away church steeple. We are part of the lively street medley that is a mark of every city or, as Walter Siebel puts it, of "the polarity of public and private life". (W. Siebel, ed., Die europäische Stadt. Suhrkamp, Frankfurt/Main, 2004).

The other extreme is the global city with its concentration of office buildings and towers in the so-called central business districts, funded by a professional management class.

The gap between rich and poor generates ever further developments of citadels, enclaves and ghettoes on urban peripheries, i.e. the suburbanization via shopping centres and entertainment parks, promoted by the commercial interests of the financial, property and developers' markets. Airports are increasingly turning into transshipment centres for the goods known as humans – people as money-spending haulage items. There is mounting pressure on the cities to hand over their abandoned industrial areas and wastelands, dockyards and factories to the property sector. This is accompanied by the privatization of infrastructures and municipal

erblicken. Wir sind Teil des lebendigen Treibens in den Straßen, das Sinnbild für die Stadt ist, oder, wie es Walter Siebel nennt: „der Polarität von Öffentlichkeit und Privatheit."[01]

Das andere Extrem ist die Global City. Die Konzentration von Bürotürmen und Bürogebäuden in den so genannten Central Business Districts, getragen von einer Klasse von professionellen Managern.

Die Kluft zwischen arm und reich führt zu immer weiteren Entwicklungen von Zitadellen, Enklaven und Ghettos an den Peripherien der Städte. Einer Suburbanisierung durch Einkaufszentren und Vergnügungsstädten, gefördert durch die kommerzielle Einflussnahme vom Finanzsektor und Immobilienwirtschaft. Flughäfen werden immer mehr zu Umschlagplätzen der Ware Mensch. Der Mensch als Geld ausgebende Transportkapazität. Der Druck auf die Städte, ihre obsolet werdenden Industriebrachen, wie Hafenanlagen, Produktionsstätten, dem Immobilienkapital zuzuführen, steigt stetig. Dieser geht einher mit Privatisierung der Infrastruktur und Dienstleistung, um die notorisch knappen Kassen des öffentlichen Sektors zu füllen oder zu entlasten. Bewirkt wird damit eine politische und ökonomische Machtverhältnisverschiebung in fast allen Städten. Angesichts dieses Szenarios, der Global City, erscheinen die Charakteristika der europäischen Stadt fast romantisch.

Die europäischen Städte stehen unter dem Druck der Globalisierung und versuchen, diesen anzupassen an die sozioökonomischen Bedingungen, denen der Stadtmensch im 21. Jahrhundert ausgesetzt ist. Oder, wie es Leonardo Benevolo formuliert: „Die Veränderungen, denen wir die Städte unterwerfen, richten sich nach unseren jeweiligen Problemen, und sie werden für viele kommende Jahre binden sein, (...)."[02] Nichteuropäische Länder, wie beispielsweise solche in Asien, und hier insbesondere China, haben es mit dem Druck einer Bevölkerung zu tun, die in die Städte will, die nicht selten so groß sind wie Hamburg, Berlin, Frankfurt und München zusammen. Dieser enorme Bevölkerungsdruck macht es notwendig, Städte aus dem Nichts zu planen. Wie plant man aber eine Stadt für 500.000 oder eine Million Menschen? Welchen Ideen von Stadt lagen vergangene Visionen von Stadtplanung zugrunde?

01 Schedel, Hartmann, Liber chronicarum, 1493.
02 Georg Braun, Civitas orbis terrarum, 1597.
03 Claude Nicolas Ledoux, Ville de Chaux, 1804.

02

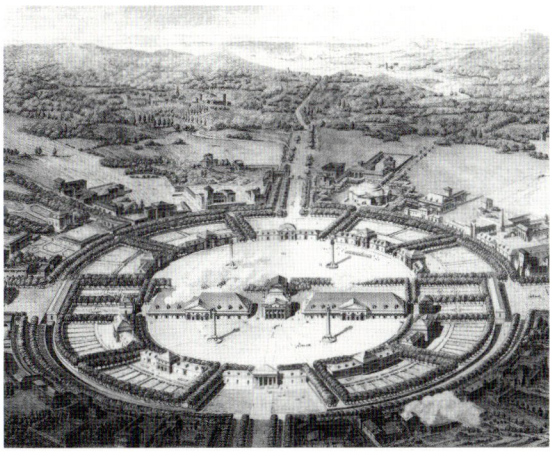
03

services to refill the notoriously empty public sector coffers. This produces a shift in the political and economic balance of power in almost every city. In view of this global city scenario, the characteristics of the European city seem almost romantic.

The cities of Europe try to conform to the mounting pressure of globalization with the socio-economic conditions the 21st-century urban dweller lives in. As Leonardo Benevolo puts it, "The changes we subject the cities to follow on from our own problems and will be binding for many years to come, [...]." Non-European countries, for example in Asia and here especially China, have to contend with the great numbers of rural migrants to cities many of which are as large as Hamburg, Berlin, Frankfurt and Munich put together. This enormous population pressure makes it necessary to plan entire cities from scratch. Yet how does one plan a city for 500,000 or one million inhabitants? What ideas formed the basis of urban planning visions in the past?

Die Idealstadt im Spiegel der Zeit

„Alles Schlechte abreißen" titelte die SZ im Januar 2003 und berief sich dabei auf ein Gespräch mit Mario Botta, in dem dieser die These vertritt: „Urbanistik der Zukunft ist eine Urbanistik der Demolierung", die die Sünden des Wirtschaftsbooms tilgt.[1]

Diese These provoziert zu den Fragen: Was ist demgegenüber das Gute? Was verdient es, erhalten zu bleiben oder neu gebaut zu werden?

Die Antwort darauf muss wohl unbeantwortet bleiben, denn Stadt ist kein statischer Zustand, sondern ein Prozess. Gedacht wurde sie von den Theoretikern immer als Harmonie, als das Einssein mit Gott, der Welt oder der Vernunft. Ob Civitas oder Polis, Idee oder Utopie, allen bekannten Ideen von Stadt ist eins gemeinsam: Ihr Ausgangspunkt ist immer ein Herrschaftsverhältnis. Ob es das Reich Gottes ist, der platonische Stadtstaat, die Kaiserstadt, ob es die faschistische, sozialistische oder demokratische Stadt ist, ohne Herrschaft und damit Macht scheint es keine Stadt zu geben.

Eine weitere Gemeinsamkeit besteht darin, dass die materiellen Bedingungen, die Ökonomie, mit dem Sinnlichen und Spirituellen, dem Ideellen versöhnt werden sollen. Sei es nun mit der Religion oder den modernen Werten, die dem Zeitalter der Aufklärung zugrunde liegen.

Stadt ist demnach immer eine Reflexion auf das jeweilige gesellschaftliche Verhältnis mit all seinen vielfältigen Abhängigkeiten und Bedingungen. Ein Architekt „muß keine persönliche Theorie aufstellen, wenn sein Handeln in den Normen der Zeit aufgeht (...) Architektur und ihre Theorie stehen in keinem kausalen Verhältnis."[2] Um es mit den Worten Thilo Schaberts zu sagen: „In den Stadtarchitekturen spiegelt sich die Architektur der Welt."[3]

Die nachfolgende Zeitreise erhebt keinen Anspruch auf Vollständigkeit. Es ist der Versuch einer Einordnung des Stadtentwurfs von Lingang New City in die Geschichte der Idealstadt.

Das Streben nach der idealen Stadt reicht schriftlich überliefert bis zurück in die Johannes-Offenbarung. Dort heißt es: „Sie hatte eine große und hohe Mauer und hatte zwölf Tore und auf den Toren zwölf Engel (...) und der mit mir redete, hatte einen Maßstab, ein goldenes Rohr, um die Stadt zu messen und ihre Tore und Mauern. Und die Stadt ist viereckig angelegt, und ihre Länge ist so groß wie die Breite."[4]

The Ideal City as Reflected through the Ages

"Everything bad should be demolished" was a headline in the *Süddeutsche Zeitung* in January 2003, thereby referring to an interview with Mario Botta, in which he stated his opinion that "urbanism of the future is an urbanism of demolition" wiping out the sins of economic booms.[1]

This thesis provokes the following questions: What on the contrary is good? What structures deserve to be maintained or newly built?

These questions shall remain unanswered, because a city is not in a constant state but in a process. Theoreticians have always perceived it as a harmony, as a unity with God, the world or rationality. Whether civitas or polis, idea or utopia, all known city concepts have one thing in common: their origin is always a system of power. Whether the Kingdom of God, the Platonic city state, the imperial city, whether fascist, socialist or democratic city, there seems to be no city without rules and consequently without power.

Another common feature is the conciliation of material conditions, the economy, with the sensory and spiritual world, that can either be religion or modern values, which form the basis of the age of enlightenment.

Consequently a city is always a reflexion of the respective social circumstances with all its manifold dependencies and conditions. An architect "does not need to establish his personal theory, if his actions are taken up by the standards of the time (...) Architecture and its theory have no causal relationship to one another."[2]

To quote Thilo Schabert: "City architectures reflect the architecture of the world."[3]

The subsequent journey through the times does not claim to be exhaustive. It is rather an attempt to categorize the urban concept of Lingang New City within the history of the ideal city.

Written documents of this striving for the ideal city reach as far back as to St. John's Revelations, where it is said: "It had a large and high wall and twelve gates and twelve angels on top of these gates (...) and the man I was talking to had a ruler, a golden pipe, to measure the city and its gates and walls. The city is laid out as a rectangle, and its length is identical to its width."[4] The Revelations could be interpreted as the first record of "heavenly architecture off the drawing-board".

In the most diverse cultures the circle and square are recurring geometric forms; whether Chinese, Indian,

Man könnte die Offenbarung als eine erste überlieferte „himmlische Reißbrett-Architektur" interpretieren. Kreis und Quadrat sind in den unterschiedlichsten Kulturen immer wiederkehrende geometrische Formen, ob chinesisch, indisch, keltisch-germanisch, peruanisch, iranisch, hellenistisch, israelitisch, islamisch oder europäisch, überall begegnen uns heute noch Zeugnisse von Stadtresten und Kultstätten, wie z. B. Stonehenge (2750 v. Chr.) oder Chanchan in Peru, eine Stadtanlage für 10.000 Menschen, oder Monte Alban, Stadt der Zapoteken in Mittelamerika. Bagdad, 760 gegründete Hauptstadt des abbasidischen Kalifats, wird von zwei Mauerringen umschlossen und ist in zwei Hauptachsen unterteilt, die sich in der Mitte rechtwinklig kreuzen.[5]

Die Idealstadt findet sich auch in Platons Werk *Die Gesetze*. Ruth Eaton schreibt darüber in ihrem Buch *Die ideale Stadt*: „Die Akropolis mit ihren runden Mauern bildet den Mittelpunkt von Platons idealer Stadt.

Strahlenförmig teilt sich die Stadt von ihr aus in zwölf Segmente, in denen die zwölf verschiedenen Bevölkerungsgruppen leben, und welche auf diese Weise die Organisation der Gesellschaft räumlich ordnen."[6]

Der Kreis verkörpert das Ideelle. Anfang ist gleich Ende. Es gibt keinen Anfang ohne Ende und umgekehrt. Die Gestirne und das Leben folgen einem fortwährenden Zyklus, einem Kreislauf ohne Anfang und Ende. Das Quadrat steht für das Rationelle. Die Konstruktion von Linien im rechten Winkel ist Ausdruck für die Gültigkeit des Willens, des Ordnens und Unterordnens.

In der Mandala-Architektur des Ostens repräsentiert der Kreis den Himmel und das Quadrat die Erde. Sinnfällig gemacht wird die Abstraktion auch in der Windrose. In der indischen

1 Maître François, Die himmlische und die irdische Macht.
2 Mandala-Architekturdarstellung und ägyptisches Zeichen für Stadt.
1 Maître François, The heavenly and the earthly lordship.
2 Mandala architecture presentation and Egyptian symbol for city.

1

Celtic-Germanic, Peruvian, Iranian, Hellenistic, Israelite, Islamic or European, everywhere we still find remains of cities and places of worship, such as for example Stonehenge (2,750 B.C.) or Chanchan in Peru, a city for 10,000 people, or Monte Alban, city of the Zapotecs in Central America. Baghdad, capital of the Abbasid caliphate founded in 760, is enclosed by two ring walls and divided into two main axes, which intersect at right-angles in the centre.[5]

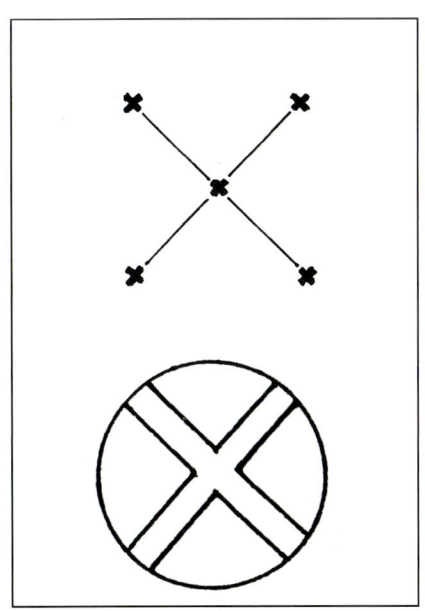

The ideal city is also mentioned in Plato's work *The Laws*. Ruth Eaton writes about this subject in her book *The Ideal City*: "The acropolis with its circular walls forms the centre of Plato's ideal city. The city radiates from this centre in twelve segments, where the twelve different sections of the population live, thus spatially organizing the social structure."[6]

The circle symbolizes the ideational world. The beginning is the end. There is no beginning without an end and vice versa. Stars and life follow a constant cycle, a cycle without a beginning or an end. The square represents the rational sphere. The construction of lines at a right angle is an expression of the validity of will, of ordering and subordination.

In the mandala architecture of the East the circle represents the sky, whilst the square symbolizes the earth. This abstraction also becomes clear in the compass card.

2

In the Indian Vastraparusha mandala architecture the square has a cosmic meaning. It is orientated according to the four directions, makes space comprehensible and is regarded as the overall symbol of the world.

In China this transcendence was expressed with the architectural positioning of the imperial palaces as focus, as centre of the world (*tichung*), "as the place where earth and sky meet, where the four seasons

Vastraparusha Mandala-Architektur hat das Quadrat eine kosmische Bedeutung. Es ist auf die vier Himmelsrichtungen ausgerichtet, macht Raum begreiflich und wird als allumfassendes Symbol der Welt angesehen.

In China fand diese Überhöhung mit den architektonischen Setzungen der Kaiserpaläste als Zentrum, als Weltmitte (ti-chung), als der „Ort, wo Erde und Himmel sich treffen, wo die vier Jahreszeiten eins werden, wo Wind und Regen beigeholt, und wo Yin und Yang in Übereinstimmung sind" ihren Ausdruck.[7]

Und wie auch in der Johannes-Offenbarung Jerusalem als Stadt mit zwölf Toren, drei in jeder Himmelsrichtung, mit gleicher Länge und Breite angelegt ist, finden sich ähnliche Aussagen in den Versen der Chou Li, den Kao-kung-Chi: „Die Hauptstadt ist ein Rechteck aus neun Quadrat-Li [1 Li = 1 chinesische Meile = 500 m]. Auf jeder Seite der Mauer finden sich drei Tore"[8]. Kreis und Quadrat, Welt und Stadt beruhen hier auf der Ordnung des Theos Tektonikos, der aus dem Chaos durch Symmetrie und Proportion Räume schuf.

In der Renaissance wird der Menschen als göttliche Schöpfung zum Maß aller Dinge. Eine vom Menschen für den Menschen zu schaffende Architektur war ihr Leitbild. Vitruv schuf das „theoretische Bild" hierzu: die anthropometrische Proportion, bestehend aus einem Kreis und einem Quadrat, deren Größe durch die ausgestreckten Arme und Beine des Menschen bestimmt wird. Durch Leonardo da Vincis Zeichnung wurde sie populär.[9]

3 Mandala aus Nepal, 1495.
4 Johann Bernhard Fischer von Erlach, Entwurf Kaiserpalast Peking, 1725.
5 Leonardo da Vinci, um 1490.
6 L' idea dell' architettura universale, Vitruvianische Figur, um 1678.
3 Mandala from Nepal, 1495.
4 Johann Bernhard Fischer von Erlach, Design for Imperial Palace, Beijing, 1725.
5 Leonardo da Vinci, around 1490.
6 L' idea dell' architettura universale, Vitruvian figure, around 1678.

become one, where wind and rain are absorbed, and where yin and yang are in accordance with each other".[7] Comparable to St. John's Revelations, according to which Jerusalem is laid out as a city with twelve gates, three towards each direction, and with identical length and width, similar statements can be found in the verses of the Chou Li, the Kao-kung-Chi: "The capital is a rectangle of nine square Li [1 Li = 1 Chinese mile = 500 m]. Three gates are located on each side of the wall".[8] Circle and square, world and city are founded on the order of the Theos Tektonikos, who generated spaces from chaos by introducing symmetry and proportion.

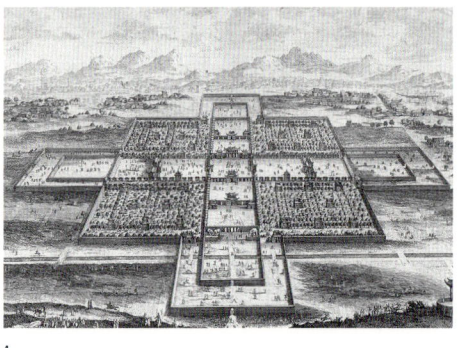

During the Renaissance mankind as divine creation became the measure of all things, its model being an architecture to be created by humans for humans. Vitruvius formed the "theoretical image" for this: the anthropometric proportion, consisting of a circle and a square with their dimension being defined by the stretched-out arms and legs of a human being. Leonardo da Vinci's drawing made this proportion popular.[9] The proportions of architecture should conform with human proportions and should therefore be in accordance with the human being. The ideal city is the polis designed accordingly, with work and life taking place in an ideal space that complies with the rhythm of human life.

Le Corbusier, one of the most significant town planners of the 20th century, regards Venice, to which he was closely connected since his youth, as the ideal anthropometric city. In a letter addressed to the participants of a town planning congress in Venice in 1962 he wrote: "There they have a treasure of human scale. Ignoring, destroying it would be grievously criminal! And this could so easily happen!"[10]

The world's uniqueness becomes lost with the discoveries of natural sciences, especially the findings of Isaac Newton. It becomes lost in the significance of the universe. How could architecture still have a scale when space is infinite? But in the infinite expanse of space the human being always remains the same. From

Dem Anspruch nach sollten die Proportionen der Architektur mit den Proportionen des Menschen übereinstimmen und so dem Menschen entsprechen. Die ideale Stadt ist die so gestaltete Polis, Arbeit und Leben finden im idealen Raum statt, der dem Lebensrhythmus der Menschen entspricht.

Le Corbusier, einer der bedeutendsten Stadtplaner des 20. Jahrhunderts, hält Venedig, die Stadt, der er seit seiner Jugend verbunden ist, für die ideale anthropometrische Stadt. In einem Brief an die Teilnehmer eines städtebaulichen Kongresses 1962 in Venedig schreibt er: „Sie haben dort einen Schatz mit menschlichen Maßen. Es wäre schmerzlich kriminell, über ihn hinwegzusehen, ihn zu zerstören! Und das kann so leicht geschehen!"[10]

Mit den Erkenntnissen der Naturwissenschaften, und hier sei insbesondere an Isaac Newton gedacht, ging die Einzigartigkeit der Welt verloren. Sie verlor sich in der Bedeutung des Universums. Wie konnte Architektur noch Maß haben, wenn der Raum unendlich ist? In der unendlichen Ausdehnung des Raumes bleibt der Mensch jedoch immer derselbe. Die Architektur im unendlichen Raum musste sich nun auf den Menschen als Architekten beziehen. Das Maß der Dinge wurde der Blick des Architekten. Er definierte die Stadt nach Maßen und Zahlen wie ein Gott in der Johannes-Offenbarung. Le Corbusier fasst dies später so zusammen, dass er die Manifestation Stadt als „die Beschlagnahme der Natur durch den Menschen" begreift.[11]

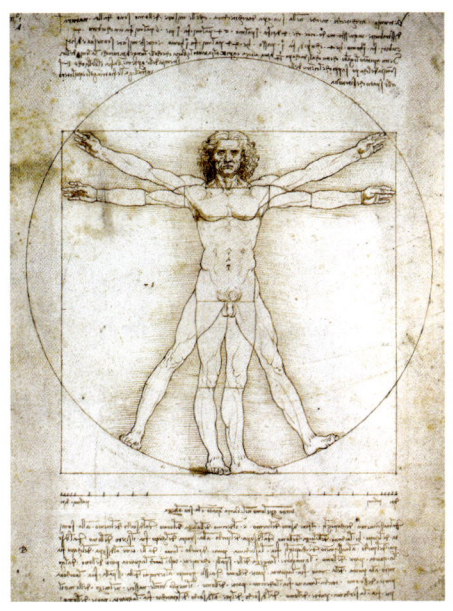

5

Macina Mundi

Mit der industriellen Revolution wird nicht nur ein Datum markiert, das darauf hinweist, dass die Menschen in einer Zeit angekommen sind, in der sie technisch so gut wie alles beherrschen, sondern in der die Weltausstellungen auch bezeugen, dass man hoch in den Himmel bauen und weitgespannte Konstruktionen erschaffen kann, die alles bis

this time on architecture in the infinite space had to refer to the human being as the architect. The eye of the architect became the measure of all things. The architect defined the city with measures and figures like God did in St. John's Revelations. At a later date Le Corbusier summarized that he sees the manifestation of "city" as "the occupation of nature by mankind".[11]

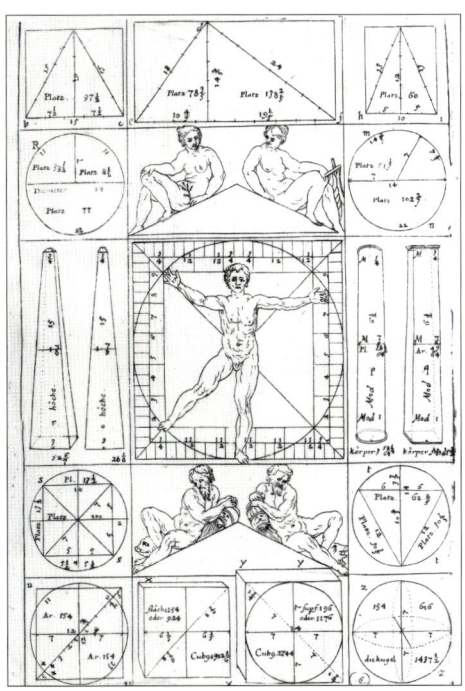

6

Macina Mundi

The industrial revolution marks a date not only indicating that humans have arrived in an era in which they can technically control almost everything, but also proving in world exhibitions that structures with an impressive vertical span and horizontal extension, surpassing anything known up to that moment, can actually be built. A contemporary witness summed up his image of ideal and reality on the occasion of his visit to the Paris world exhibition in 1855: "We should not be surprised that our industrial jubilee has not generated any results in the intellectual (...) field. Being a splendid spectacle to the eyes, an instructive educational work for the practitioner and expert, it has little to offer to the mind. Where in all this lies the sentiment for the superior designation of mankind? Our century neither develops towards the better nor worse, but towards mediocrity".[12]

But this is also the time of misery, of typhus and cholera, a time in which "city" has got nothing in common with the traditions of the ideal cities of the ancient world. It is a time in which Charles Dickens in his novel *Hard Times* and Friedrich Engels in *The Question of Housing* described the city as the most inhospitable place on

dahin Bekannte übertreffen. Ein Zeitzeuge fasst sein Bild von Ideal und Wirklichkeit anlässlich des Besuchs der Weltausstellung 1855 in Paris so zusammen: „Wir dürfen uns nicht wundern, dass unser industrielles Jubiläum nichts auf geistigem (...) Gebiet hervorgebracht hat. Ein großartiges Schauspiel für die Augen, ein lehrreiches Unterrichtswerk für den Praktiker und Fachmann, hat es dem Gedanken wenig zu sagen. Wo ist in all dem das Gefühl für die höhere Bestimmung der Menschheit enthalten? Unser Jahrhundert entwickelt sich weder zum Guten noch zum Bösen hin, sondern zur Mittelmäßigkeit".[12]

Es ist aber auch die Zeit des Elends, des Typhus und der Cholera, eine Zeit, in der Stadt nichts mehr gemein hat mit den Überlieferungen der Idealstädte der Antike. Eine Zeit, in der Charles Dickens in seinem Roman *Hard Times* und Friedrich Engels in *Zur Wohnungsfrage* Stadt als den unwirtlichsten Ort auf Erden beschreiben. Diese Unwirtlichkeit war in allen europäischen Industriemetropolen zu finden.

Es war Ebenezer Howard, der 1898 in England ein neues Konzept der idealen Stadt begründete, die Gartenstadtbewegung. Ihm war es ein Anliegen, Stadt wieder als lebbare Einheit der Harmonie von Mensch und Natur zu gestalten.

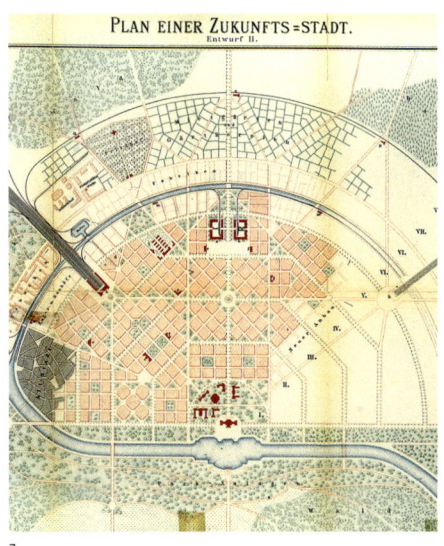

Doch schon zwei Jahre zuvor, 1896, konzipierte der Deutsche Theodor Fritsch ein Konzept der idealen Stadt. Ausgangspunkt für sein Ideal der Gartenstadt war die Kritik an der Bodenspekulation.

„Eine Stadt muss etwas mehr sein als ein Konglomerat von Gebäuden und Menschen. Sie sollte ein organisches Wesen

7 *Die Stadt der Zukunft*, Theodor Fritsch, 1895.
8 Schaubild, Ebenezer Howard, 1898.
9 *Gartenstädte von Morgen*, Ebenezer Howard, 1898.
7 *City of Tomorrow*, Theodor Fritsch, 1895.
8 Chart, Ebenezer Howard, 1898.
9 *Garden Cities of Tomorrow*, Ebenezer Howard, 1898.

7

earth. This inhospitableness existed in the European industrial metropolis.

It was Ebenezer Howard who in 1898 established a new concept of the ideal city in England, the garden city, aiming to return to the design of a city as a viable unity in harmony between mankind and nature.

Two years earlier, in 1896, the German Theodor Fritsch had conceived an image of the ideal city. The initial point for his ideal of the garden city was the criticism of real estate speculation. "A city must be slightly more than a conglomerate of buildings and people. It should be an organic being with sensible structures and equipped with the ability to extend by growth without losing its fundamental nature and becoming disloyal to the laws of its development. Presently several houses that are well habitable are demolished, in order to replace them by a factory. In ten years this factory has to give way because a market hall or railway station needs to be realised in this location (...) An economic distortion of oneself is the characteristic of these aimless heaps of houses. The purpose of this short report is the search for basic rules for future town planning as well as the design of the most important human domiciles according to improved plans and with the introduction of sense and form. What would be the sensible layout of a new city? Part of a sensible order is that same adjoins same and related things are combined. What would be more natural than a spatial division of buildings according to their type and designation? Is it a realistic situation that smoking factories are built next to theatres, museums and churches? How much more economical could the transport between factories and production workshops be if they were located closely together in dense quarters and would be interconnected with roads, rails or maybe even waterways?" [13]

Fritsch designs the ideal of a radial city organized by the division into sectors and functions. He differentiates seven different zones: zone 1—monumental public buildings, zone 2—villas with monumental character, zone 3—better residential buildings, zone 4—residential and commercial buildings, zone 5—working-class dwellings and small workshops, zone 6—factories, building yards and stockyards, zone 7—nurseries, allotments etc.

In the epilogue of the 1912 edition Fritsch however declared his support for the national thought that regards the city as the destruction of the national renewal.[14]

The idea of designing a radially laid out ideal city also existed in Italy in the 1920s and 1930s. In 1928 the

sein mit vernünftiger Gliederung und mit der Fähigkeit ausgestattet, wachsend sich zu erweitern, ohne im Grundwesen zu verlieren und dem Gesetz ihrer Entwicklung untreu zu werden. Heute reißt man einige noch recht wohlbewohnbare Häuser nieder, um eine Fabrik an ihrer Stelle zu errichten. In zehn Jahren muss die Fabrik wieder weichen, weil eine Markthalle oder ein Bahnhof notwendigerweise an diese Stelle kommen muss (...) Ein ökonomisches Sich-Selbst-Verzerren ist ein Merkmal dieser planlosen Häuserhaufen. Der Zweck dieses Schriftchens soll es sein, nach Grundregeln für die Städtebauten der Zukunft zu suchen und die wichtigsten Wohnsitze des Menschen nach besseren Plänen zu gestalten als bisher, ihnen Sinn und Form zu geben. Wie wäre nun eine neue Stadt vernünftig anzulegen? Zu einer vernünftigen Ordnung gehört, dass Gleiches an Gleiches sich anschließt, Verwandtes mit Verwandtem sich paart. Was wäre natürlicher, als dass man eine räumliche Scheidung der Gebäude nach ihrer Bauart und Bestimmung vornähme? Ist es ein realer Zustand, dass man neben den Theatern, Museen und Kirchen rauchende Fabrikflut errichtet? Wie viel sparsamer könnte der Verkehr unter den Fabriken und Produktionswerk-

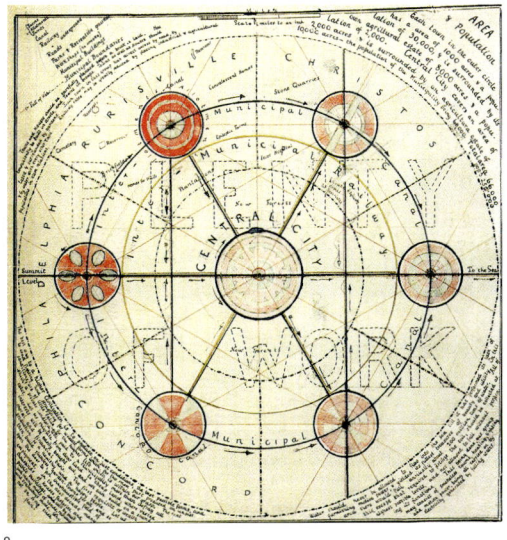
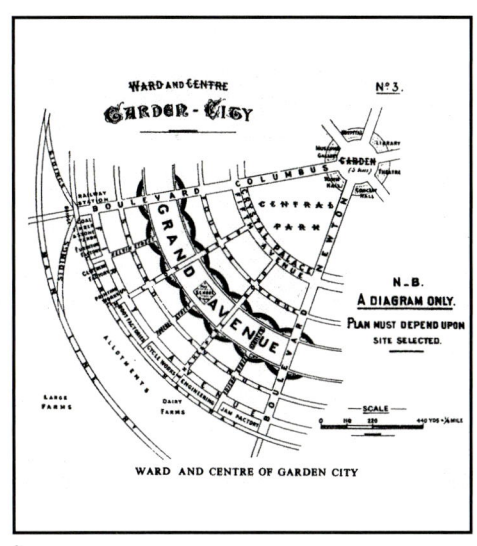

8 9

Pontine Marshes located south of Rome were drained of water over an area totalling 18,000 ha in order to realise this concept. The former Littoria, today called Latina, is one of the cities that were designed on the drawing board and realised. It was adopted by the "Duce" and combined the demand of a social-political presentation with the self-portrayal of Italian Fascism. This becomes especially apparent with the gigantic party forum built on the city's periphery, its plan resembling an "M", and which was therefore referred to as "Palazzo M". This unusual plan was designed in honour of Mussolini.

It took only six months from the decision for the foundation of the city in April 1932 till the settlement of the first 19 families from northern Italy.

The city designed by the planners Frezzotti and Savoia became the provincial capital in 1934. Renowned architects such as Angiolo Mazzoni, who amongst other things planned the Venice railway station, have immortalised themselves in Latina.[15]

Le Corbusier turned to the study of town planning in the 1920s. He regarded town planning as a challenge, which "he dedicated himself to with splendid visions of South American cities: Rio, São Paulo, Montevideo, Buenos Aires, the plan for Algiers (...), where he translated his theoretical concepts into applied projects".[16]

In 1929 Le Corbusier paid a visit to Brazil, during which he took a sightseeing flight over São Paulo that clarified for him the problem of inner-city density and transport, which Le Corbusier called "city centre disease".

A habitable viaduct-like street intersection, located in the city centre, was his visionary answer to reconcile city and individual transport.[17]

It may result from functional correlations as well as a cosmologic "language reflecting the world" that modern architectural foundations of cities again refer to the geometry of the coordinate system and circle.[18]

The most renowned and cited newly founded cities of the last century are Brasilia and Canberra. Both are ideal cities, designed on the drawing board and requiring realisation.

Canberra, Australia's capital, was designed by the architect Walter Burley Griffin and is organised with the help of a cross derived from a land axis and a water axis. The city districts have a circular layout and are divided into rectangles. The capital of Brazil, Brasilia, is also based on the form of a cross, its north-south axis

stätten sein, wenn sie in engen Vierteln dicht beieinander lägen, durch Verkehrswege, Schienengleise, vielleicht sogar durch Wasserstraßen miteinander verbunden?" [13]

Fritsch entwirft das Ideal einer radialen Stadt, die nach Sektoren und Funktionen gegliedert ist. Er unterscheidet sieben Zonen: Zone 1 – monumentale öffentliche Gebäude, Zone 2 – Villen monumentalen Charakters, Zone 3 – bessere Wohnhäuser, Zone 4 – Wohn- und Geschäftshäuser, Zone 5 – Arbeiterwohnungen und kleine Werkstätten, Zone 6 – Fabriken, Bauhöfe und Lagerplätze, Zone 7 – Gärtnereien, Mietgärten etc.

Im Nachwort der Ausgabe von 1912 bekennt sich Fritsch jedoch zum völkischen Gedanken, der Stadt als Vernichtung von völkischer Erneuerung ansieht.[14]

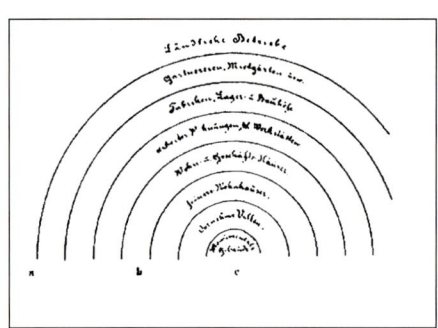

Die Idee einer Neuschöpfung der radial angelegten Idealstadt gab es auch in den 20er und 30er Jahren des 20. Jahrhunderts in Italien. Dafür wurden 1928 die südlich von Rom gelegenen Pontinischen Sümpfe auf einer Fläche von 18.000 ha trockengelegt. Das ehemalige Littoria, heute Latina genannt, ist eine der am Reißbrett entworfenen, realisierten Städte. Sie stand unter Patenschaft des „Duce"

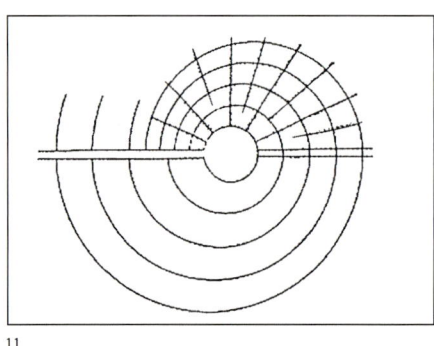

10

10 Zoneneinteilung nach Fritsch.
11 Spiralförmig sich erweiternde Zonen.
12 Erstes Stadium der Bebauung.
13 Th. Fritsch, Stadt mit hunderten Fabrikvorstädten.
14 Stadtplan von Latina.
15 Ansicht Latina.
10 Zone arrangement according to Fritsch.
11 Zones, spirally expanding.
12 First stage of building development.
13 Th. Fritsch, City with hundreds of factory suburbs.
14 City map of Latina.
15 View of Latina.

11

"swinging" upwards, whilst its monumental axis has a west-east orientation.

Brasilia, synonym for Oscar Niemeyer, although the master plan was designed by his mentor Lucio Costa, is regarded as one of the most outstanding examples of town planning of the Modern Age. A drawing-board-architecture that is in our time discussed as a blessing and a curse alike. In those days it was the response to the demand for a city suited for car traffic.

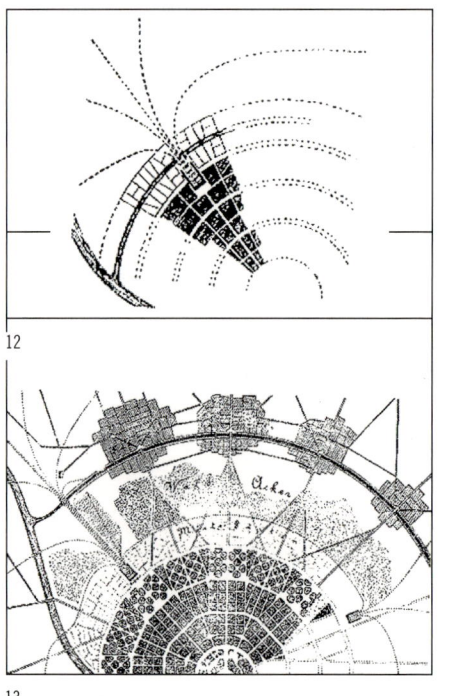

Oscar Niemeyer, who was able to realise many parts of Brasilia, assesses the city project in retrospect as follows: "Initially there was a plan, and now the city is what it is. That is why I am sad. He [Lucio Costa] designed a significant part of the architecture in the monumental area as well as several buildings in the city, and subsequently the people have disorganised the whole creation. The architecture in Brasilia's side streets is appalling. Long gone are the times when the place had an architectural unity (...) In Brasilia the banks tried to assert dreadful conditions, I was very disappointed".[19]

The concept of the city suited for motor traffic as well as the separation of residential and working areas lasted until the 1970s. Oscar Niemeyer has still not given up his dream of the ideal city, when he muses: "We can always dream a little and present our modest proposal for a city of the future." Nevertheless he soberingly admits: "When considering town planning, the young architect becomes very frustrated, especially when he is confronted with a site being cut up into small parts and merely intended for the profit of real estate agencies." [20]

Today we know that the ideal of the city suited for car traffic was a mistake; whether it is new cities such as

30

und verband den Anspruch einer sozialpolitischen Darstellung mit der Selbstdarstellung des italienischen Faschismus. Dies zeigt sich insbesondere dadurch, dass an der Peripherie der Stadt ein gigantisches Parteiforum gebaut wurde, welches im Grundriss ein M darstellt und daher auch „Palazzo M" genannt wurde. Dieser ungewöhnliche Grundriss wurde zu Ehren von Mussolini entworfen.

Von der Entscheidung zur Stadtgründung im April 1932 bis zur Besiedelung durch die ersten 19 Familien aus Norditalien vergingen nur sechs Monate.

Die von den Planern Frezzotti und Savoia konzipierte Stadt wurde 1934 Provinzhauptstadt. Namhafte Architekten wie Angiolo Mazzoni, der auch den Bahnhof in Venedig geplant hat, haben sich in Latina verewigt.[15]

Le Corbusier wendet sich in den 20er Jahren dem Studium des Städtebaus zu. Stadtplanung ist für ihn eine Herausforderung, „der er sich mitgroßartigen Visionen südamerikanischer Städte widmet: Rio, São Paulo, Montevideo, Buenos Aires, der Plan für Algier (...), bei denen er seine theoretischen Konzepte in angewandte Projekte umwandelt".[16]

Im Jahr 1929 besuchte Le Corbusier Brasilien. Ein Rundflug über São Paulo verdeutlichte ihm die Problematik der innerstädtischen Verdichtung und des Verkehrs, von ihm „Stadtmittelpunktkrankheit" genannt.

14

15

Brasilia and Chandighar in India or European metropolises attesting this mistake, which has cut up our cities with broad "divisions". Tunnels and bridges presently try to mitigate these divisions for car traffic. At the close of the 20th and the beginning of the 21st century, urban renewal projects are one of the most essential characteristics of town planning.

What do the concepts, the ideals of the 21st century city look like? How strongly the ideas of the ideal city of the future presently differ shall be representatively verified by two significant opinions.

Frei Otto, renowned for his roof over of the Munich Olympic Stadium, questions past town planning: "Look at our cities; we cannot progress with the usual repertoire of architecture, which is outdated. Especially the grid network, which the antiquity is responsible for, cannot be applied to building lively cities. It's about time to test something new."[21]

The building historian Wolfgang Schäche has pleaded for the city of the future during the UIA World Congress 2002 in Berlin: "The traditional middle-class city, however, proved and proves to be a model generating urbanly that principally withstood all social processes and movements. It is the only realistic model for the city of the 21st century."[22] The conceptions of the future city cannot be expressed more diametrically opposed.

Meinhard von Gerkan's design for the ideal city of Luchao takes reference from the failed concepts of the past. His ideal vision of a city reconciles the elements of the garden city with urbanity. The car deserves respect just as do the pedestrian. The city's centre as an open space, a lake, is a generous centre for the citizen, there-

Ein bewohnbares viaduktartiges Straßenkreuz, das seinen Schnittpunkt in der Mitte der Stadt hat, war seine visionäre Antwort, Stadt und Individualverkehr miteinander zu versöhnen.¹⁷

Dass sich auch die Stadtgründungen moderner Architektur auf die Geometrie, des Achsenkreuzes und des Kreises beziehen, mag sich zum einen aus funktionellen Zusammenhängen ergeben und zum anderen aus einer kosmologischen „Sprache, die die Welt spiegelt".¹⁸

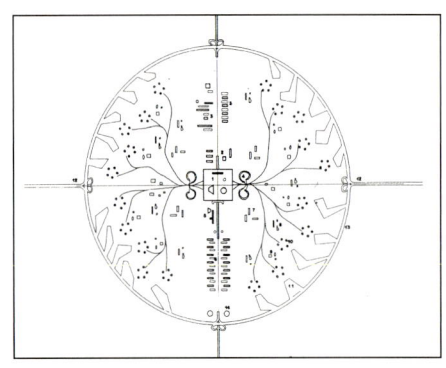

16

Die uns bekannten und wohl am meisten zitierten Stadtneugründungen des letzten Jahrhunderts sind Brasilia und Canberra. Beides Idealstädte, am Reißbrett entworfen, mit dem Anspruch, sie zu realisieren.

Canberra, die Hauptstadt Australiens, entworfen von dem Architekten Walter Burley Griffin, ist durch ein Kreuz aus einer Landachse und einer Wasserachse gegliedert. Die Stadtteile sind kreisförmig angelegt und in Rechtecke unterteilt. Auch der Hauptstadt Brasiliens, Brasilia, liegt die Form eines Kreuzes zu Grunde. Die Nord-Südachse des Kreuzes „schwingt" dabei nach oben, während die Monumentalachse von Westen nach Osten verläuft.

Brasilia, Synonym für Oscar Niemeyer, der Masterplan jedoch von seinem Lehrer Lucio Costa entworfen, gilt als eines der herausragenden Beispiele des Städtebaus der Moderne. Eine Reißbrettarchitektur, die man heute gleichermaßen als Fluch und Segen diskutieren kann. Damals war es die Antwort auf die Forderung nach einer autogerechten Stadt.

Oscar Niemeyer, der viele Teile Brasilias realisieren

16 Oscar Niemeyer, Entwurf für die Stadt von Morgen, 1979.
17 Le Corbusier, Skizze São Paulo, 1929.
18 Le Corbusier, Masterplan Chandigarh, 1922.
19 Stadtplan Brasilia, „südlicher Flügel".
20 Brasilia-Skizze von Lucio Costa.
21 Umfahrbare Stadt in der Negev-Wüste, Oscar Niemeyer, 1964.
22 Friedhelm Fischer, Stadtplan Canberra, 1911.
16 Oscar Niemeyer, Design for the city of tomorrow, 1979.
17 Le Corbusier, Sketch of São Paulo, 1929.
18 Le Corbusier, Masterplan of Chandighar, 1922.
19 City map of Brasilia, "southern wing".
20 Brasilia sketch by Lucio Costa.
21 City in the Negev desert, Oscar Niemeyer, 1964.
22 Friedhelm Fischer, City map of Canberra, 1911.

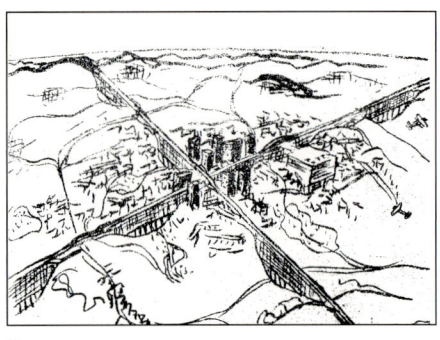

17

fore sparing Lingang New City the "city centre disease", as Le Corbusier called it. Residential and working areas are separated where it is inevitable and combined where it is necessary to generate an urban density.

Meinhard von Gerkan's reasoning is that: "The city has to be a pulsating organism, with short distances that can be covered by foot or by train." ²³

"In the model the planned harbour city appears like the revival of past city utopias, it is reminiscent of

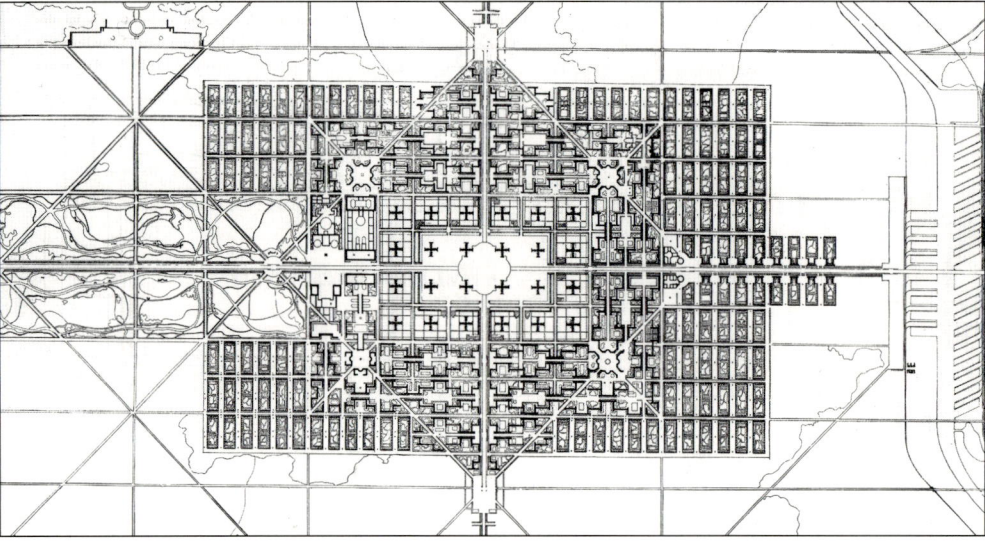

18

konnte, bewertet das Stadtgründungsprojekt im Nachhinein wie folgt: „Am Anfang gab es einen Plan, und nun ist die Stadt wie sie ist. Deswegen bin ich traurig. Er [Lucio Costa] entwarf einen wichtigen Teil der Architektur im monumentalen Bereich und einige andere Gebäude in der Stadt, dann haben die Menschen das ganze Gebilde in eine große Unordnung gebracht. In Brasilias Nebenstraßen ist die Architektur schrecklich. Die Zeiten, als der Ort eine architektonische Einheit aufwies, sind lange vorbei (...) In Brasilia versuchen die Banken, einen fürchterlichen Zustand durchzusetzen, ich bin sehr enttäuscht gewesen".[19]

Die Konzeption der autogerechten Stadt sowie der Trennung von Wohnen und Arbeiten reichte noch bis in die 70er Jahre des 20. Jahrhunderts hinein. Den Traum von der idealen Stadt hat Oscar Niemeyer bis heute nicht aufgegeben, wenn er sinniert: „Aber wir können immer ein wenig träumen und unseren bescheidenen Vorschlag für eine Stadt der Zukunft präsentieren." Gleichwohl gibt er ernüchternd zu: „Was die Stadtplanung angeht, so wird hier der junge Architekt ganz besonders frustriert, nämlich besonders dann, wenn er den Boden in kleinen Teilchen zerschnitten sieht und dieser allein für den Profit der Immobiliengesellschaften vorgesehen ist."[20]

Heute wissen wir, dass das Ideal der autogerechten Stadt ein Irrweg war, seien es neue Städte wie Brasilia und Chandighar in Indien oder die europäischen Metropolen, die diesen Irrweg bezeugen, der unsere Städte durch breite „Schneisen" zerschnitten hat; Schneisen für den Autoverkehr, die man heute mit Tunneln und Brücken zu entschärfen sucht. Stadtreparatur ist eines der wesentlichsten Merkmale des Städtebaus am Ende des 20. und zu Beginn dieses Jahrhunderts.

Doch wie sehen die Konzepte, die Ideale der Stadt für das 21. Jahrhundert aus? Wie weit auch heute die Vorstellungen der idealen Stadt der Zukunft auseinander gehen, sollen hier stellvertretend zwei Auffassungen von bedeutenden Zeitzeugen belegen.

Frei Otto, bekannt durch die Überdachung des Olympiastadions München, stellt den vergangenen Städtebau in Frage: „Schauen Sie sich unsere Städte an; mit dem üblichen Repertoire der Architektur kommen wir da nicht mehr weiter, das ist veraltet. Gerade mit dem Rasternetz der Straßen, das uns die Antike eingebrockt hat, kann man keine lebendigen Städte bauen. Es wäre an der Zeit, etwas Neues zu erproben."[21]

Der Bauhistoriker Wolfgang Schäche hat sein Plädoyer für die Stadt der Zukunft auf dem UIA-Kongress 2002 in Berlin gehalten: „Die traditionelle bürgerliche Stadt erwies und erweist sich hingegen als ein nach wie vor urbani-

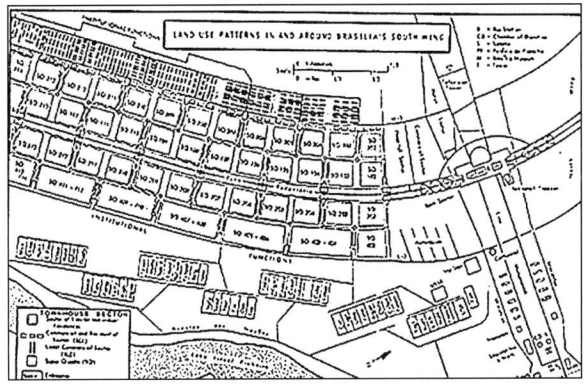
19

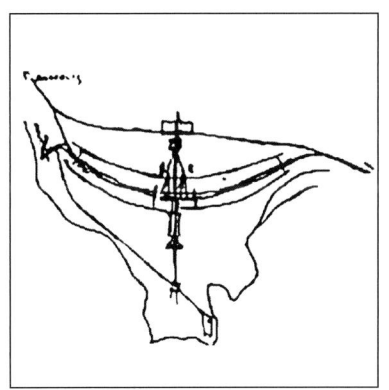
20

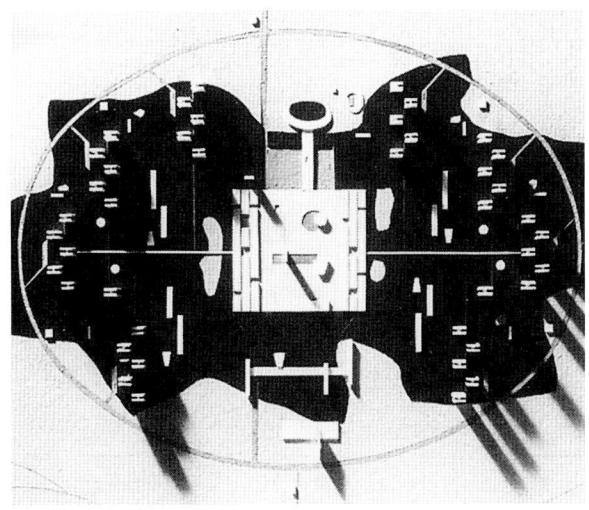
21

22

tätsschaffendes Modell, das allen gesellschaftlichen Prozessen und Bewegungen im Prinzip standgehalten hat. Es ist das einzig realistische Modell für die Stadt des 21. Jahrhunderts." [22]

Diametraler können die Vorstellungen über die zukünftige Stadt nicht zum Ausdruck gebracht werden.

Meinhard von Gerkans Entwurf für die ideale Stadt Lingang New City reflektiert die gescheiterten Konzepte der Vergangenheit. In seiner idealen Stadtvision versöhnt er Elemente der Gartenstadt mit Urbanität. Das Auto bekommt seine Berechtigung genauso wie der Fußgänger. Die Mitte der Stadt, ein See, ist als großer Freiraum eine Mitte für den Bürger, so dass Luchao von der „Stadtmittelpunktkrankheit", wie Le Corbusier es bezeichnet, verschont bleibt. Wohnen und Arbeiten sind getrennt, wo es unvermeidlich ist, und zusammengefügt, wo es notwendig ist, eine urbane Dichte zu erzeugen.

Denn, so Meinhard von Gerkan: „Die Stadt muss ein pulsierender Organismus sein, mit kurzen Wegen, die man zu Fuß oder mit der Bahn zurücklegen kann." [23]

„Im Modell wirkt die geplante Hafenstadt wie die Wiederbelebung vergangener Stadtutopien, sie erinnern an Vitruvs kreisförmige Idealstadt, auch an das klassische Bagdad, die vorhellenistischen, iranisch-mesopotamischen Stadtmodelle", schreibt Niklas Maak in seinem Artikel über die Wiedergeburt der Idealstadt. „Doch das Zentrum von Gerkans Idealstadt ist kein kosmisches Sternornament mit dem Bild des Herrschers (...) sondern ein kreisrunder See." [24]

So nennt der Architekt denn auch seine Stadt: „Lingang New City – Aus einem Tropfen geboren".

Bernd Pastuschka

Vitruvius's circular ideal city, also of the classic Baghdad, the pre-Hellenistic, Iranian-Mesopotamian city models", writes Niklas Maak in his article on the rebirth of the ideal city. "The centre of von Gerkan's ideal city does not however resemble a cosmic star pattern with the ruler's image (...) but is a circular lake." [24]

As a consequence the architect names his city: "Lingang New City – Born from a Drop".

Bernd Pastuschka

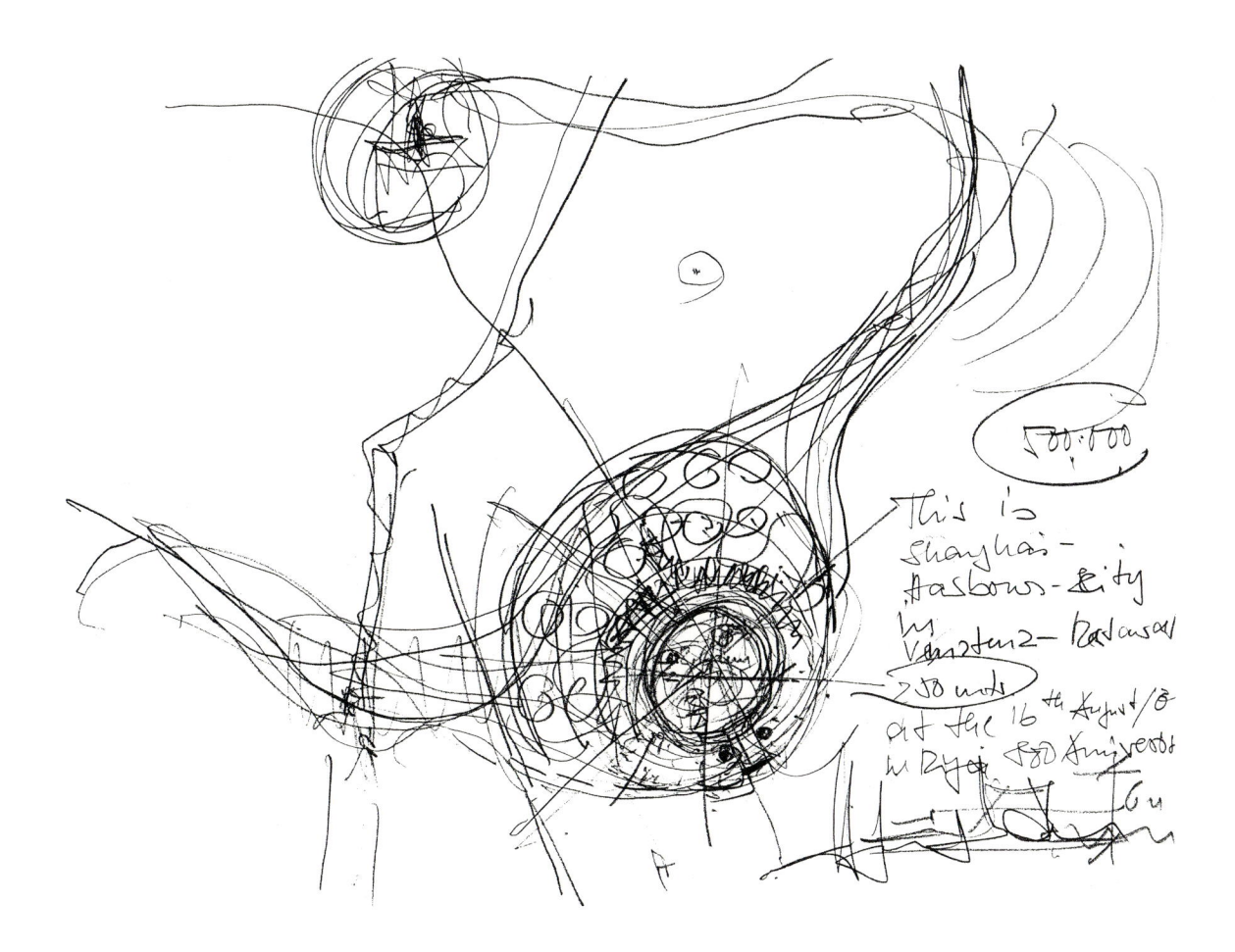

Anmerkungen/Literatur

01 W. Siebel, Hrsg., Die europäische Stadt,, Frankfurt am Main 2004

02 Leonardo Benevolo, Die Stadt in der Europäischen Geschichte, München 1993

1 H. Klüver, Alles Schlechte abreißen, in: Süddeutsche Zeitung, München, 4./5./6. Januar 2003

2 H.W. Kruft, Geschichte der Theorie, München, 1991, S. 16

3 T. Schabert, Stadtarchitektur – Spiegel der Welt, Zürich, 1990

4 Offenbarung des Johannes, Kap. 21, Vers 10–14 (Luther-Übersetzung)

5 vgl. T. Schabert, a.a.O., S. 25

6 R. Eaton, Die ideale Stadt. Von der Antike bis zur Gegenwart, Berlin, 2001, S. 12 f.; Abb. 1, 5, 7, 8

7 T. Schabert, a.a.O., S. 27; Abb. 2, 3

8 ebd., S. 27

9 H.W. Kruft, a.a.O., S. 28; Abb. 4, 6, 9

10 G. Jaaks, Der Traum von der Stadt am Meer. Hafenstädte aus aller Welt, Hamburg, 2003, darin: Valerio Casali, Le Corbusier in Venedig, S. 154

11 T. Schabert, a.a.O., S. 96

12 L. Benevolo, Geschichte der Architektur des 19. und 20. Jahrhunderts, Bd. 1., München, 1994, S. 185 f.

13 Th. Fritsch, Die Stadt der Zukunft, Leipzig, 1895, vgl. auch: www.idg.de; Abb. 10, 11, 12, 13

14 Ch. Kühberger, Faschistische Selbstdarstellung, Berlin, 2001

15. vgl. auch: Associazione culturale Novecento, www.Nonsololatina.it; Abb. 14, 15

16 G. Jaaks, a.a.O., S. 147

17 O. Niemeyer, Eine Legende der Moderne, Frankfurt, 2003, S. 38; Abb. 16, 17, 21

18 T. Schabert, a.a.O.

19 O. Niemeyer, a.a.O., S.41

20 ebd., S. 43, vgl. auch: Hamburger Architektur Sommer 1997, Veranstaltung BDB Werkstattgespräch, Prof. Sharma
und Prof. Lambert Rosenbusch, Le Corbusiers Konzept für Chandighar, www.tu-harburg.de

21 H. Rauterberg, Der Herr des Augenblicks, in: Die Zeit, Hamburg, 2. Januar 2003

22 W. Schäche, Es funktioniert einfach nicht, in: Die Welt, Hamburg, 21. Oktober 2002

23 M. Wellershoff, Wollen Sie hier leben?, in: Kulturspiegel, Heft 4, April 2003

24 N. Maak, Wiedergeburt der Idealstadt, in: Frankfurter Allgemeine Zeitung, 7. Oktober 2002

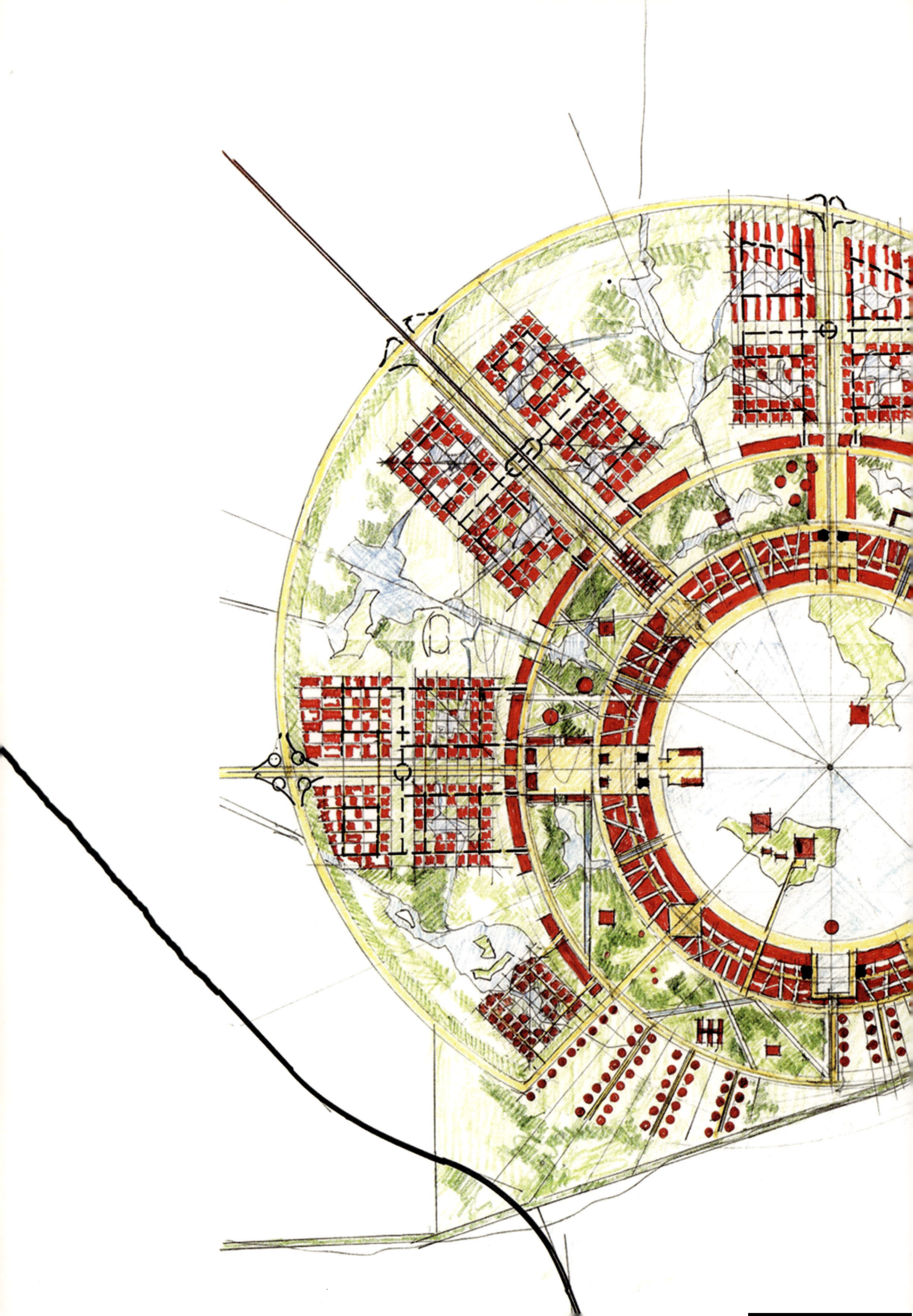

„Jede Lösung hat für mich jedoch etwas mit Dialog zu tun, die gestellte Frage muss analysiert werden: erstens Shanghai, zweitens neuer Hafen, Seefahrt, Handel und zum Dritten die exponierte Lage an der Küste, d.h. die Auseinandersetzung mit dem Wasser."

"Each solution has something to do with dialogue, the asked question has to be analyzed: first Shanghai, secondly the new harbour, seafaring, trade and as thirdly the exposed location on the coast – to be in dialogue with the sea."

„Wir schlagen einen zentralen See vor, darum wird sich ringförmig der Central Business Bereich legen. Die Form des Sees folgt exakt der Kreisform, wir haben es ja mit künstlichen Setzungen zu tun, brauchen keine natürlichen Formen zu klonen, sondern nutzen die Metapher eines Tropfens, der ins Wasser fällt und konzentrische Kreise zieht."

"We propose a central lake, around which the central business area will be built. The form of the lake will be a precise circle. As we are dealing with an artificial feature, there is no need to clone natural forms. Instead we will use the metaphor of a drop falling into the water and creating concentric ripples."

Unten links: Satellitenaufnahme vor der Landgewinnung.
Bottom Left: Satellite photo before the land reclamation.
Unten Rechts: Satellitenaufnahme von der Landgewinnung für Lingang New City, 2003.
Bottom right: Satellite photo of the land reclamation for Lingang New City, 2003.

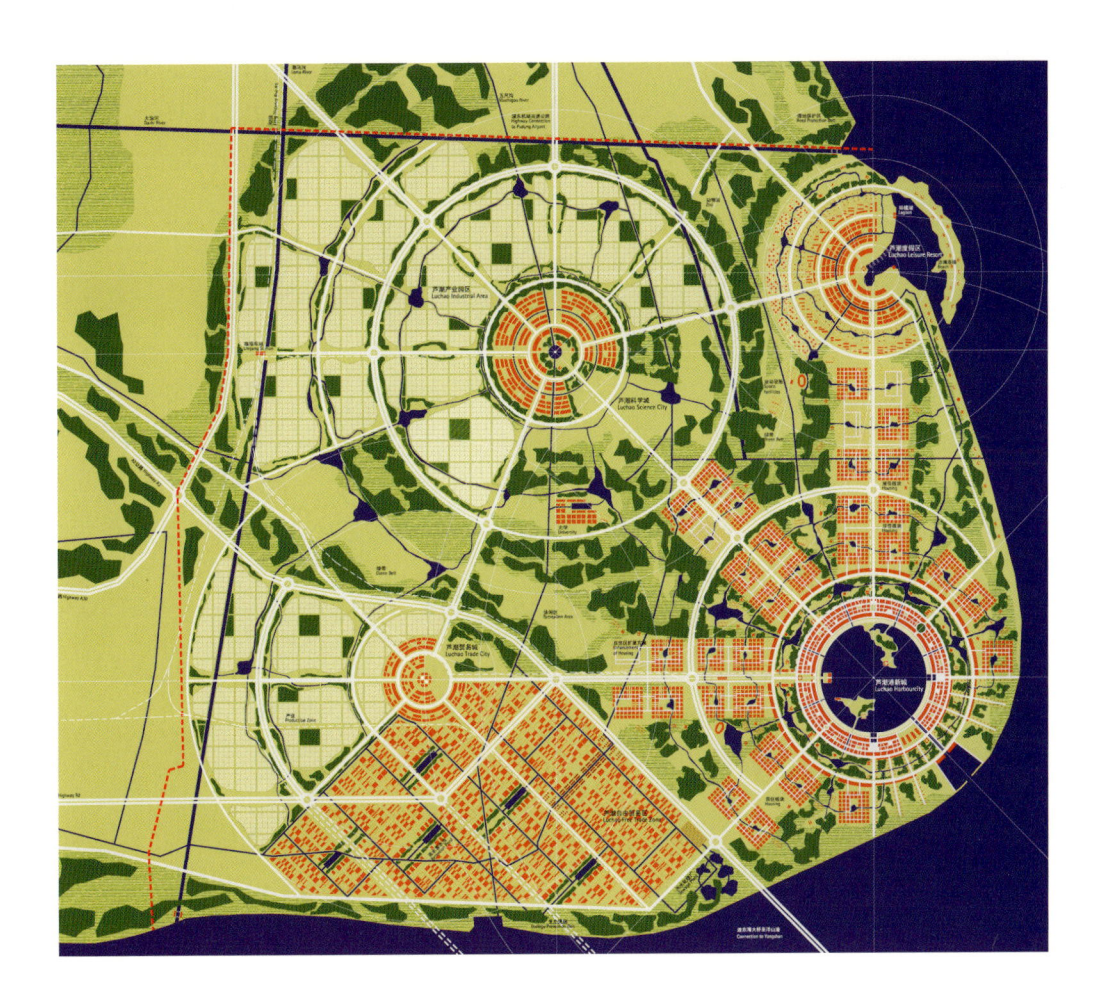

Lingang New City – Eine Großstadt im Chinesischen Meer

Shanghai

Shanghai ist ein wichtiges Wirtschaftszentrum und zugleich Verkehrsknotenpunkt innerhalb Chinas. Als historisch und kulturell bedeutende Stadt soll sich Shanghai zukünftig zu einer internationalen Wirtschafts-, Finanz- und Handelsmetropole weiterentwickeln.

Die rasch zunehmende Einwohnerzahl Shanghais von heute fast 13 Millionen wird im Jahr 2020 bereits 16 Millionen betragen, darin enthalten allein eine städtische Bevölkerungszahl von 13,6 Millionen. Das Stadtzentrum Shanghais

Lingang New City – A Metropolis in the East China Sea

Shanghai

Shanghai is both a significant commercial centre and at the same time a traffic junction within China. There are plans to develop Shanghai, a historically and culturally important city, into an international commercial, financial and trade metropolis in the future. The rapidly increasing population of Shanghai, today nearly 13 million, will reach 16 million by 2020, 13.6 million of which will live in the city. Shanghai's city centre will then have an estimated surface area of 600 km^2 and approximately eight million inhabitants.

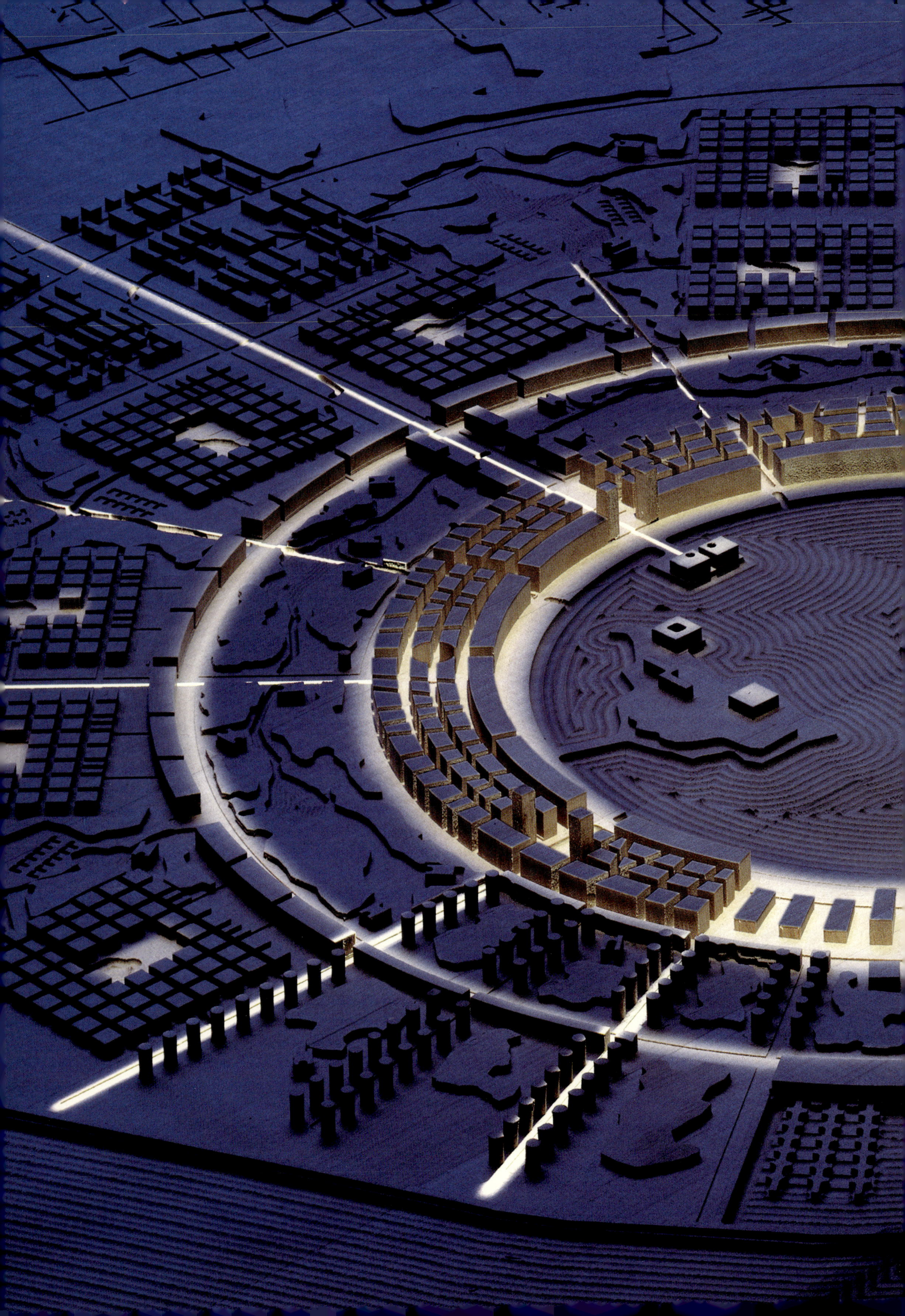

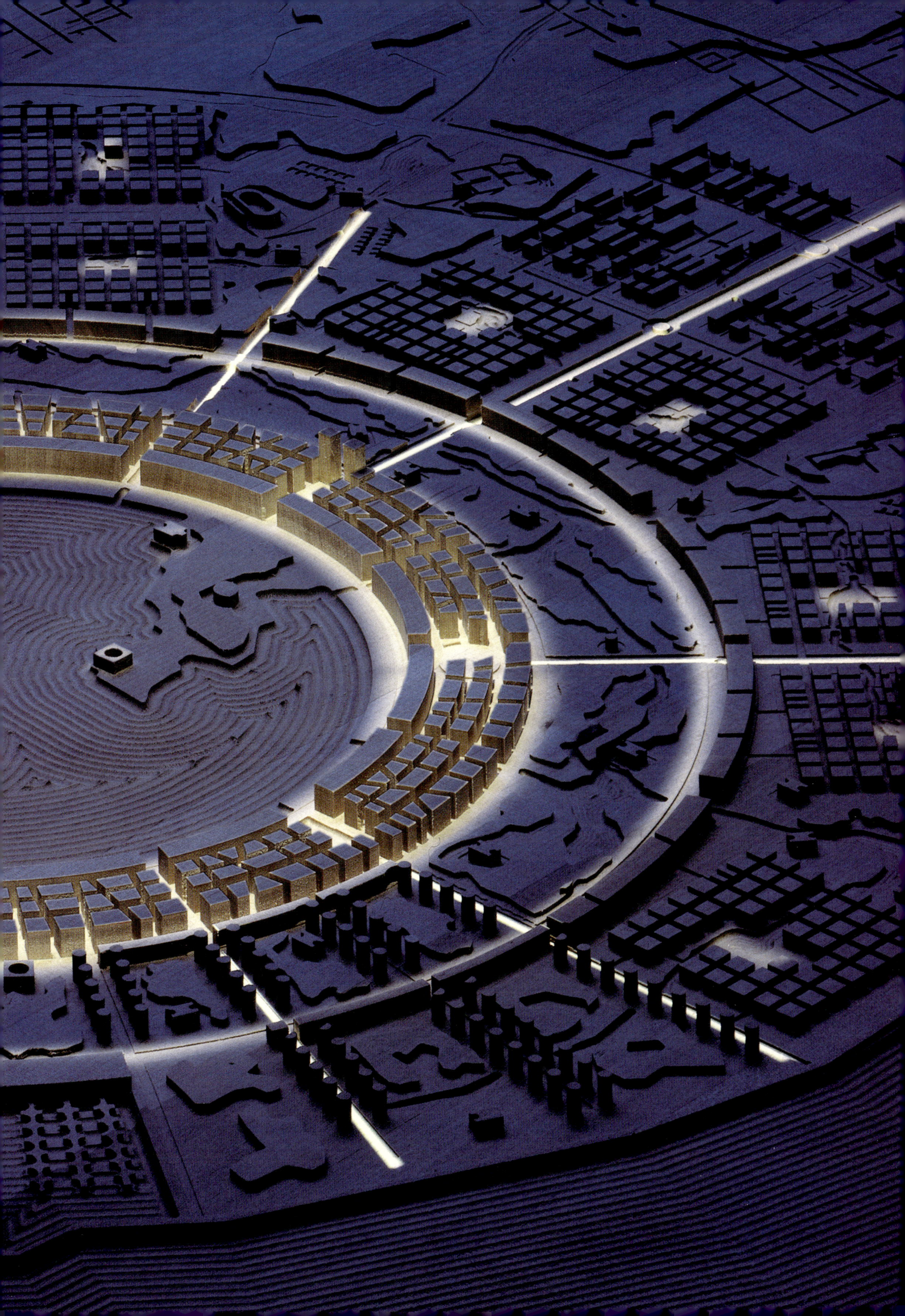

wird im Jahr 2020 eine geschätzte Fläche von 600 km² und ca. acht Millionen Einwohner haben.

Um das enorme Bevölkerungs- und Industriewachstum von Shanghai aufzunehmen, lobte das dortige Stadtplanungsamt einen internationalen Wettbewerb zur Planung einer neuen Hafenstadt in Zusammenhang mit dem internationalen Container-Tiefseehafen Yangshan aus. Der erste Preis des mehrstufigen Wettbewerbs ging an das Hamburger Architekturbüro gmp – von Gerkan, Marg und Partner.

Die neugeplante Satellitenstadt Lingang New City soll auf ca. 74 km² Platz für 450.000 Einwohner bieten und stellt neben Chandighar, Brasilia und Canberra die einzige Stadtneugründung dieser Größenordnung während der letzten hundert Jahre dar.

Städtebauliches Konzept

Das Konzept von Lingang New City greift die Ideale der tradierten europäischen Stadt auf und verbindet sie mit einer „revolutionären" Idee: Den Mittelpunkt bildet – anstelle eines baulich verdichteten Stadtzentrums – ein kreisrunder See von 2,5 km Durchmesser und eine 8 km lange Seepromenade mit einem Badestrand à la Copa Cabana im Herzen der Stadt. Kulturbauten und Freizeitangebote sind auf Inseln situiert und per Schiff erreichbar.

Die Stadt Alexandria als eines der sieben Weltwunder stand Pate für den Entwurf; die Lebensqualität durch die Nähe zum Wasser bezieht sich auf Referenzen aus Hamburg.

Das Bild konzentrischer Wellen, die durch einen ins Wasser fallenden Tropfen gebildet werden, ist das metaphorische Leitbild der ganzen Stadtstruktur. Dieser Allegorie entsprechend gliedern sich die Nutzungsstrukturen in konzentrischen Ringen von innen nach außen um den zentralen Lake Luchao: von der Promenade über einen Businessdistrikt mit hoher Verdichtung, einen 500 m breiten, ringförmigen Stadtpark mit solitär eingelagerten öffentlichen Bauten bis hin zu den blockartigen Wohnquartieren für jeweils 13.000 Menschen.

Der Stadtring zwischen Seepromenade und Grüngürtel, der Businessdistrikt, bildet das Zentrum des städtischen Lebens. Hier befinden sich in Mischnutzung Büros, Geschäfte, Einkaufspassagen, Fußgängerzonen und verdichtetes Wohnen.

Die konzentrische Struktur wird von radialen Strahlen in Form von Straßen und Wegen nach dem Prinzip einer Windrose überlagert. Sie geben der Stadt ein klares Ordnungsprinzip und unterteilen die bebauten Ringe in

In order to accommodate the huge growth of population and industry in Shanghai, the city-planning department conducted an international competition for the planning of a new harbour city that incorporates the international deep-sea container harbour Yangshan. The first prize of the competition, which took place in several stages, was awarded to the Hamburg architects' office gmp – von Gerkan, Marg und Partner.

The newly-planned satellite city Lingang New City is intended to provide space for 450,000 inhabitants in an area of 74 km² and represents, alongside Chandighar, Brasilia and Canberra, the only city of this scale to be founded in the past hundred years.

Urban Planning Concept

The concept for Lingang New City takes up the ideals of the traditional European city and combines it with a "revolutionary" idea: instead of a high-density centre, the focal point will be a circular lake with a diameter of 2.5 km and an 8 km lakeside promenade with a bathing beach à la Copa Cabana in the heart of the city. Cultural buildings and leisure facilities are located on islands which can be accessed by boat.

The design was inspired by the city of Alexandria, one of the Seven Wonders of the World; the quality of life provided by the close proximity to water draws its references from Hamburg.

The whole city structure is based on the metaphor of an image of concentric ripples, formed by a drop falling into water. In line with this allegory, the utility structures are ordered in the form of concentric rings spreading outwards from the central Lake Luchao: from the promenade, through to the extremely dense business district, a circular city park, 500 m in width which incorporates solitary public buildings, to the block-like living quarters for 13,000 inhabitants respectively.

The city ring between the lakeside promenade and the green belt, the business district, forms the centre of city-life. A mix of offices, shops, arcades, pedestrian precincts and dense living space is located here.

The concentric structure is layered following the principle of a compass rose, the streets and pathways radiate out from the centre. These provide the city with a clear, ordered structure and divide the built-up rings into separate sectors. In this way, an ideal network of access is created, within which the city can also expand above and beyond the planned scale. The countryside penetrates like wedges as far as the second ring.

einzelne Sektoren. Auf diese Weise entsteht ein ideales Erschließungsnetz, innerhalb dessen sich die Stadt auch über das geplante Maß hinaus erweitern kann. Die Landschaft dringt keilförmig bis zum zweiten Ring vor. Wasserläufe und kleine Seen durchdringen alle Quartiere und thematisieren das „Wohnen am Wasser" in zahlreichen Varianten. Das öffentliche Verkehrssystem mit Light-Trains auf Straßenniveau funktioniert als Ringbahn mit angehängten Schleifen.

Realisierung

Im Jahr 2006 soll bereits der erste Bauabschnitt der neuen Stadt für 80.000 Einwohner auf dem Gebiet des heutigen Festlandes abgeschlossen sein. Zweiter und dritter Bauabschnitt folgen bis zum Jahr 2020. Das hierfür benötigte Areal wird durch Aufschüttung dem Ozean abgerungen. Im Zuge dieser Landgewinnung entsteht auch der Dishui Lake– heute noch Teil des Ozeans – als Mittelpunkt der neuen Hafenstadt.

Unser Büro ist zurzeit mit den Planungen der Wolkennadel (Seite 61), des ersten Abschnittes mit einer Länge von 2 Kilometern des sogenannten Neuen Bundes (Seite 76), der Insel der Arbeit, der Western Island (Seite 54) sowie des Marinemuseums (Seite 100) und des ihm gegenüberliegenden Rathauses (Seite 104) befasst.

Meinhard von Gerkan

Waterways and small lakes extend into all quarters, underlining the central theme of "waterside living" in a wide variety of forms. The public transport system with light-trains at street level functions as a circular railway with adjoining loops.

Realisation

The first construction phase of the new city for 80,000 inhabitants in the present mainland area should be completed by 2005. The second and third phase of construction will follow until 2020. The area required for this will be dragged up from the ocean by means of an earth bank. In the process of obtaining this land, the Dishui Lake – today still part of the ocean – will be formed as the central point of the new harbour city.

At present our practice is planning the Cloud Needle (page 61), the first segment with a length of 2 kilometres of the so called New Bund (page 76), the Island of Work, the Western Island (page 54) as well as the Maritime Museum (page 100) and the opposite Shanghai Nanhui District Administration Centre (page 104).

Meinhard von Gerkan

Dishui Lake, August 2004.
Dishui Lake, August 2004.

Nutzungsverteilung Maps of Use

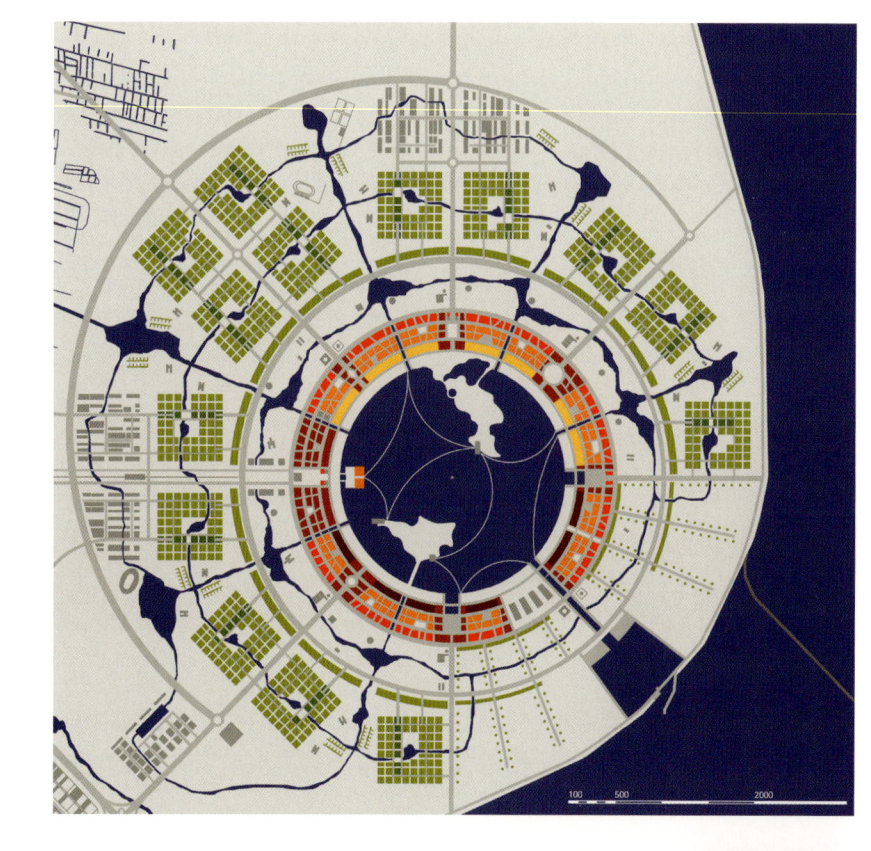

100% Dienstleistung
100% service

60% Dienstl., 40% Büro
60% service, 40% office

40% Wohnen, 30% Dienstl., 30% Büro
40% resid., 30% service, 30% office

50% Dienstl., 50% Büro
50% service, 50% office

100 % Büro
100 % office

85% Wohnen, 15% Dienstl.
85% residential, 15% service

100% Wohnen
100% residential

Konzerthalle
Concert hall

Museum
Museum

Theater
Theatre

Mehrzweckhalle
Multipurpose hall

Industrieausstellung
Industrial exhibition

Bücherei
Library

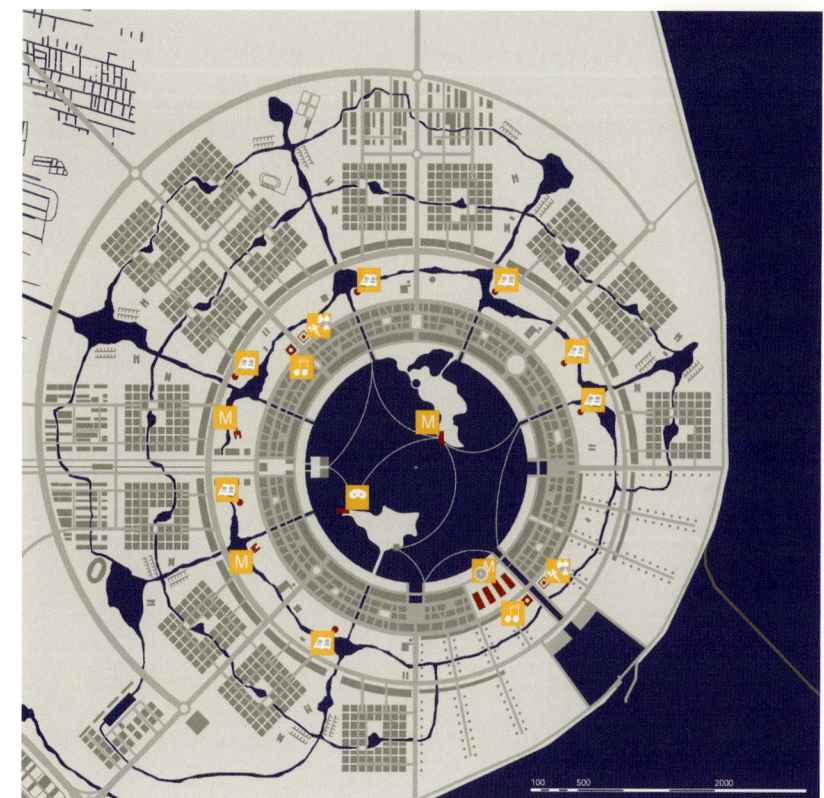

44

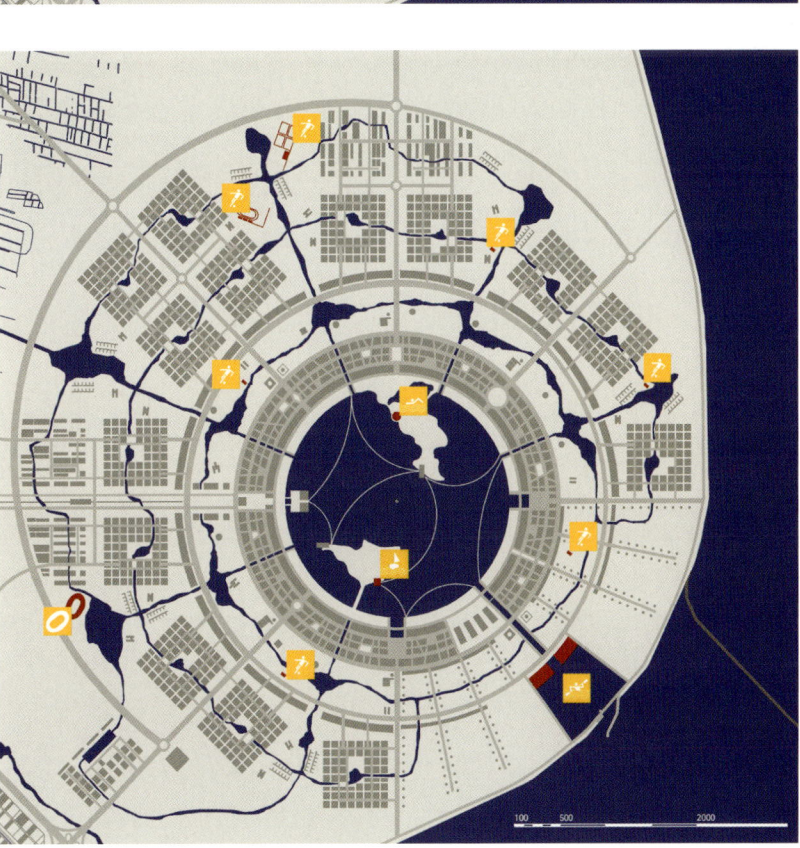

●	**Kindergarten** / Kindergarten
●	**Grundschule** / Primary school
●	**Weiterführende Schule** / Secondary school
●	**Berufsschule** / Vocational school
●	**Universität** / University

⛹	**Sportplatz** / Sports field
🏟	**Stadion** / Stadium
🏊	**Schwimmbad** / Swimming pool
⚓	**Yachthafen** / Marina
🏄	**Wassersport** / Aquatic sport

Lingang New City

45

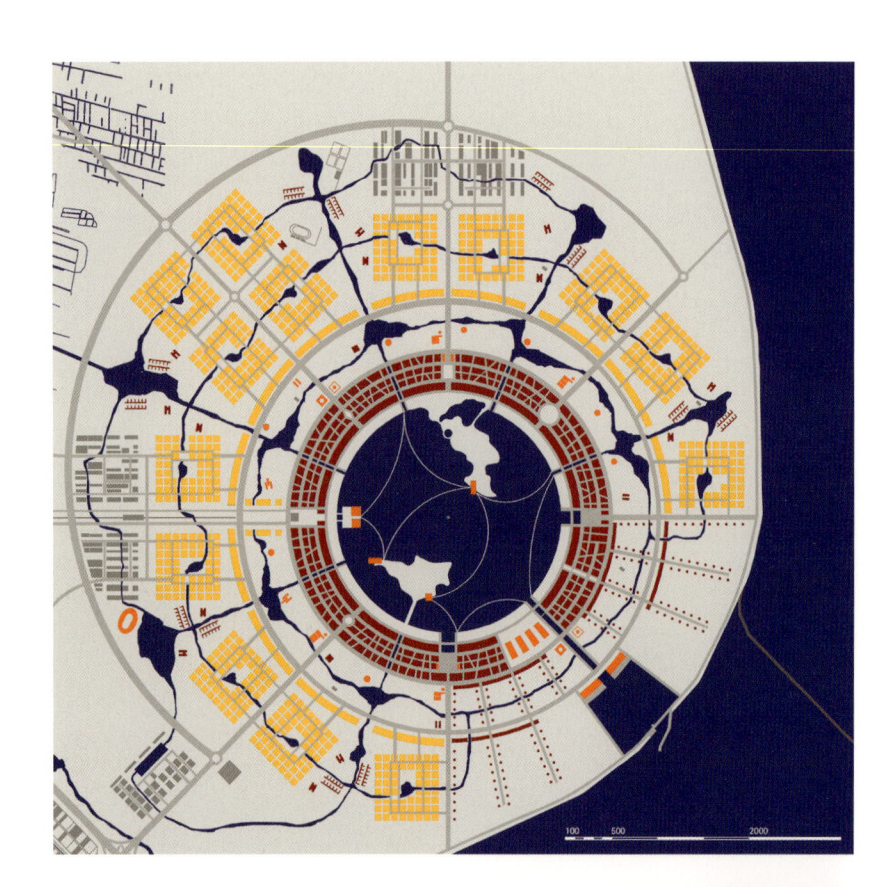

Glas, Stahl
Glass, steel
Ziegel
Brick
Putz und Naturstein
Plaster and natural stone

Stadteingänge und Plätze
City accesses and squares

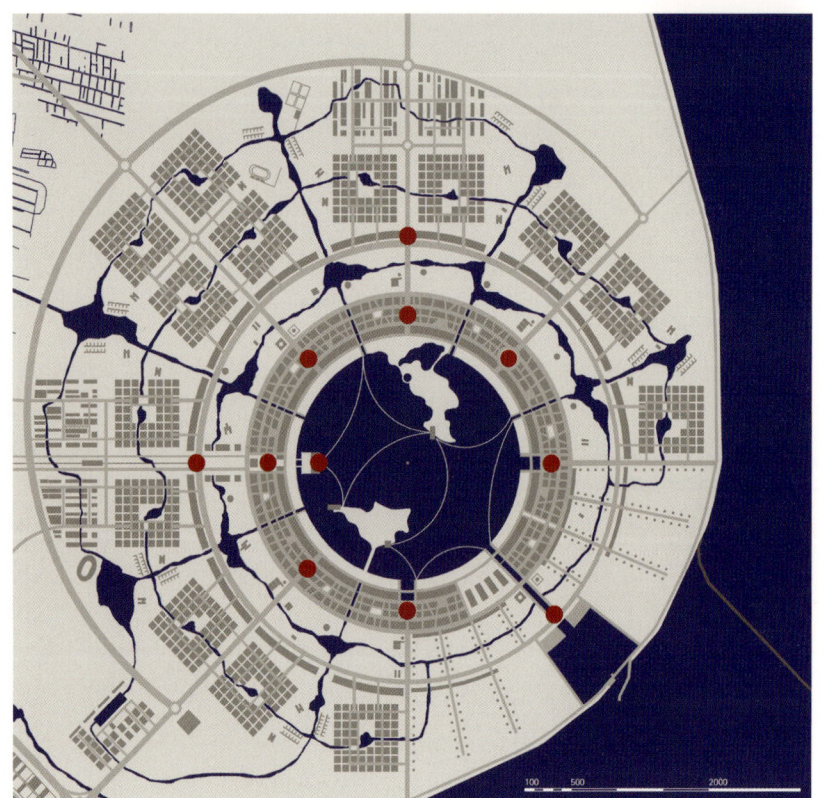

46

Materialkonzept **Materials**
Nutzungsverteilung **Maps of Use**

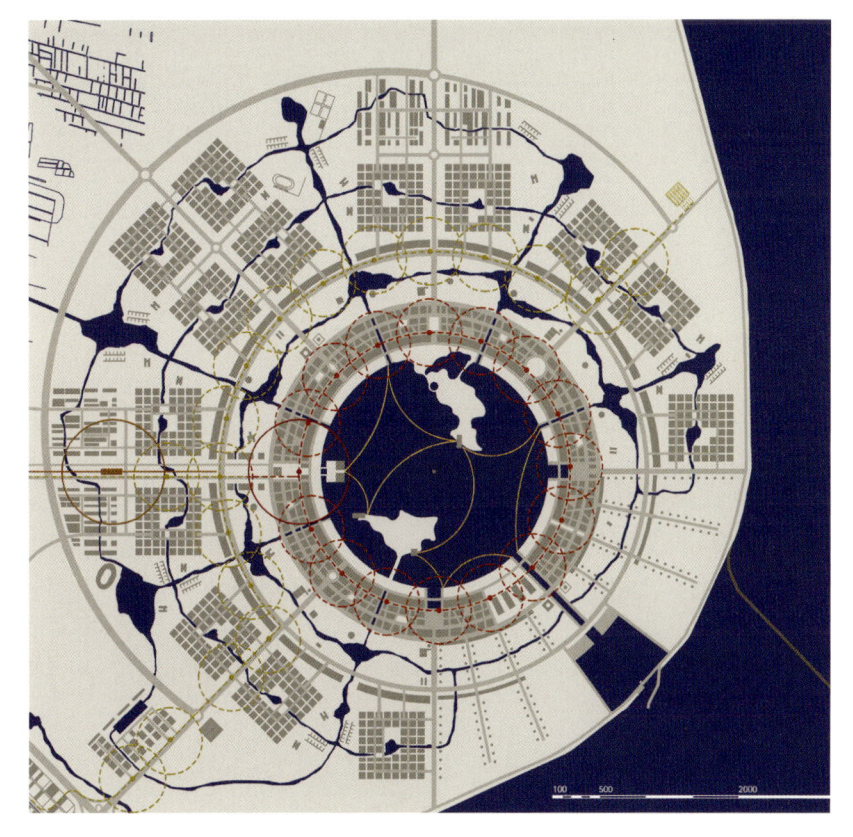

Linie 1 mit Haltestellen
Line 1 with stops

Linie R mit Haltestellen
Line R with stops

Umsteigebahnhof für Linie R
Linien 1 und 2/Busbahnhof
Station to change for line R
lines 1 and 2/bus station

Fährverbindungen
Ferry connections

Linie 2 mit Haltestellen
Line 2 with stops

Lingang New City

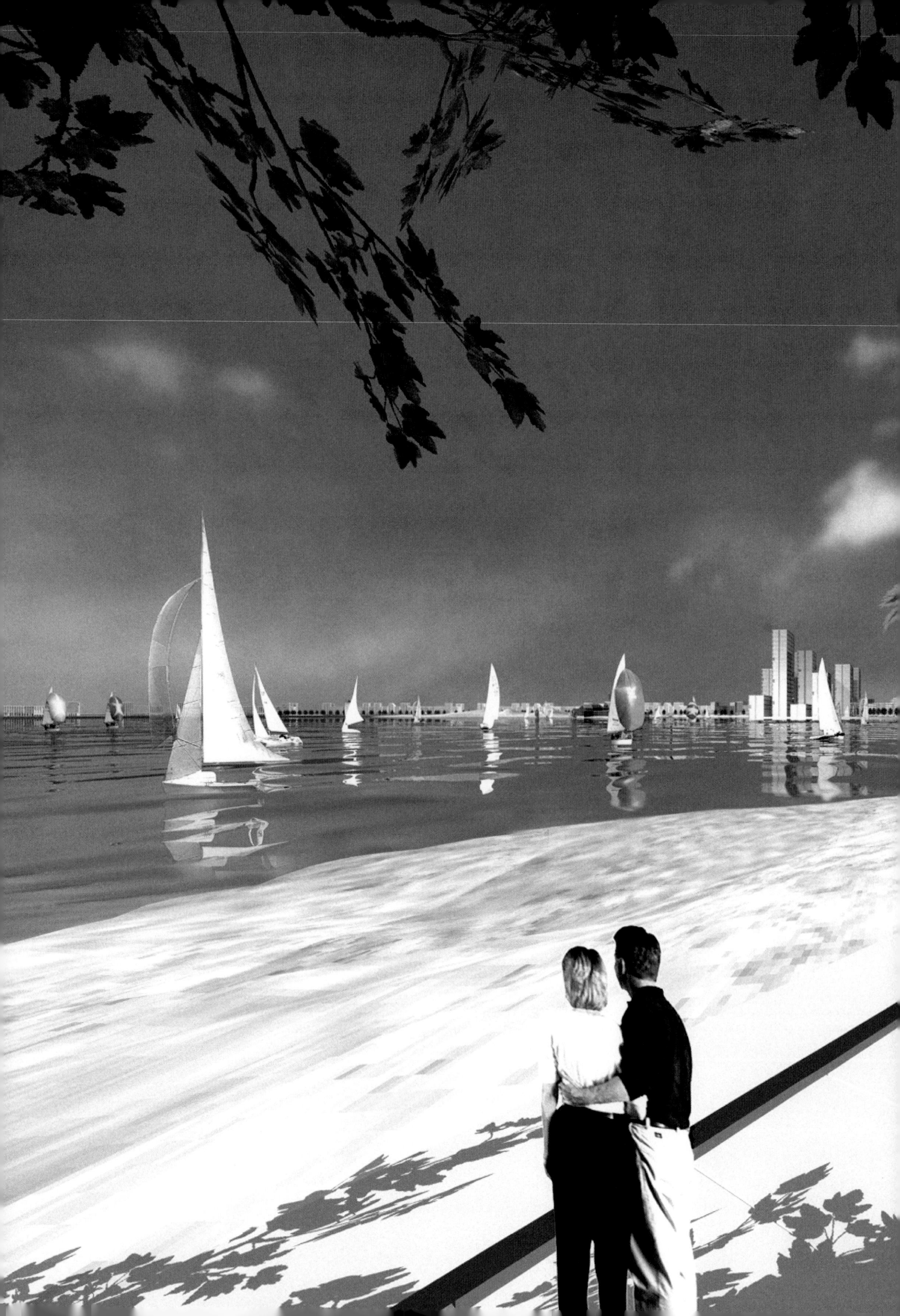

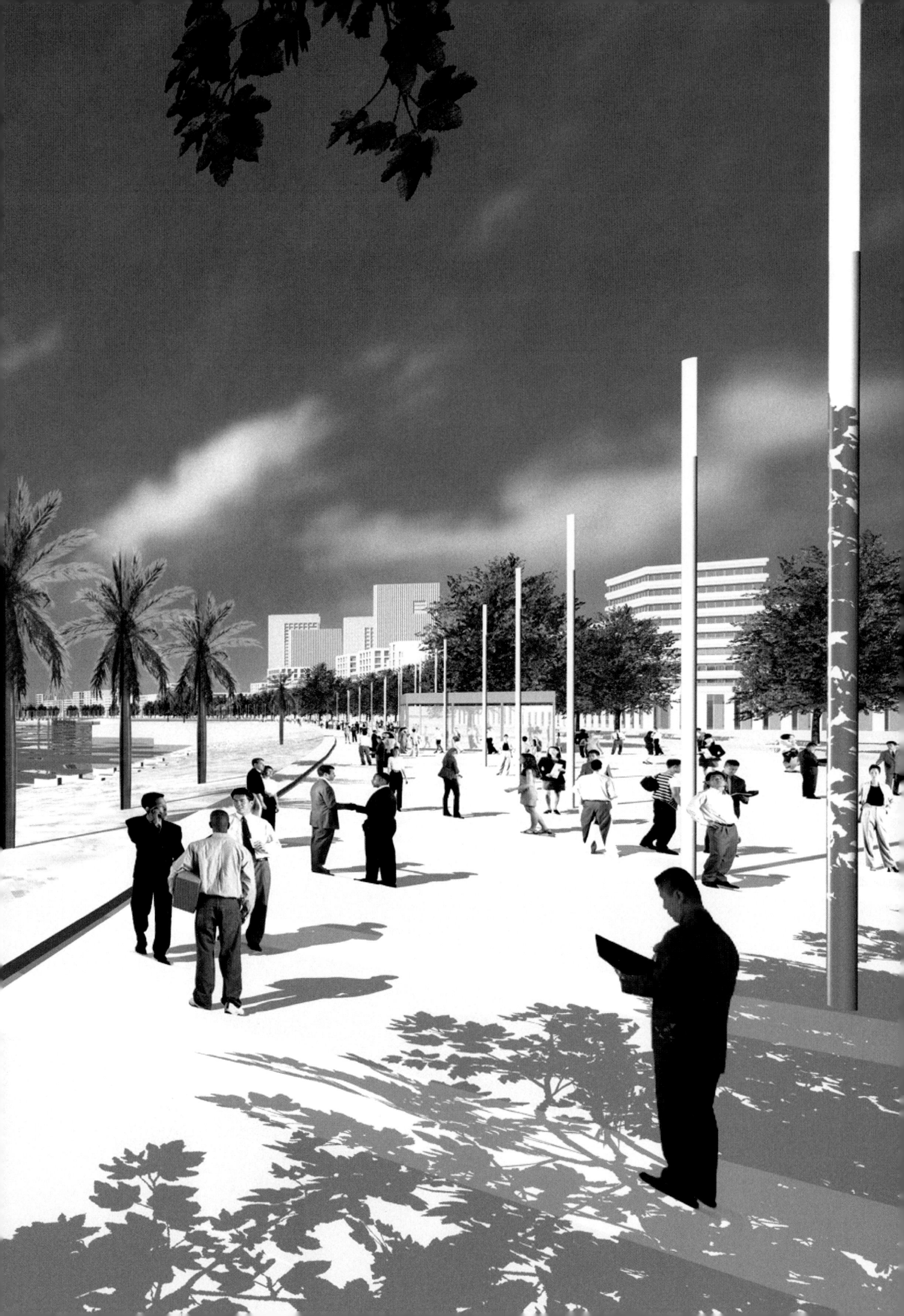

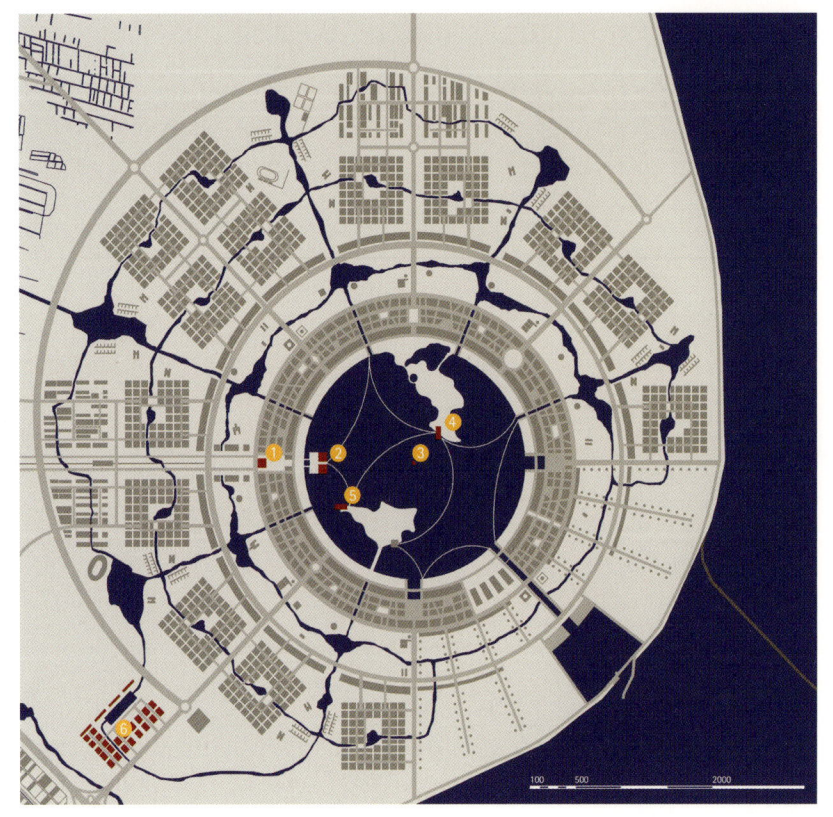

①	**Haus der Ströme**	House of Streams
②	**Insel der Arbeit**	Island of Work
③	**Wolkennadel**	Cloud Needle
④	**Großes Dock**	Large Dock
⑤	**Umspültes Riff**	Water-Washed Reef
⑥	**Atoll des Wissens**	Atoll of Knowledge

Landmarken

Die Landmarken sind weithin sichtbare Repräsentanten des Seins und des Inhaltes von Lingang New City. In ihnen manifestieren sich wirtschaftliche Quelle, Herkunft und Kultur der Stadt. Als solitäre Bauten sind sie in ihrer Materialität filigran und gläsern. Wie leuchtende Kristalle stehen sie sinnbildlich für die urbane Gemeinsamkeit und geben somit dem Stadtzentrum architektonische Identität.

Landmarks

The landmarks are representatives, visible from afar, of the essence and the substance of Lingang New City. The economic source, origin and culture of the city are manifested in them. They are solitary buildings, filigree and glass in their materiality. Like glowing crystals, they are allegories of the urban community and thus provide the city centre with an architectural identity.

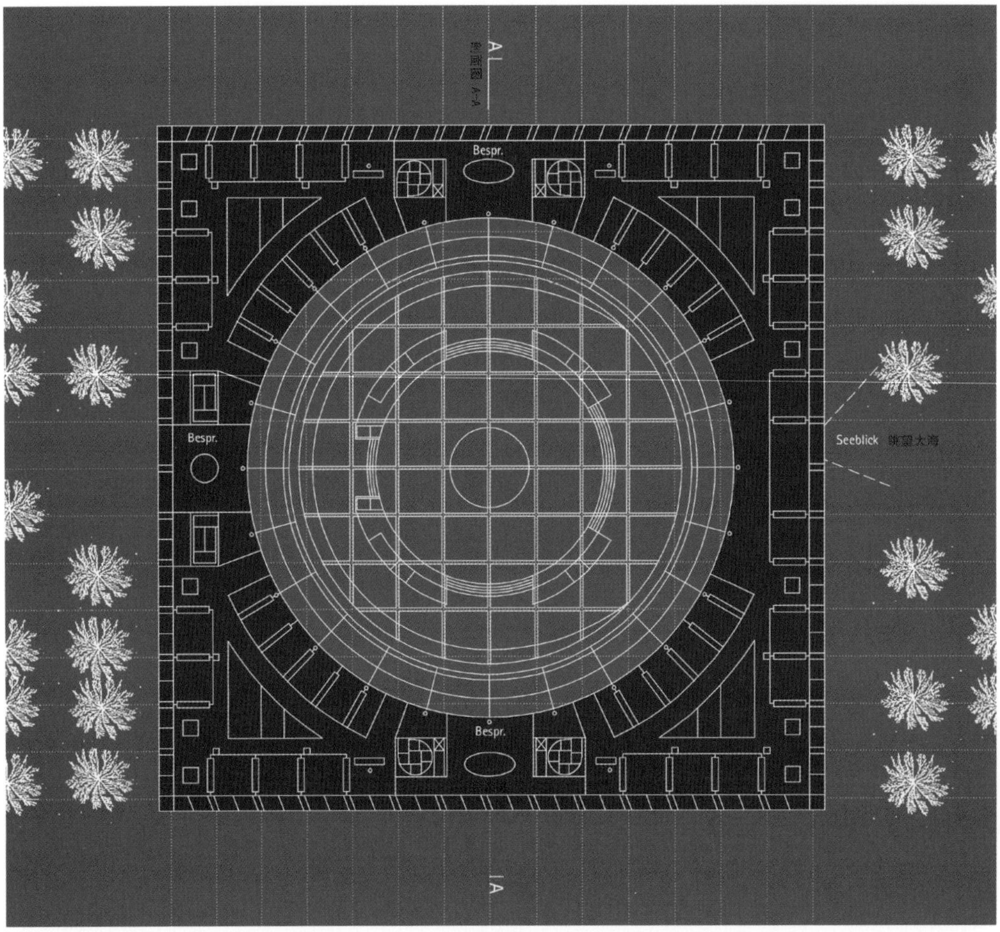

A
剖面图 A–A
Bespr.
Bespr.
Seeblick 眺望大海
Bespr.
A

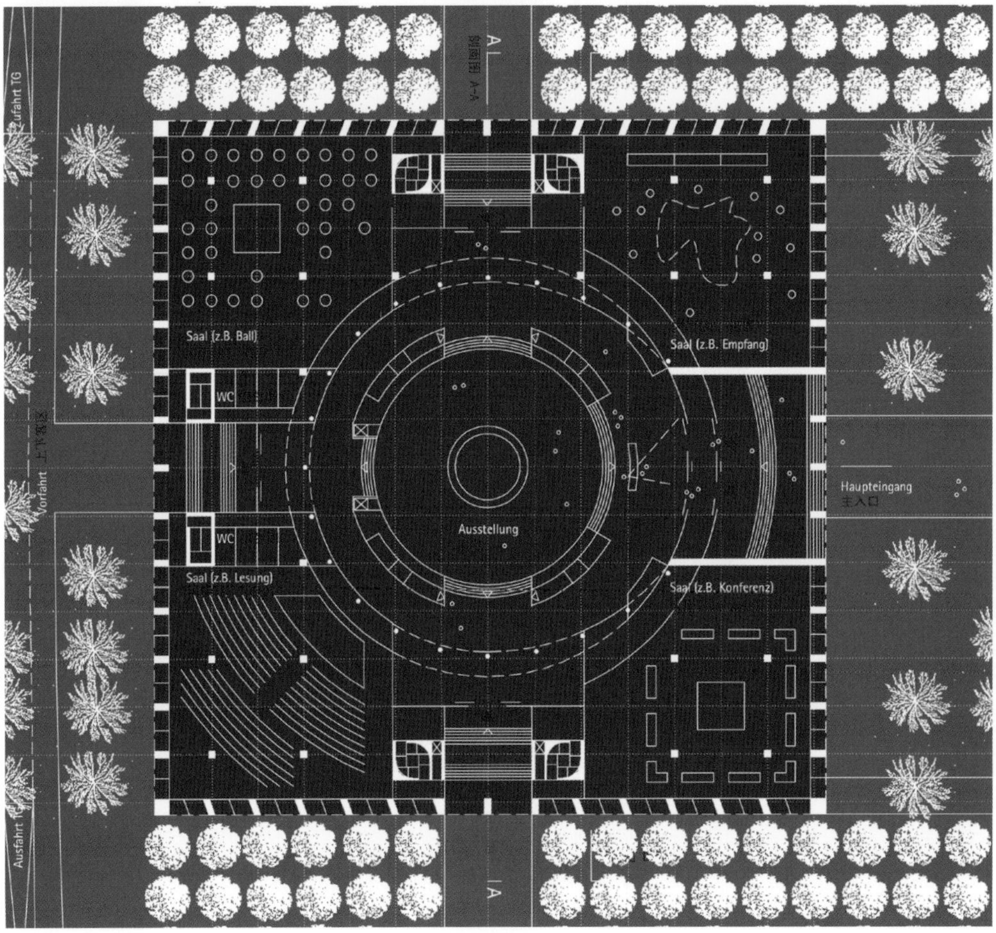

A
剖面图 A–A
Zufahrt TG
Saal (z.B. Ball)
Saal (z.B. Empfang)
WC
WC
Vorfahrt 上下客区
Ausstellung
Haupteingang
主入口
Saal (z.B. Lesung)
Saal (z.B. Konferenz)
Ausfahrt
A

„Für mich ist es die Balance von Vielfalt und Einheit, die Gemeinsamkeiten und die Individualität. Die Bindung daran hat Vorrang – das Ausbrechen muss man nicht beschreiben."

"For me, it is the balance of variety and unity, the similarities and the individuality. The obligation to this takes priority – dropping out of it does not have to be described."

Haus der Ströme (Kommunikationszentrum)

Die Positionierung des Gebäudes im Kreuzungspunkt der Haupterschließungsachse mit dem urbanen Ring unterstreicht die Schlüsselfunktion des Hauses der Ströme im Stadtgefüge von Lingang New City. Durch die gleichmäßige Ausbildung der transparenten Fassaden öffnet sich das Gebäude in alle vier Richtungen mit der gleichen Geste. Das Haus der Ströme ist Schaltzentrale und Schnittstelle, es fungiert als Mittler im Austausch der Wirtschaftsinteressen und deren Verzweigungen. Es übernimmt den Vorsitz im dichten baulichen Ring Lingang New City's, dem „Runden Tisch" des globalen Seehandels.

House of Streams (Communication Centre)

The positioning of the building at the intersection of the main circulation axes with the urban ring emphasizes the key function of the House of Streams within Lingang New City's urban fabric. The consistent formation of the transparent façades opens up the building towards all four directions with an identical gesture. The House of Streams is control centre and vierface; it functions as an intermediary in the exchange of economic interests and their various branches. It dominates within Lingang New City's dense built-up ring, the "round table" of the global maritime trade.

Western Island

Die Stadtinsel bildet den einprägsamen Schlusspunkt der Ost-West-Achse von Lingang New City. Die exponierte Lage der Grundstücke auf der somit im Westen des Sees liegenden Insel erfordert daher eine ebenso einzigartige architektonische Komposition.

Als Hochhauspaar sprechen beide Gebäude, Bürohaus und Hotel, dieselbe architektonische Sprache, die unterschiedlichen Nutzungen werden jedoch sowohl in der Formensprache des Gebäudes als auch in der Fassadengestaltung eingearbeitet.

Western Island

The city island forms the memorable termination of the east-west axis of Lingang New City. The exposed location of the plots on the island in the western part of the lake therefore calls for an equally unique architectural composition.

As a pair of high-rise buildings, both towers, the office tower and the hotel, speak the same architectural language, the differing utilisations are, however, integrated both in the use of shapes in the building and also in the design of the façade.

Whereas the base of the northern building accommodates the central sections of the hotel such as restau-

Während der Sockelbau des nördlichen Gebäudes die zentralen Bereiche des Hotels, wie Restaurants, Bankettsäle, Konferenzzentrum sowie alle weiteren Sondernutzungen beinhaltet, befinden sich die Zimmergeschosse in dem eigentlichen Hochhausturm. Die exklusiven Suiten sind den obersten Ebenen vorbehalten.
Im Süden der Insel befindet sich der Büroturm, dessen Büroeinheiten flexibel aufteilbar sind.
Den Abschluss der Twin Towers bilden jeweils die zweigeschossigen Skybars, welche einen grandiosen Ausblick über den Dishui Lake bieten.

rants, banqueting halls, conference centre and all further special function areas, the hotel rooms are located on the various floors of the tower itself. The uppermost floors are reserved for the exclusive suites.
The office tower, in which the office units are flexible in their layout, is located in the southern part of the island.
The top of each of the Twin Towers is formed by a two-storey Skybar offering breathtaking views over Dishui Lake.

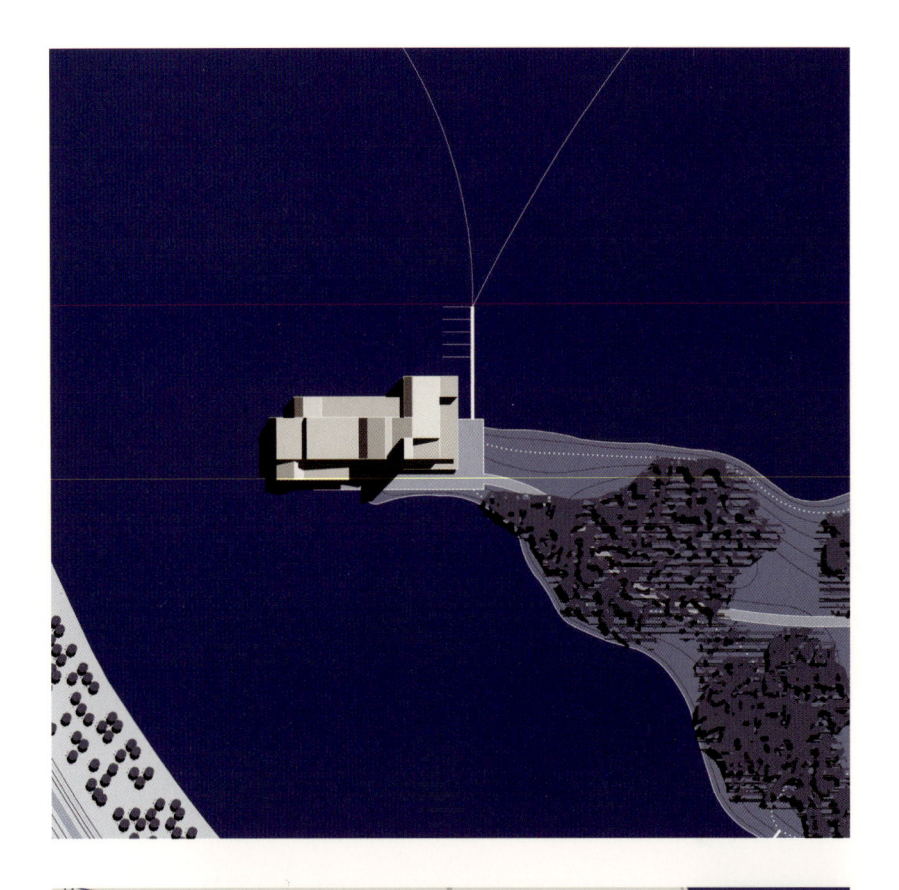

„Jeder Ort birgt Risiken, weil jedes Stück neuer Architektur einen Eingriff bedeutet, der den Ort verändert."

"Every location holds risks, because every piece of new architecture means intervention that alters the place."

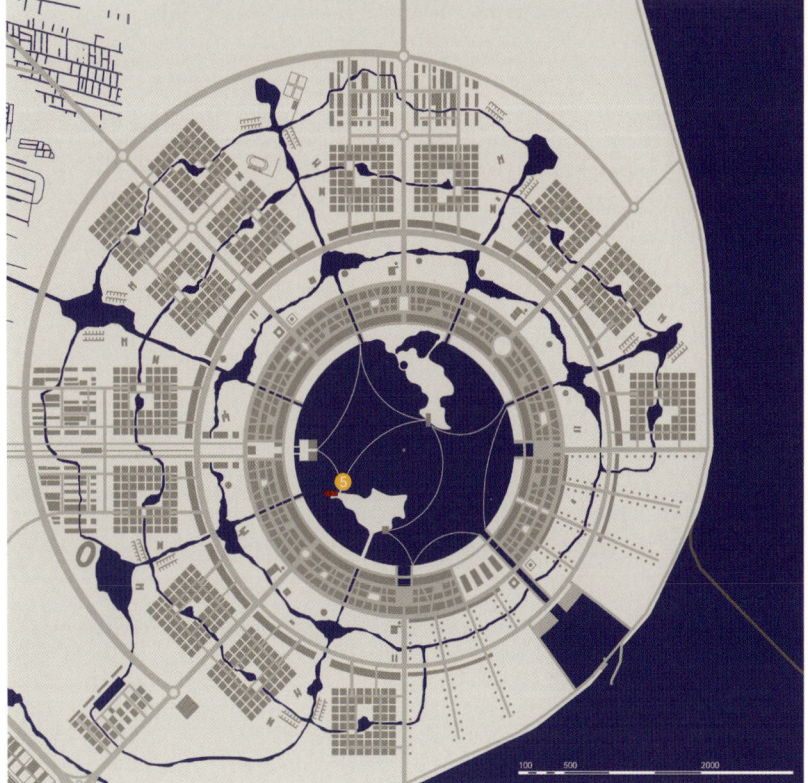

Umspültes Riff

Das umspülte Riff beherbergt das Theater Lingang New City's und ist darüber hinaus zentraler Ort des kulturellen Lebens.
In seiner Materialität filigran und gläsern, repräsentiert es als kristalliner Solitär die Kultur und den Genuss des Lebens. Das expressive und dynamische Äußere und die exponierte Position auf der Insel des Vergnügens machen das Umspülte Riff zu einer zentralen Landmarke der Stadt.

Water-Washed Reef

The Water-washed Reef houses Lingang New City's theatre and is simultaneously the focus of cultural activity. With its delicate and transparent materiality the theatre as a crystalline solitaire symbolises the culture and the enjoyment of life. The expressive and dynamic exterior and the exposed positioning on Pleasure Island make the Water-washed Reef a central landmark of the city.

Umspültes Riff
Water-Washed Reef

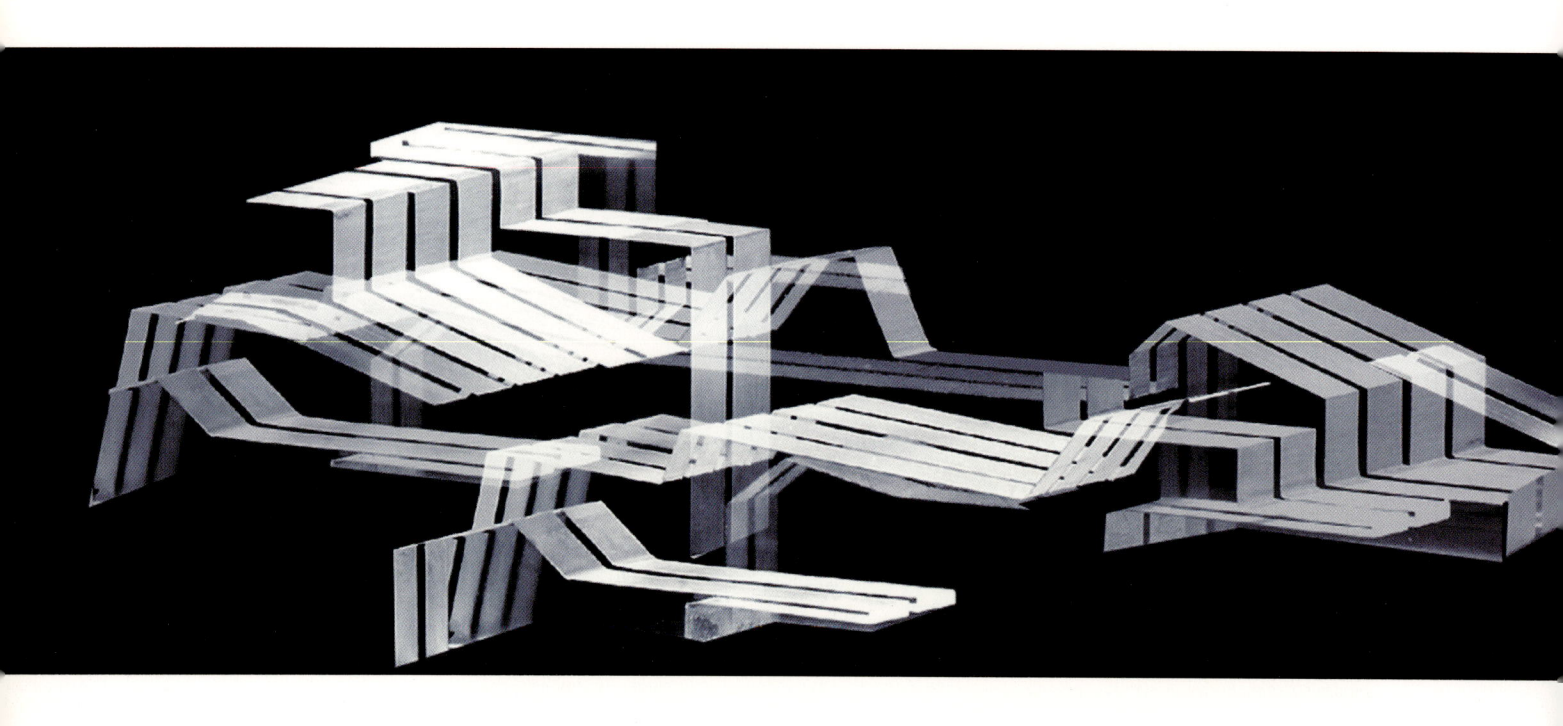

„Es gibt immer einen Dialog zwischen Umwelt und Architektur."
"There is always a dialogue between the environment and architecture."

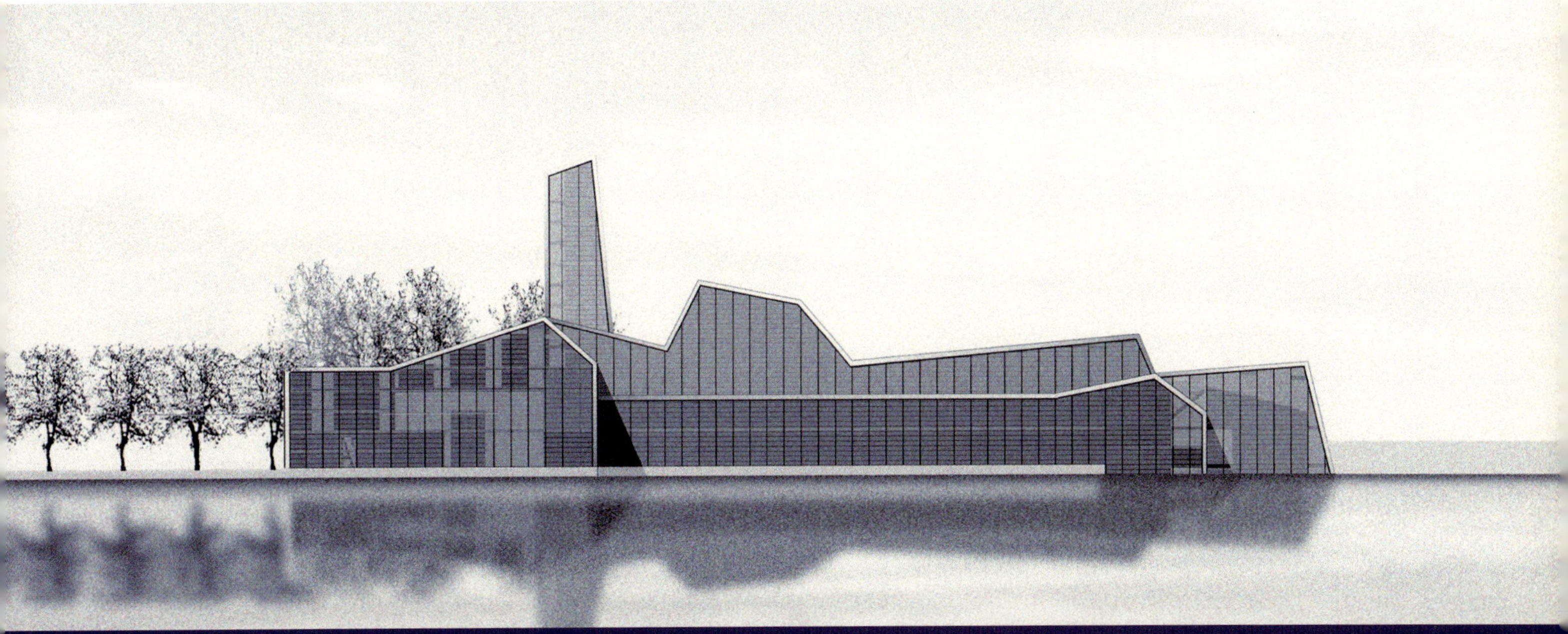

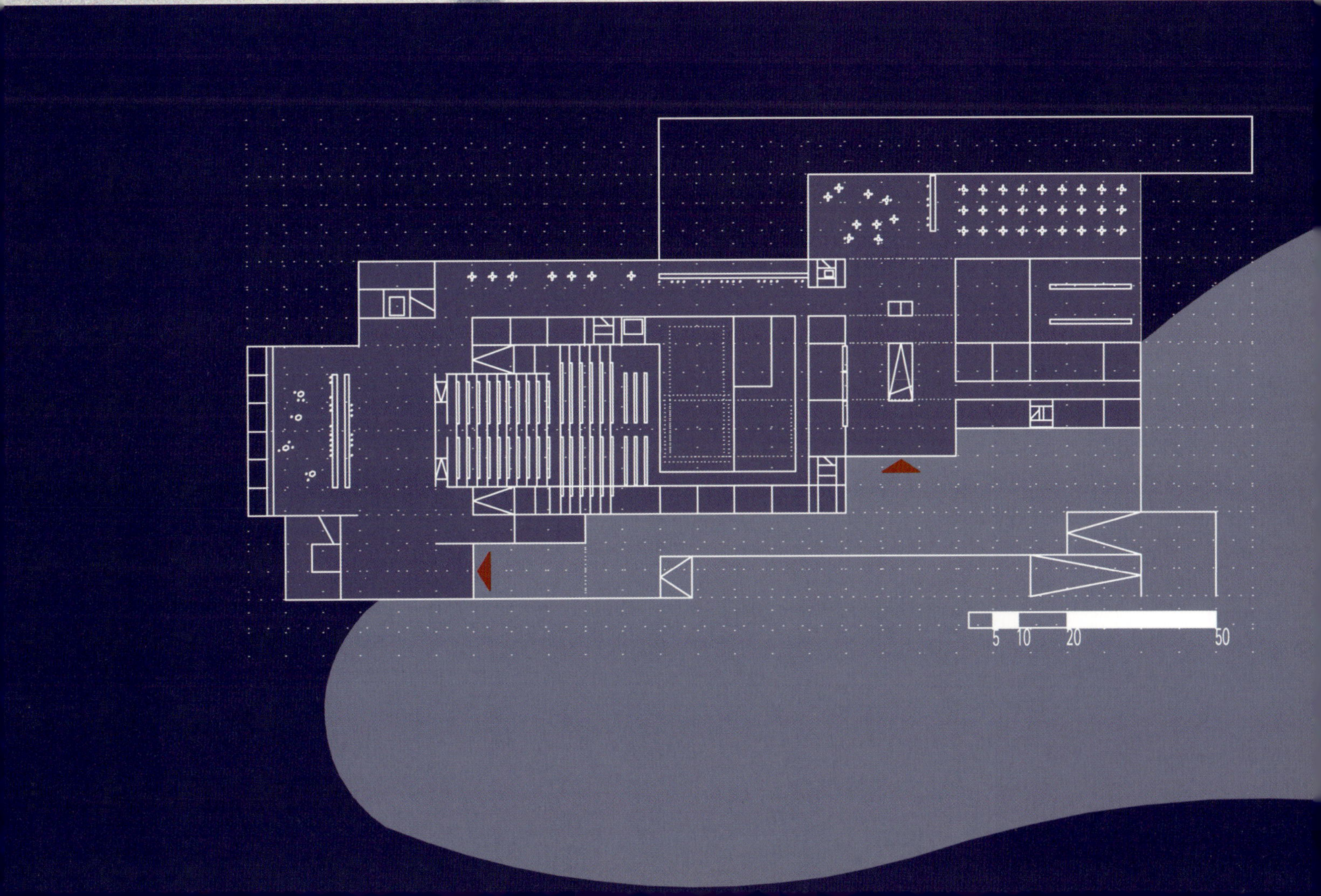

5 10 20 50

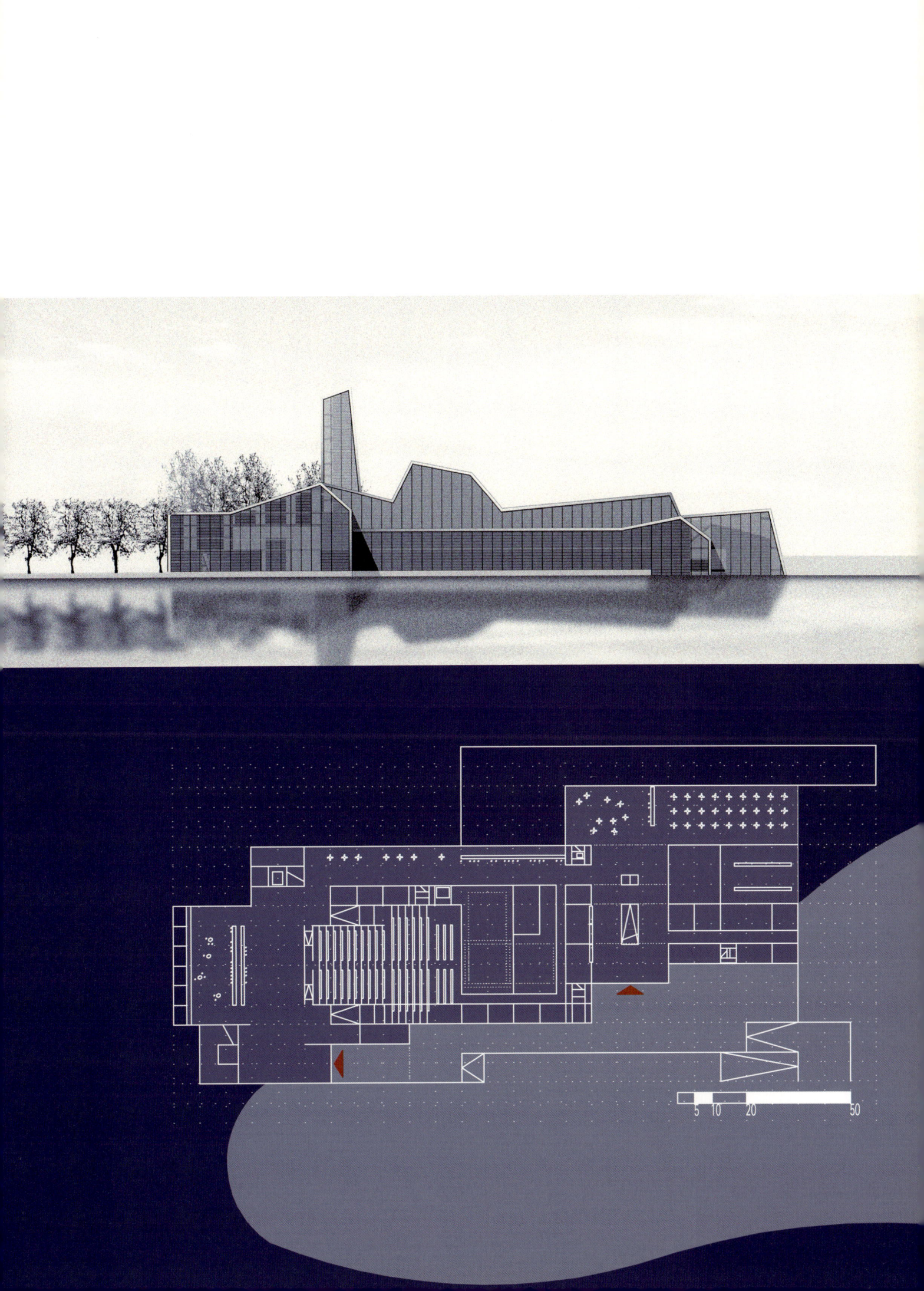

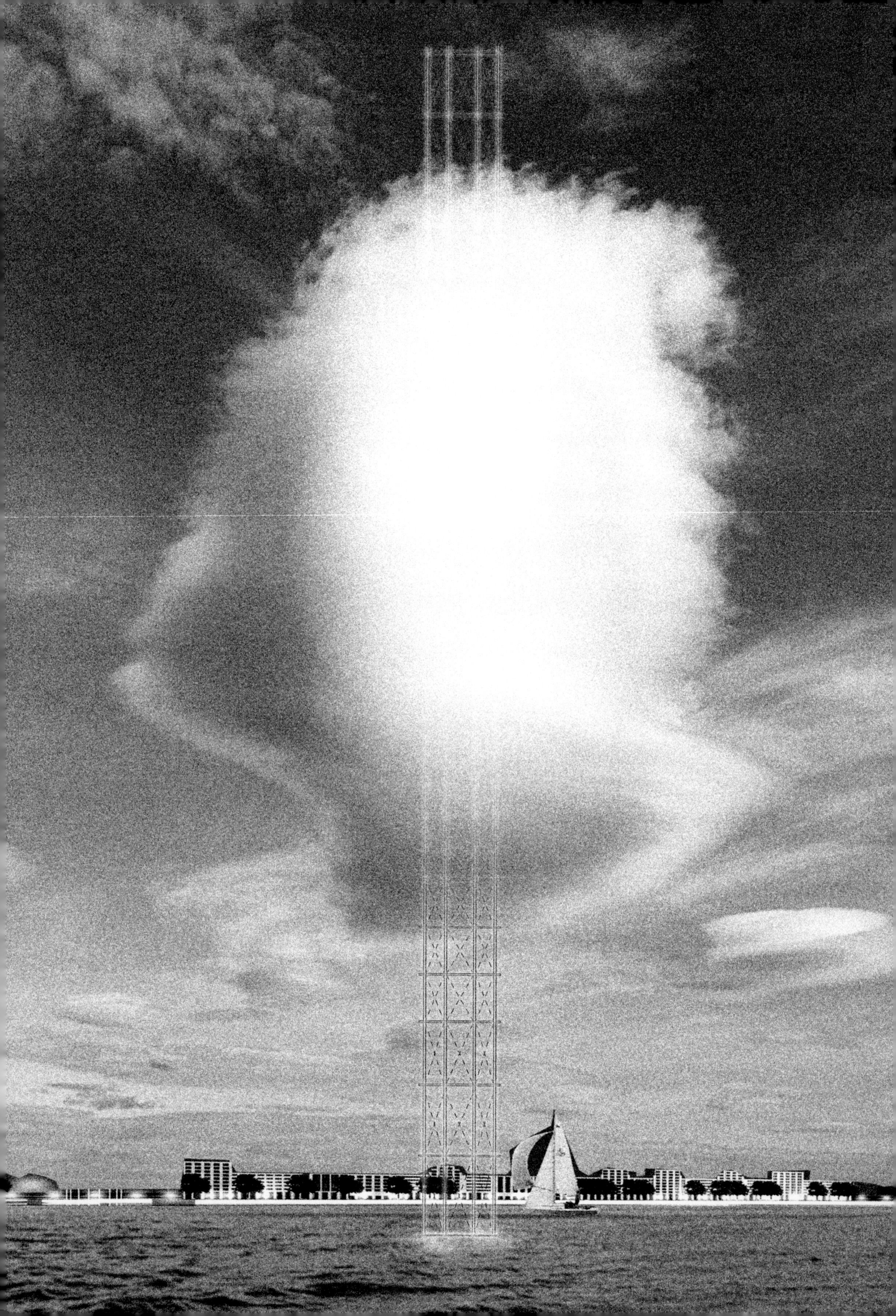

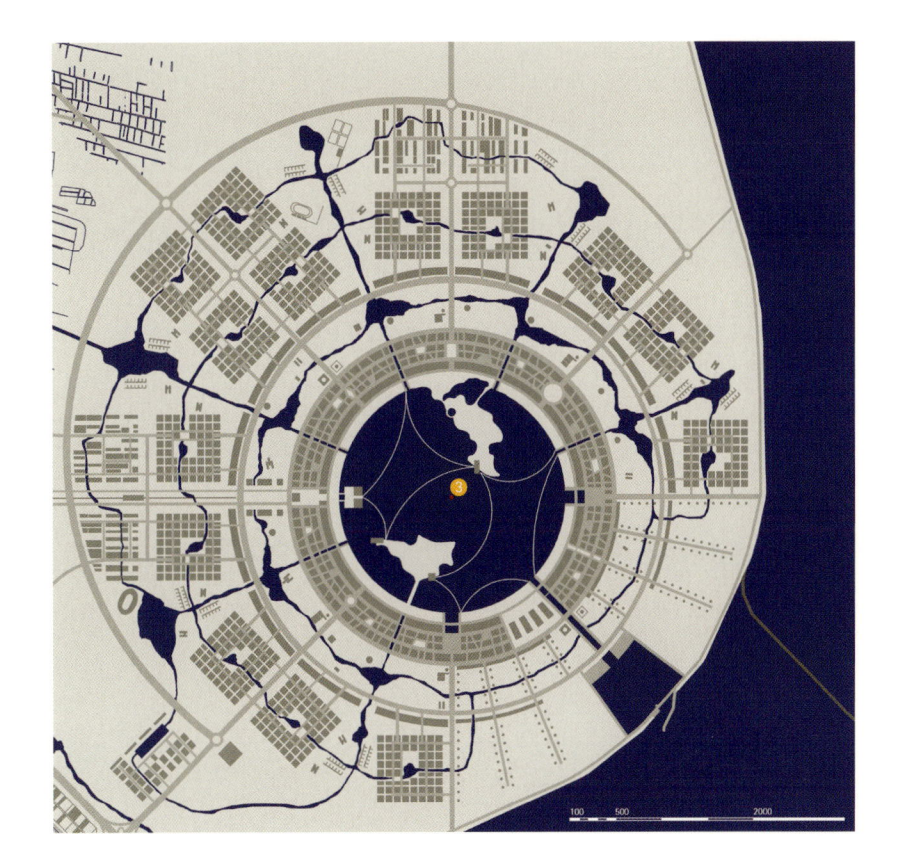

"Freier Raum, der keine Rendite bezieht, wertet die Gebiete auf, die an das Wasser andocken, das allgegenwärtig ist."

"Open space, that does not obtain a rate of return, upgrades those areas adjoining the water, which is omnipresent."

Wolkennadel

Die Wolkennadel steht als Wahrzeichen von Lingang New City im Mittelpunkt des zentralen Sees. Sie markiert die Falllinie des Tropfens und die Stelle, an der er die Wasseroberfläche berührt. An den Kreuzungspunkten der vertikalen und horizontalen Konstruktionselemente erzeugen Hochdruckwasserdüsen Nebel, der bei Dunkelheit angestrahlt wird. Die filigrane Stahlkonstruktion ist weitgehend zurückgenommen und verdichtet sich lediglich zum Schwerpunkt der Wolke hin.

Cloud Needle

The Cloud Needle ascends from the middle of the central lake as Lingang New City's primary landmark. It marks the path of the drop of water and the place where it touches the water surface. At the intersections of the vertical and horizontal structural elements, high-pressure water jets generate mist which is illuminated in the dark. The light-weight steel structure is minimized and concentrates purely towards the centre of the cloud.

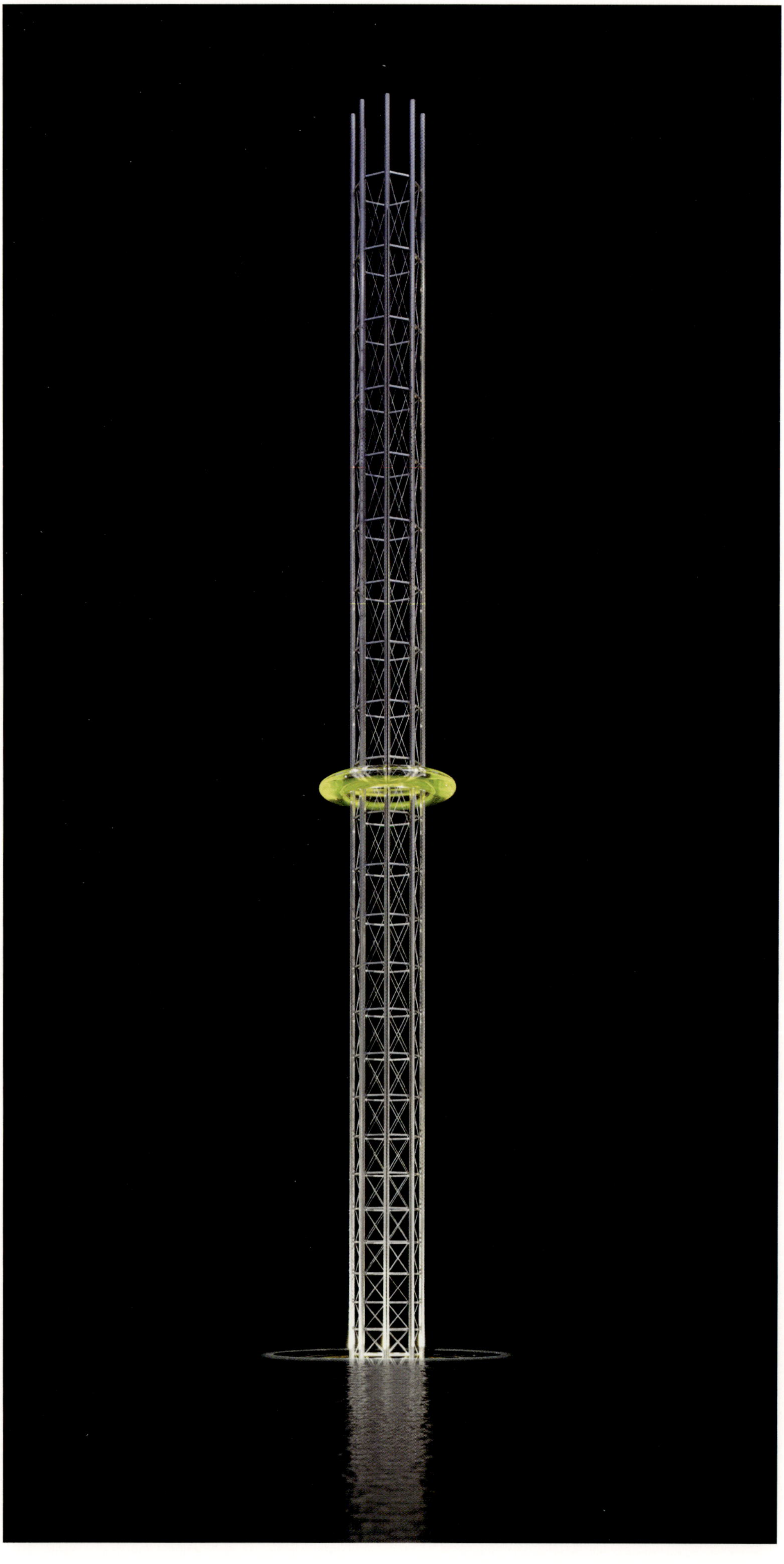

Wolkennadel
Coud Needle

Lingang New City

63

„Zwölf Monate Badezeit ist eine wunderbare Geschichte als Freizeitangebot für die dort lebenden Menschen."

"Twelve months of swimming season is a wonderful thing as a leisure facility for the people who live there."

Stahlbrücke
Steel bridge

Betonbrücke
Concrete bridge

Holzbrücke
Timber bridge

Steinbrücke
Stone bridge

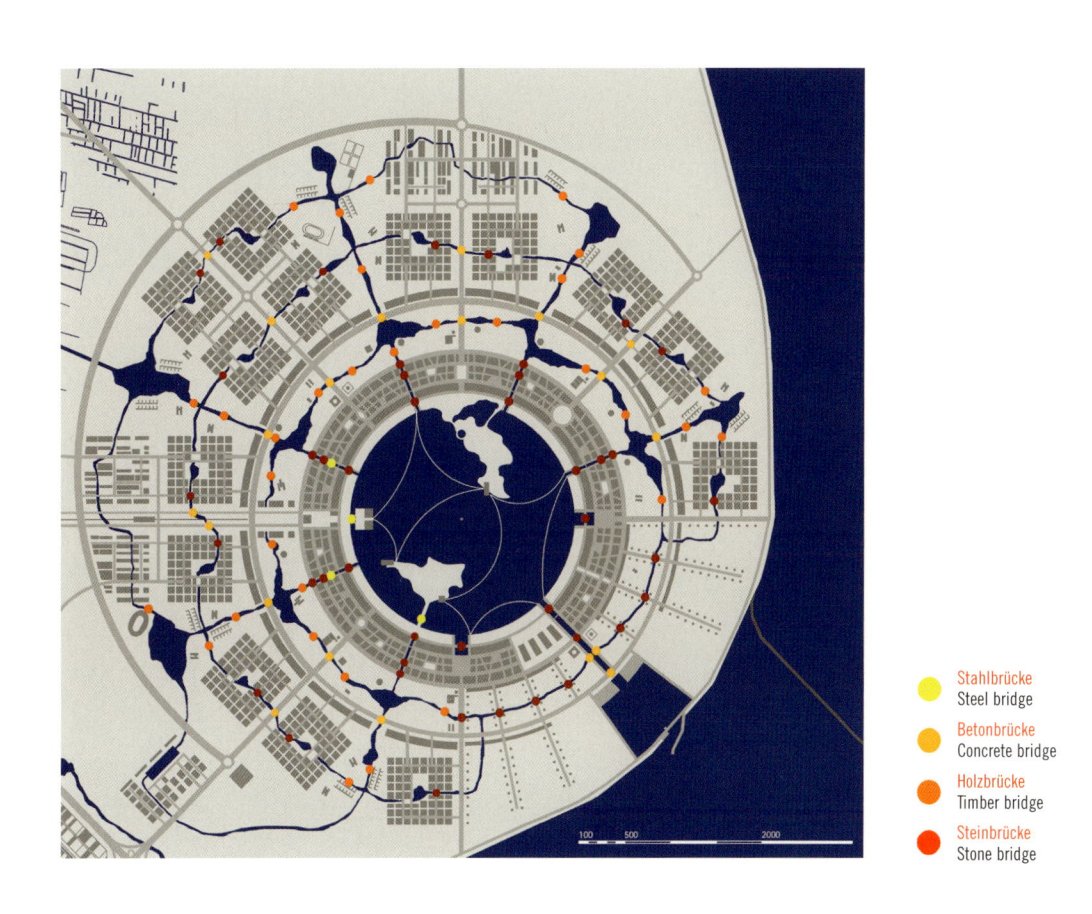

Brücken

Die Brücken über die vielen Wasseradern von Lingang New City fügen sich in ihrer Gestaltung und Materialität in die jeweiligen Stadtbereiche ein – so sind vorwiegend hölzerne Brücken im Parkgürtel zu finden und monolithische Steinbrücken im bebauten Ring. Stahlkonstruktionen mit teilweise verglasten Laufflächen verbinden die Inseln im zentralen See mit der Promenade – sie stellen in ihrer Materialität eine direkte Verbindung zu den filigranen, gläsernen Landmarken im Zentrum der Stadt dar.

Bridges

The design and material of the bridges across Lingang New City's numerous watercourses blend into the respective urban areas: consequently timber bridges predominate in the park belt and monolithic stone bridges in the built-up ring. Steel constructions with partially glazed walking areas connect the islands in the central lake with the promenade, the nature of their material forming a direct connection to the delicate, glazed landmarks in the city centre.

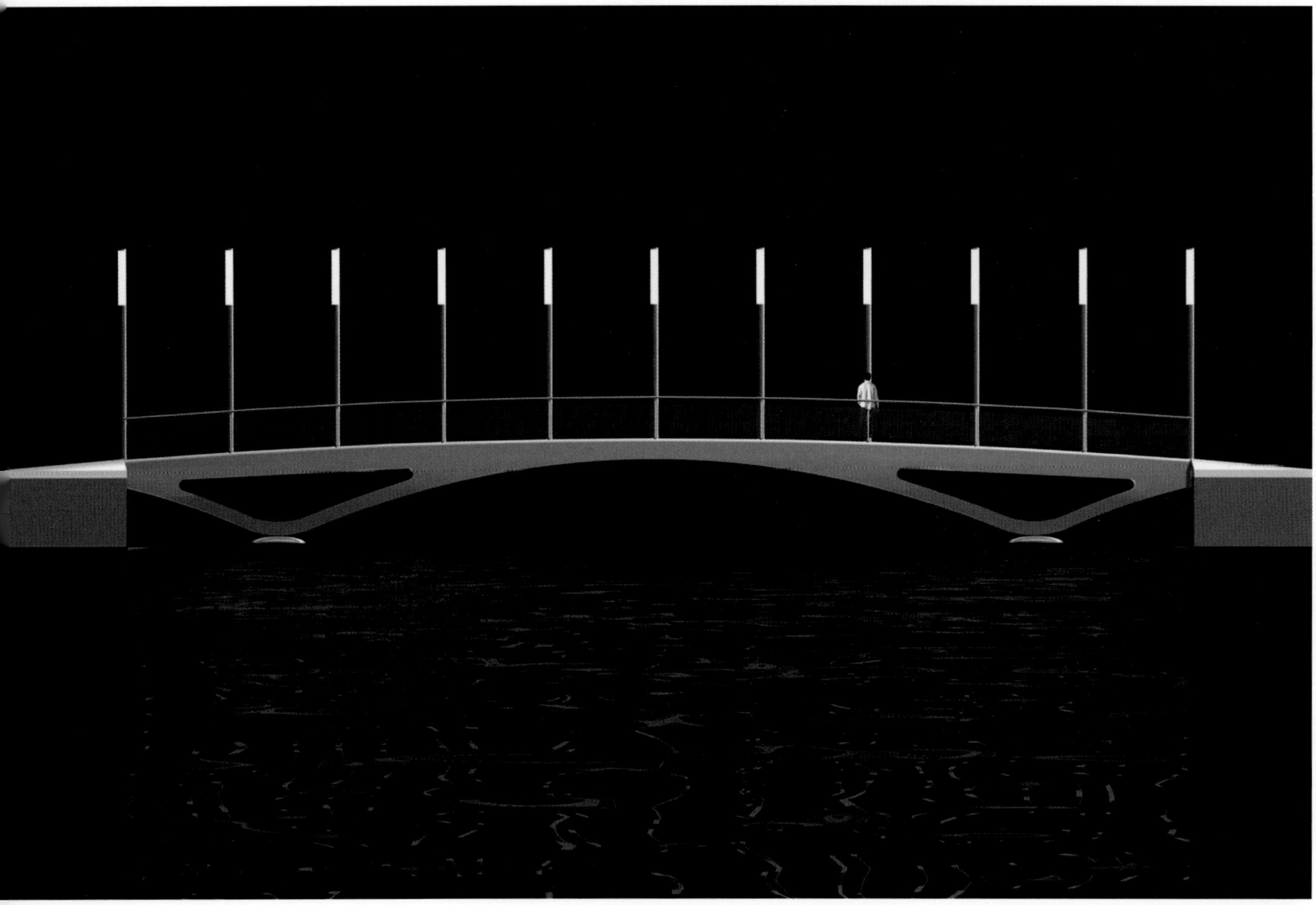

Brücken
Bridges

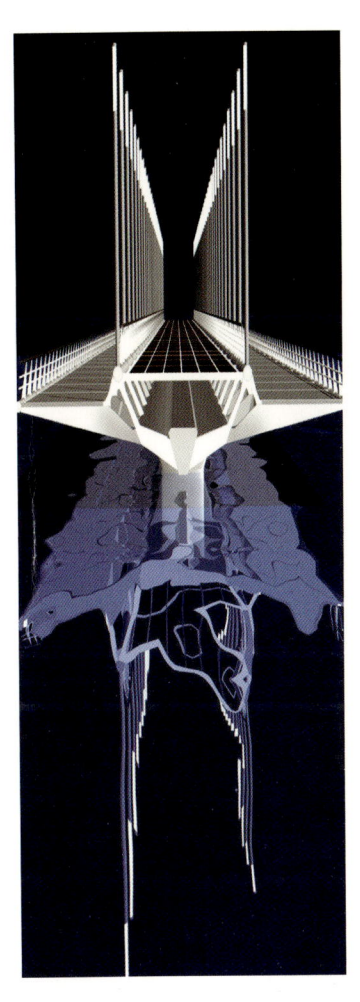

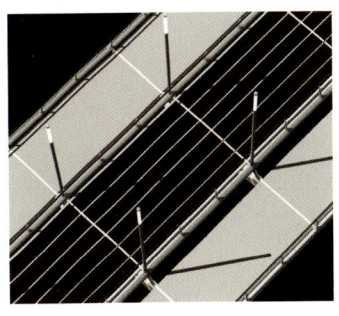

Lingang New City

67

Geschäft/Büro Shop/office

Kaufhaus/Kino Department store/cinema

Mall Mall

Büro Office

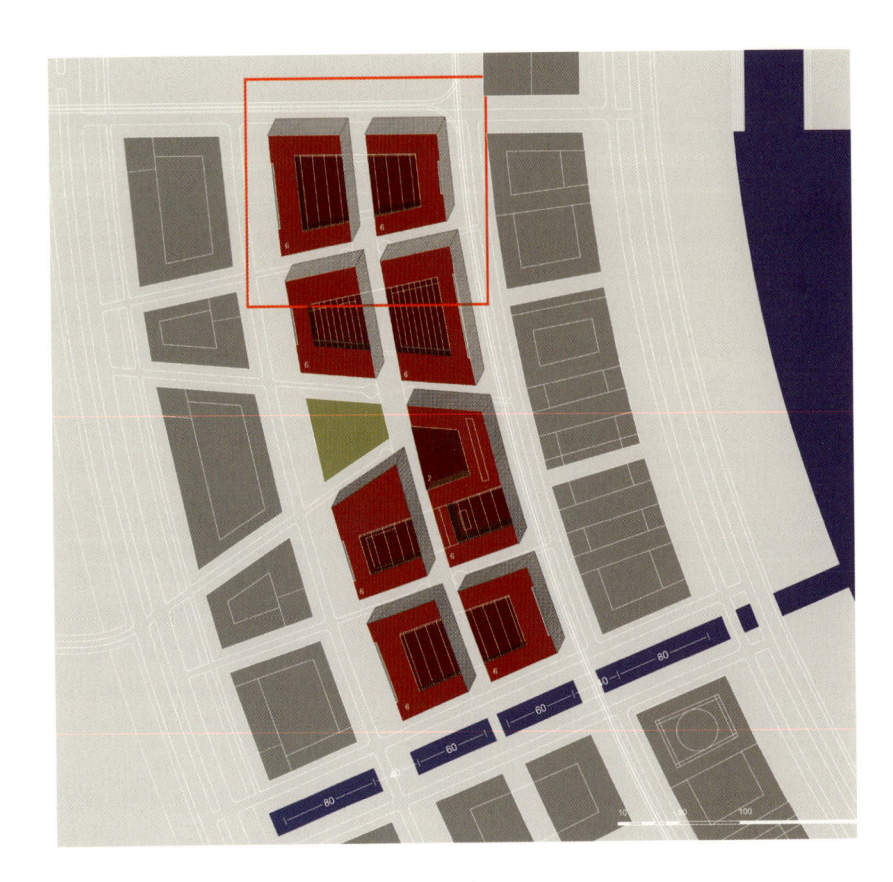

70

Ringbebauung
Ring Development

„Für uns steht das Anliegen, urbane Lebensqualität durch maßstäbliche Straßen und Platzräume zu schaffen, stark im Vordergrund."

"Our most important aim is to create urban quality of life by providing streets and open spaces on a human scale."

men städtebaulichen Kanon, der die einzelnen Bauten plausibel und nachvollziehbar als Teile eines Ganzen zu einem Ensemble fügt.
Um die geeigneten Materialien für Lingang New City auszuwählen, ist ein Blick auf die alte Bautradition Chinas und insbesondere der Region Shanghai wichtig. Eine gelungene Mischung aus kultureller Tradition und modernen europäischen Architekturstilen wird Lingang New City seine unverwechselbare Identität geben.

all fit a common city-planning canon and the individual buildings can be plausibly seen as part of the whole, forming an ensemble.
In the selection of the building materials for Lingang New City, it is important to consider the ancient building tradition of China, in particular of the Shanghai region. A successful mixture of cultural tradition and modern European architectural styles will give Lingang New City an unmistakable identity.

Ringbebauung
Ring Development

Lingang New City

1.1. Baukörper/Proportionen

1.1.1 Typen: Als Bautyp werden um innere Höfe angeordnete Bebauungen (z.B. Hofhaus) und geschlossene Blockkanten festgelegt.

1.1.2 Proportionen: Die Größe der Module (Parzellengröße) wird auf 28,00 m +Fugen (Fugenbreite 70 cm) festgelegt. Eine Zusammenlegung bzw. Unterteilung einzelner Module ist möglich, um funktionell gute Grundrisse zu erreichen.

1.1.3 Achsmaße und Raster: Aus funktionalen und gestalterischen Gründen empfehlen wir, ein kontinuierliches Gebäuderaster festzuschreiben. Dieses Raster baut auf dem Grundmodul von 1,35 m auf. Daraus ergibt sich eine Stützweite von 8,10 m, die für sämtliche Funktionen der Gebäude (Laden, Büro, Hotelzimmer, Garagen etc.) gut geeignet ist.

1.1.4 Geschossigkeit: Es wird eine Dreiteilung der Fassade in Sockelzone, Hauptzone und Turmzone festgelegt.

1.1.5 Sockelzonen: Es wird die Ausbildung einer hohen Sockelzone mit zwei Geschossen à 4,50 m Geschosshöhe festgelegt.

1.1.6 Hauptgeschosse: Es wird die Ausbildung einer Zone mit fünf Hauptgeschossen à 3,50 m Geschosshöhe festgelegt.

1.1.7 Turmgeschosse: In Ausnahmefällen kann eine Zone mit max. drei Turmgeschossen à 3,50 m Geschosshöhe ausgebildet werden. Der Anteil der Turmgeschosse darf dabei 40% nicht übersteigen.

1.1.8 Traufhöhen: Die zulässige Traufhöhe beträgt +27,50 m ab Oberkante Gelände. Turmgeschosse haben eine zulässige Traufhöhe von +38,00 m ab Oberkante Gelände.

1.1.9 Baulinien und Baufluchten: Baulinien und Baugrenzen sind einzuhalten. Es wird eine hintere sowie eine vordere Bauflucht festgelegt.

1.2. Fassaden

1.2.1 Gliederung der Fassaden: Die Fassaden sind als Lochfassade mit rechteckigen, stehenden Fensterformaten auszubilden.

1.2.2 Fassadenmaterialien: Die Fassaden müssen straßenseitig als Putzfassaden ausgebildet werden. Erdgeschossverblendungen, Gebäudesockel oder Gliederungselemente der Fassade aus Naturstein sind zulässig. Alternativ kann eine Fassadenverkleidung aus Naturstein mit stumpfer Oberfläche verwendet werden. Verspiegelte Verglasungen werden ausgeschlossen.

1.2.3 Farben: Es sind gebrochene Weiß- und Ockertöne zu verwenden. Das Farbspektrum liegt zwischen hellem Ocker, Gelb und Grau.

1.2.4 Fenster und Türen: Fenster und Türen haben rechteckige, stehende Formate. Der Fassadenöffnungsanteil beträgt 50%. Die max. zulässige Größe der Fensteröffnungen ist 40 m^2.

1.2.5 Arkaden: In den markierten Bereichen sollen Arkaden ausgebildet werden.

Lingang New City

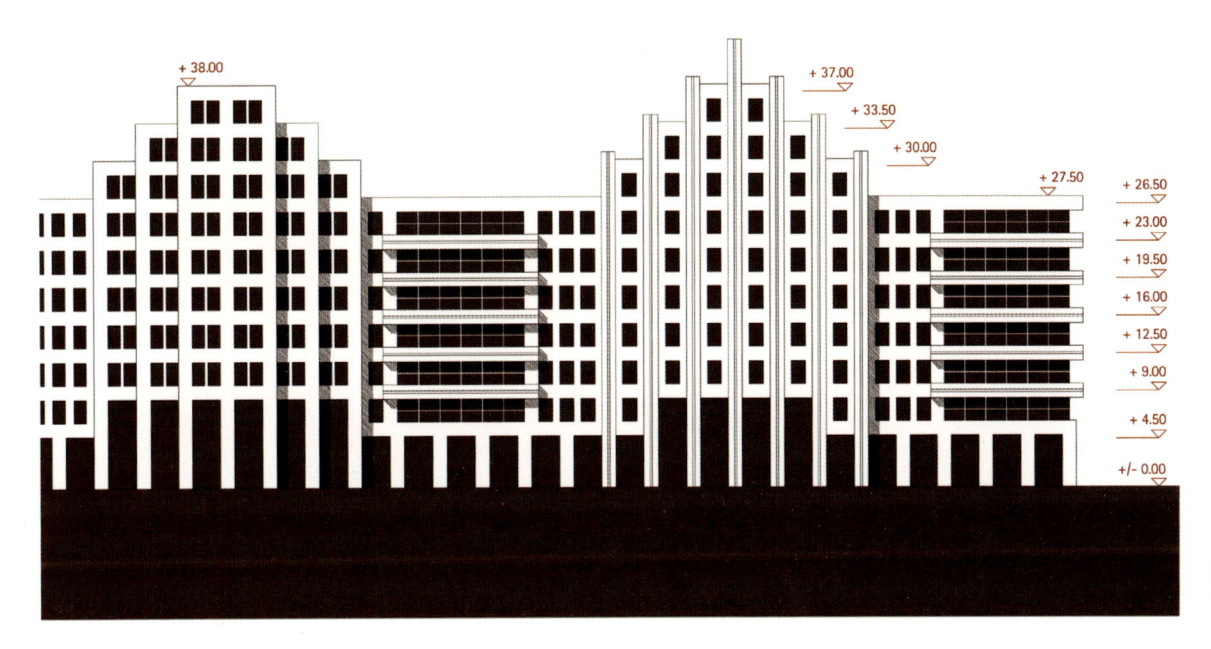

Der neue Bund
The New Bund

In der Natur sind die hierarchischen Prinzipien
von der Einheit des Ganzen und der Mannigfaltigkeit
des Einzelnen in unerschöpflicher Vielzahl verkörpert:
das Prinzip eines Baumes.
In nature, the hierarchical principles of the unity
of the whole and the diversity of the individual are
manifest in inexhaustible multiformity.
The principle of a tree.

Im Mittelalter bedingten Bautechnik und beschränkte
Verfügbarkeit von Materialien, dass Städte eine große
Familie von individuellen Häusern und gemeinschaftlicher Typologie jedes „Familienmitgliedes" die so
hochgeschätzte Vielfalt in der Einheit schufen.
The construction techniques and limited availability of
construction materials in medieval times meant that
cities became large "families" of individual houses
with shared typologies and "family" characteristics that
formed their much appreciated unity in diversity.

Vielfalt und Einheit: Schaffe die Einheit in der Vielfalt. Erzeuge die Vielfalt in der Einheit.

Variety and uniformity:
Create uniformity within variety.
Create variety within uniformity.

Die mittelalterliche oberitalienische Stadt in der Toskana entstand nach strengen Regeln einer von der Stadtkommune vereinbarten Gestaltungsordnung. Häuser, die an der „zentralen Plaza", dem Campo, diesen Regeln nicht entsprachen, mussten wieder abgerissen werden. Diese Konsequenz macht den Platz zu einem Weltkulturerbe.
The medieval Tuscan town of Siena was built according to the strict design rules laid down by the community. Houses on the central square, the Campo, that did not comply with these rules, had to be demolished. Due to this rigour, the Campo has become a world heritage.

An der Hamburger Binnenalster waren die Regeln liberaler, aber trotzdem dominiert das gemeinsame gegenüber dem Individuellen.
Darin liegt das Geheimnis jeder zeitlosen Wertschätzung von städtischen Qualitäten.
The rules governing the buildings around Hamburg's Binnenalster were more liberal, but still determined by common features, instead of individuality. This is the secret behind every timeless urban quality.

Lingang New City

77

Der neue Bund
The New Bund

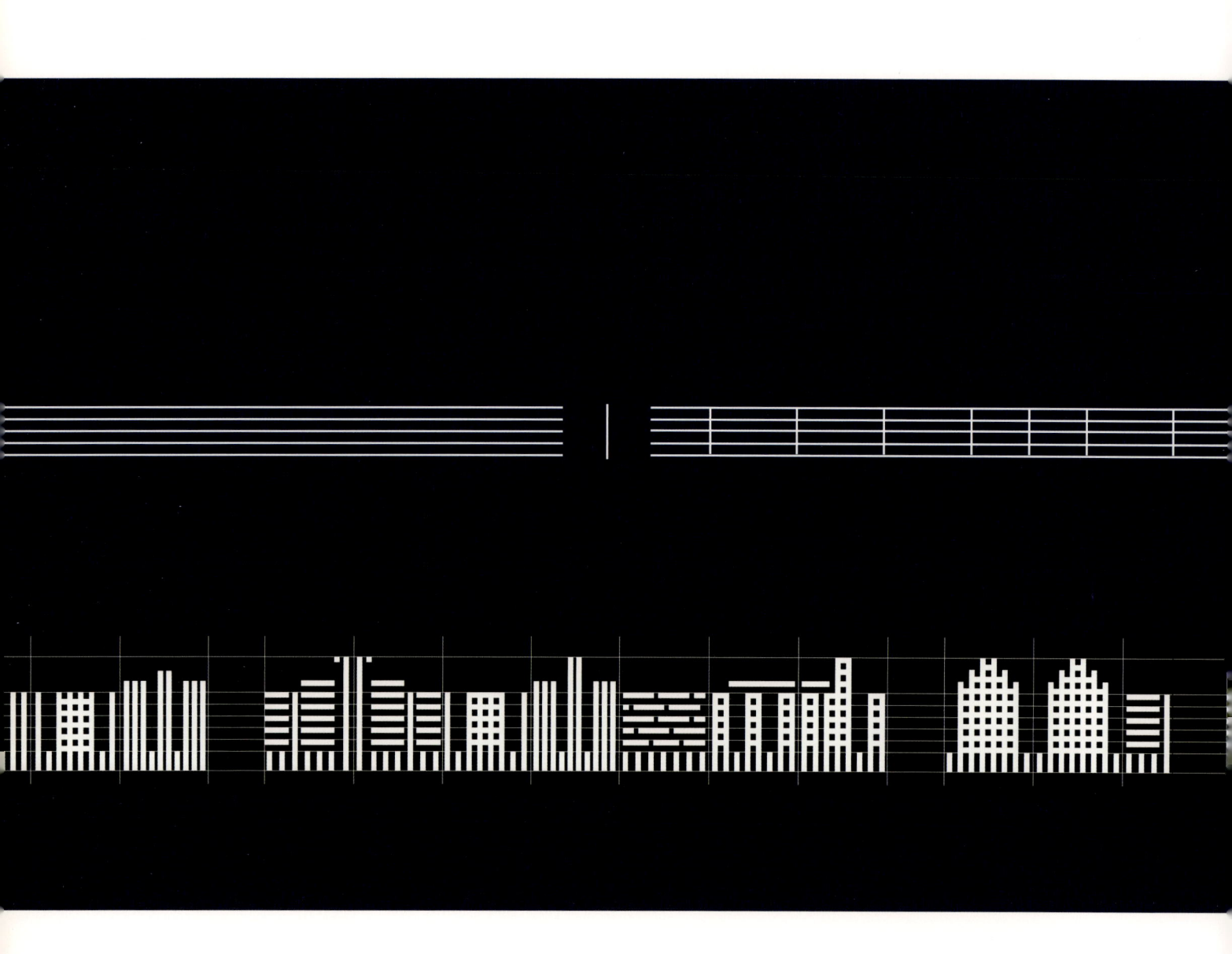

Struktur und Gestalt einer Stadt haben analoge Gesetzmäßigkeiten wie die Musik.
Urban structures and forms are subject to the same laws as music.

Die Notenlinien sind in der Musik die ordnende Struktur. Analog dazu ordnen Baulinien und Höhenfestlegungen die Struktur einer Stadt.
In music, lines of notation represent the ordering structure. In analogy, fixed frontage and height lines determine the structure of a city.

Der Takt gibt die Gliederung der Parzellen vor. Rhythmus ist die Bewegung der Silhouette und die Differenzierung der Fronten.
The beat determines the structuring of the plots of land. Rhythm is the kinetic shaping and differentiation of building contours and façades.

Die Wahl der Materialien bestimmt die Tonart, die Gestaltung der Fassaden ist schließlich die Melodie einer Gebäudereihe.
The choice of materials determines the key, while the façade design represents the melody of a row of buildings.

Die Stadt als Ganzes gleicht dem Werk einer Partitur. Damit wird jedes einzelne Instrument in die übergreifende Komposition eingebunden.
Oberstes Ziel ist die Harmonie einer Stadtsymphonie, in der die Balance des Einzelnen zum Rahmen des Ganzen gefügt wird.
The city as a whole resembles a musical score which orchestrates the sounds of every instrument as the individual parts of the whole composition. The main aim is to achieve the harmony of an urban symphony in which every individual building contributes to the whole framework.

Der neue Bund
The New Bund

Dominanz der Vielfalt.
Dominance in diversity.

Die Symbiose aus Vielfalt und Einheit ist das Geheimnis der urbanen Qualität.
The symbiosis of unity in diversity is the secret of urban quality.

Dominanz der Gleichheit.
The dominance of similarity.

Lingang New City

81

Der neue Bund
The New Bund

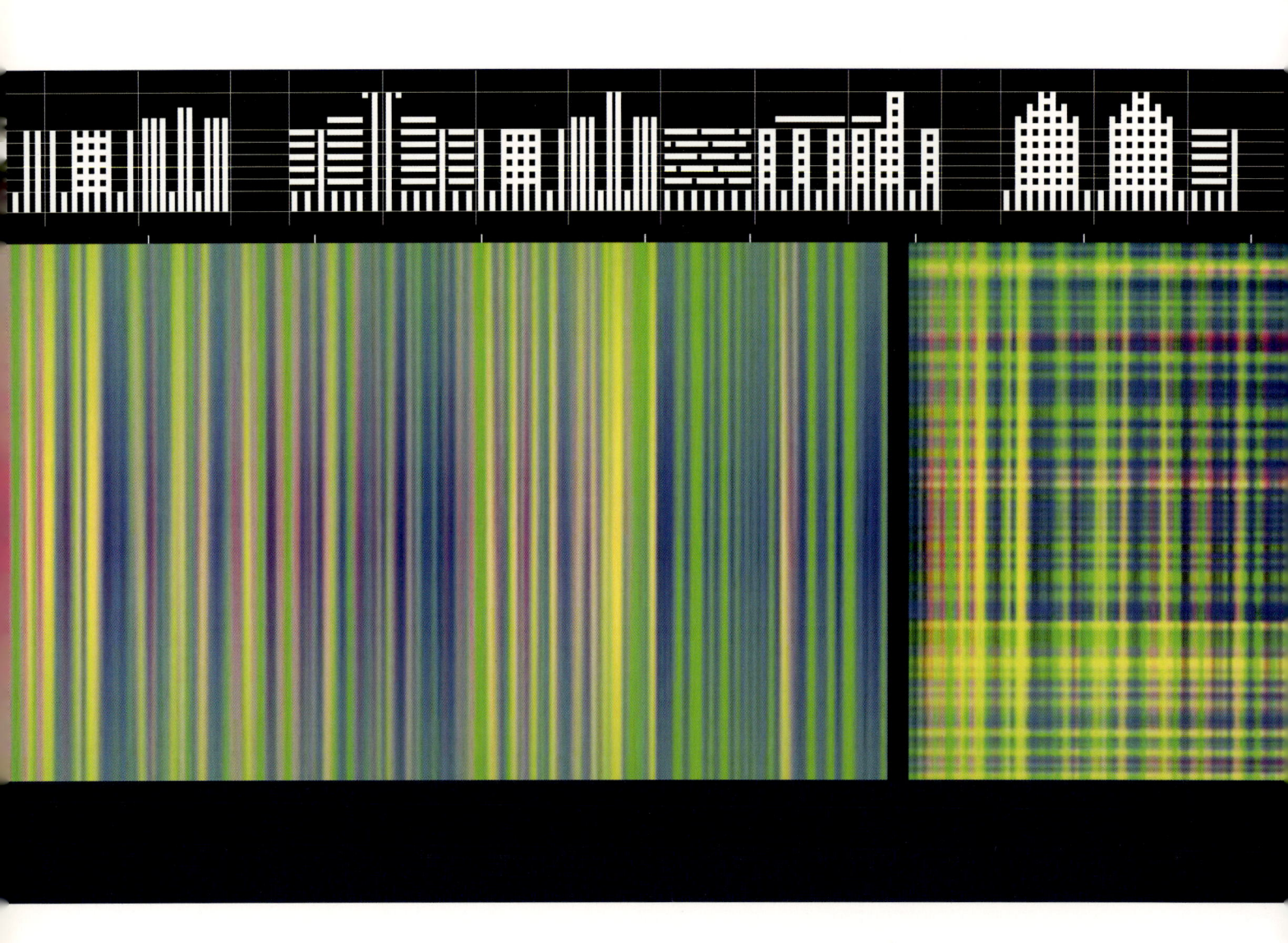

Vertikalität und Horizontalität,
Männlichkeit und Weiblichkeit
bilden die Pole gestalterischer Fügung,
die in der harmonischen Verschmelzung
die Basis des Lebens darstellen.
Verticality and horizontality,
masculinity and femininity form
the opposite poles of design structures
which, in their harmonious fusion,
represent the basis of all life.

Lingang New City

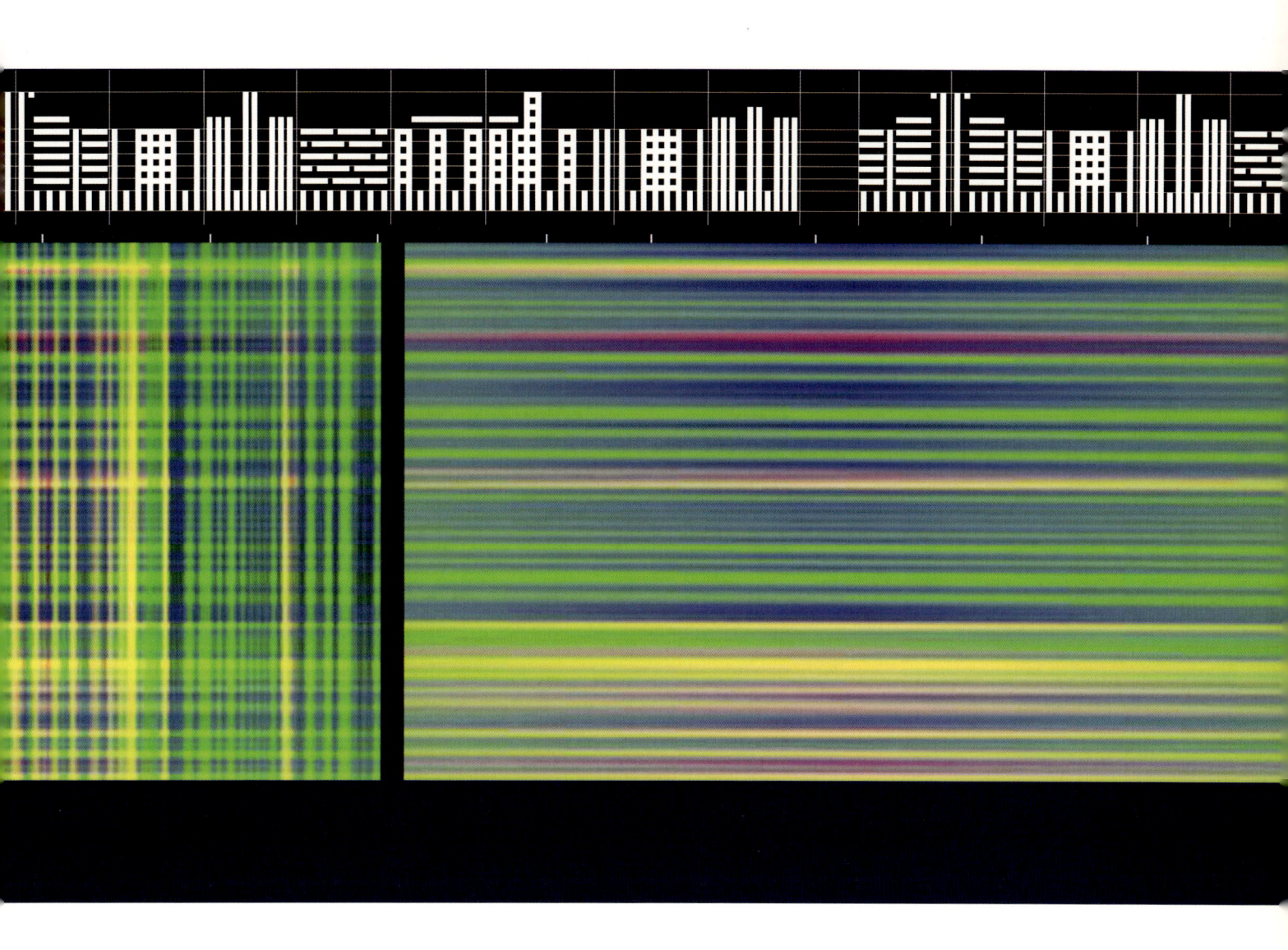

Der neue Bund
The New Bund

Lingang New City

Der neue Bund
The New Bund

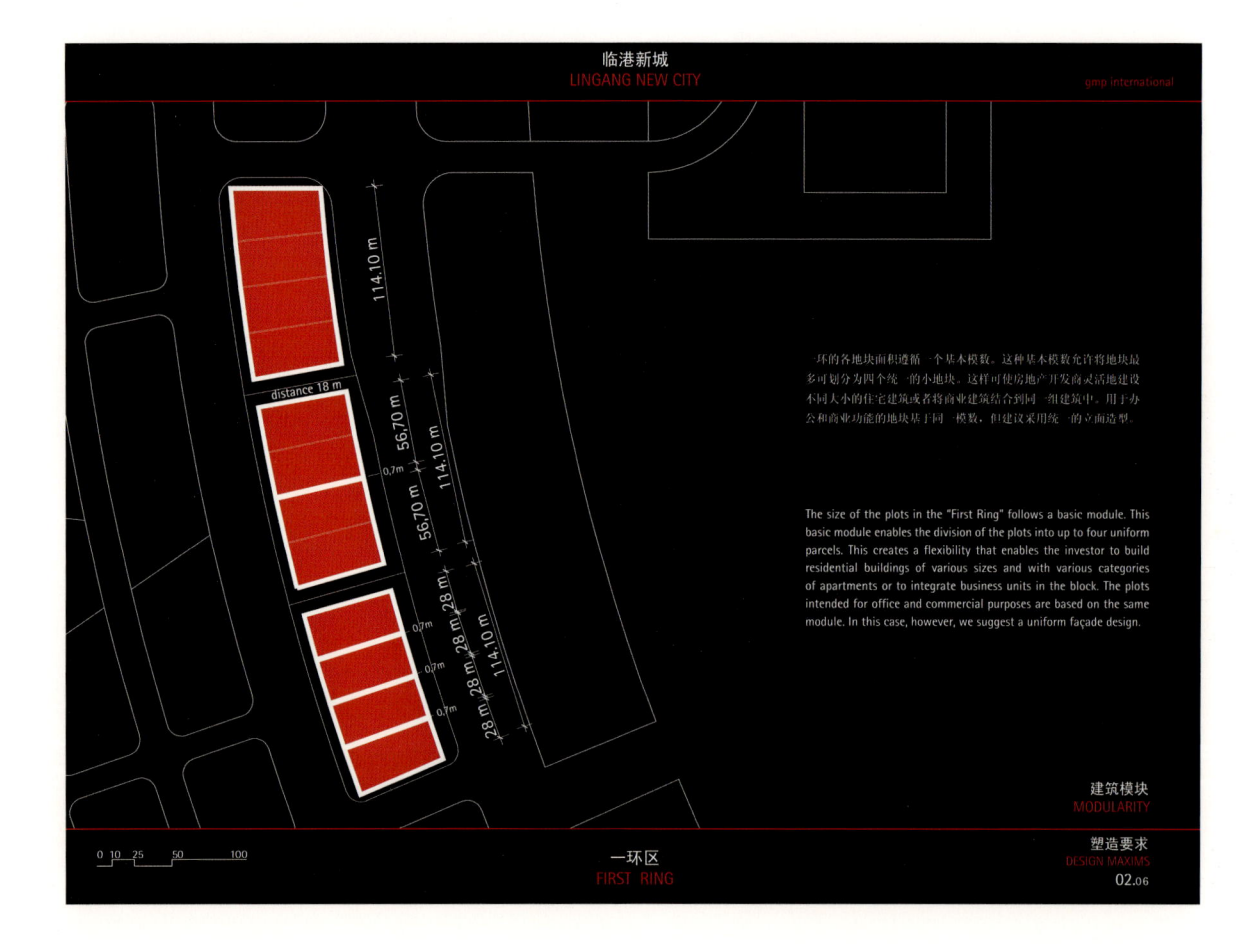

Die Gliederung der Parzellen basiert auf einem modularen Prinzip.
Zoning of the lots is based on the modular principle.

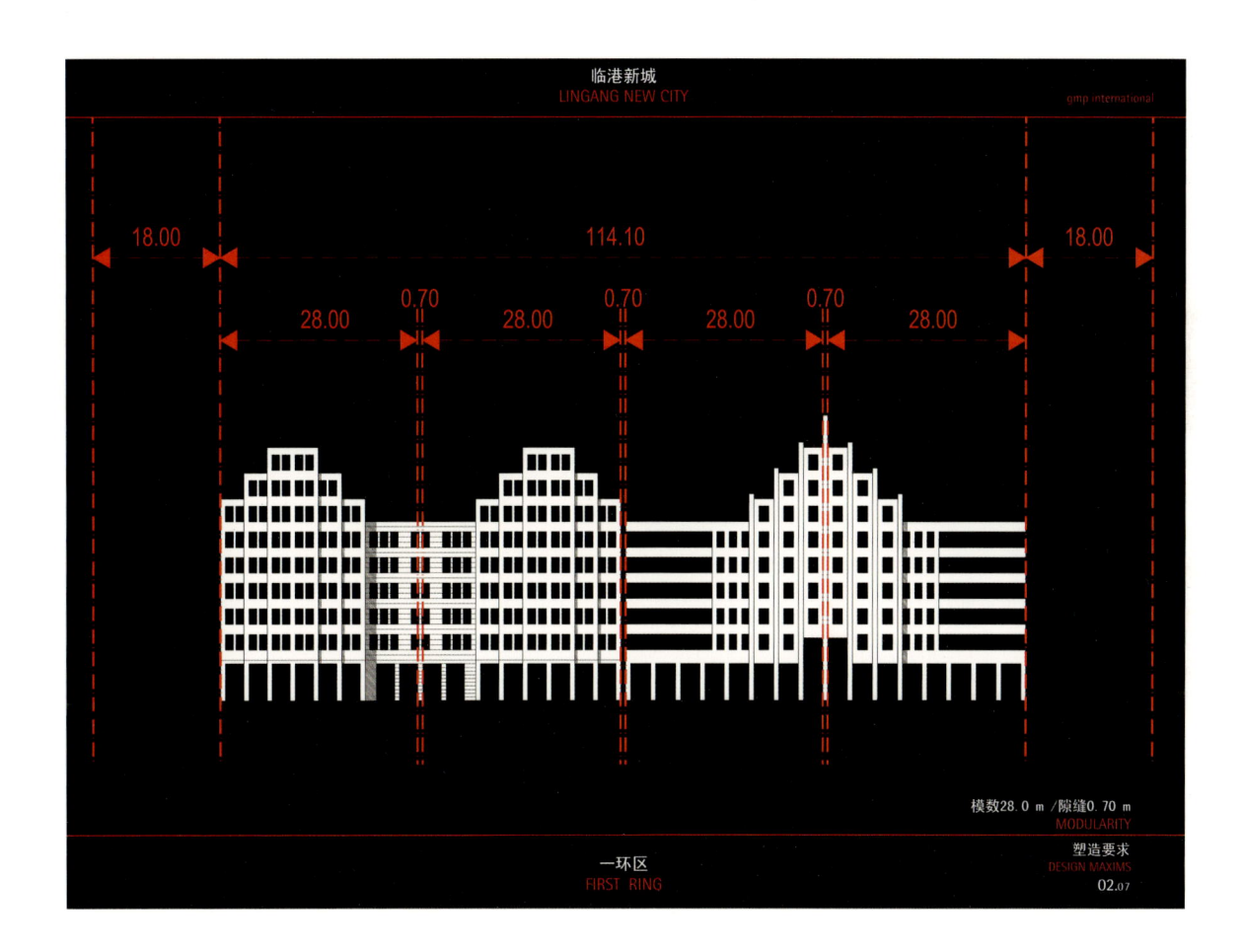

Parzellen im Aufriss.
Lots, elevations.

Der neue Bund
The New Bund

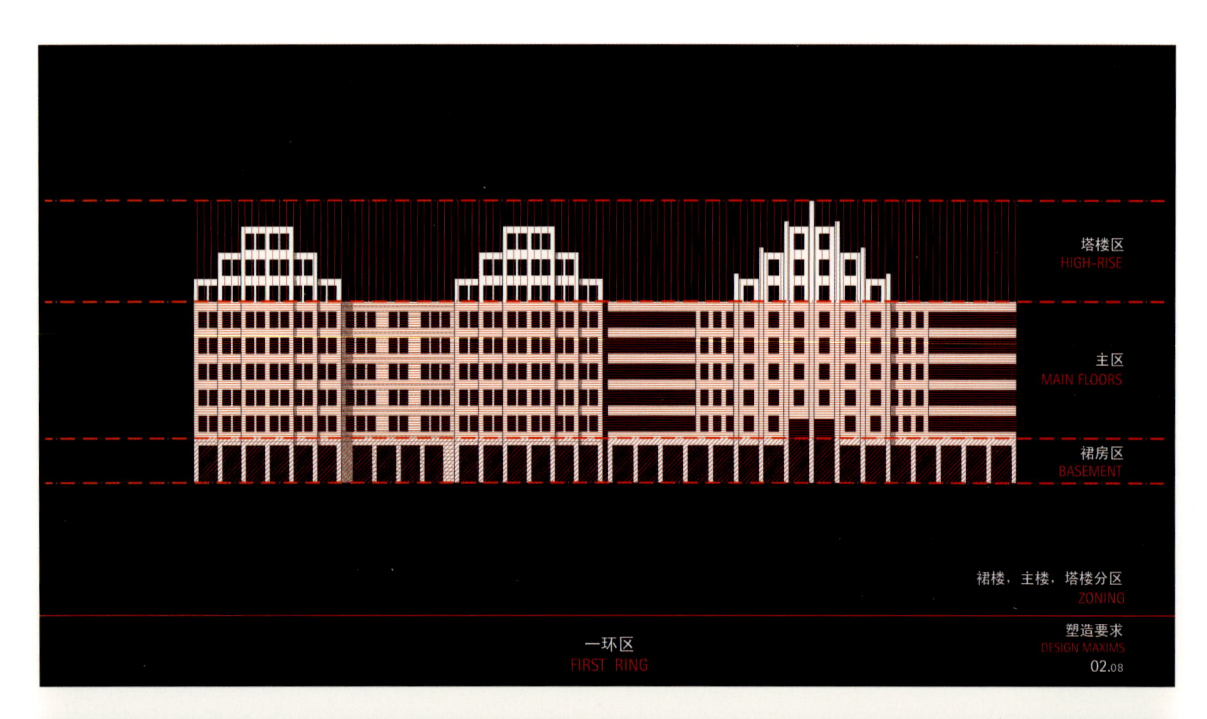

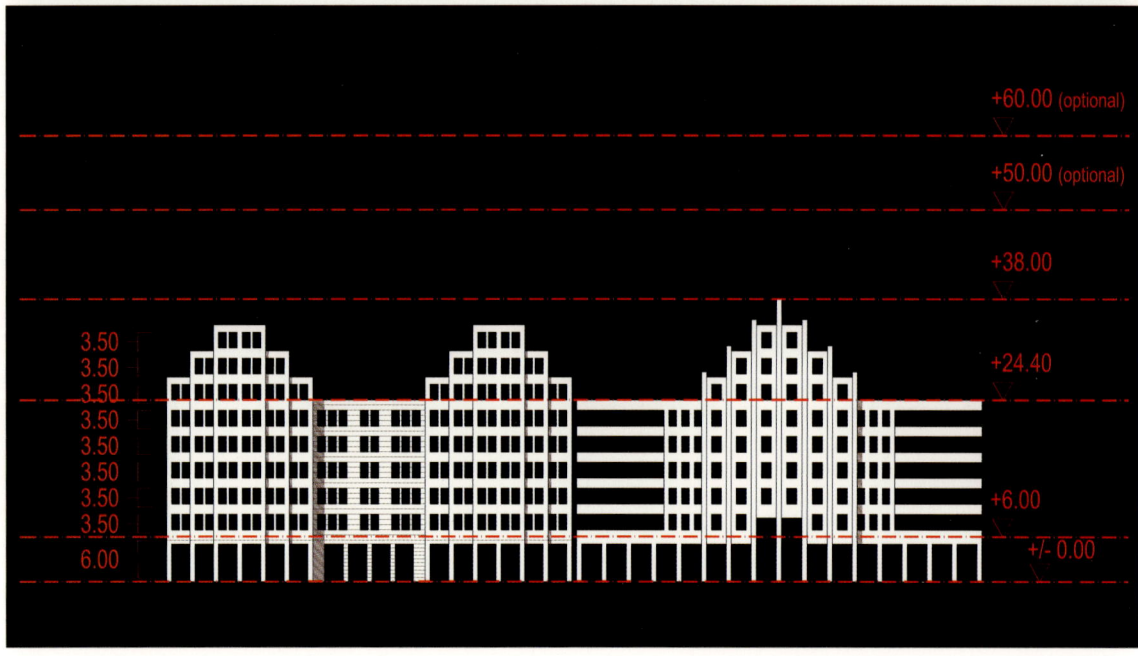

Oben: Jedes Gebäude hat eine zonierte Höhengliederung.
Basement, Hauptgeschosse, Dachaufbau.
Top: Every building is vertically divided into three sections, i.e.
basement, main floors, roof/attic.
Unten: Die Höhenstaffelung regelt den Rhythmus der Gebäudeprofile.
Bottom: The staggered heights regulate the rhythm of the building profiles.

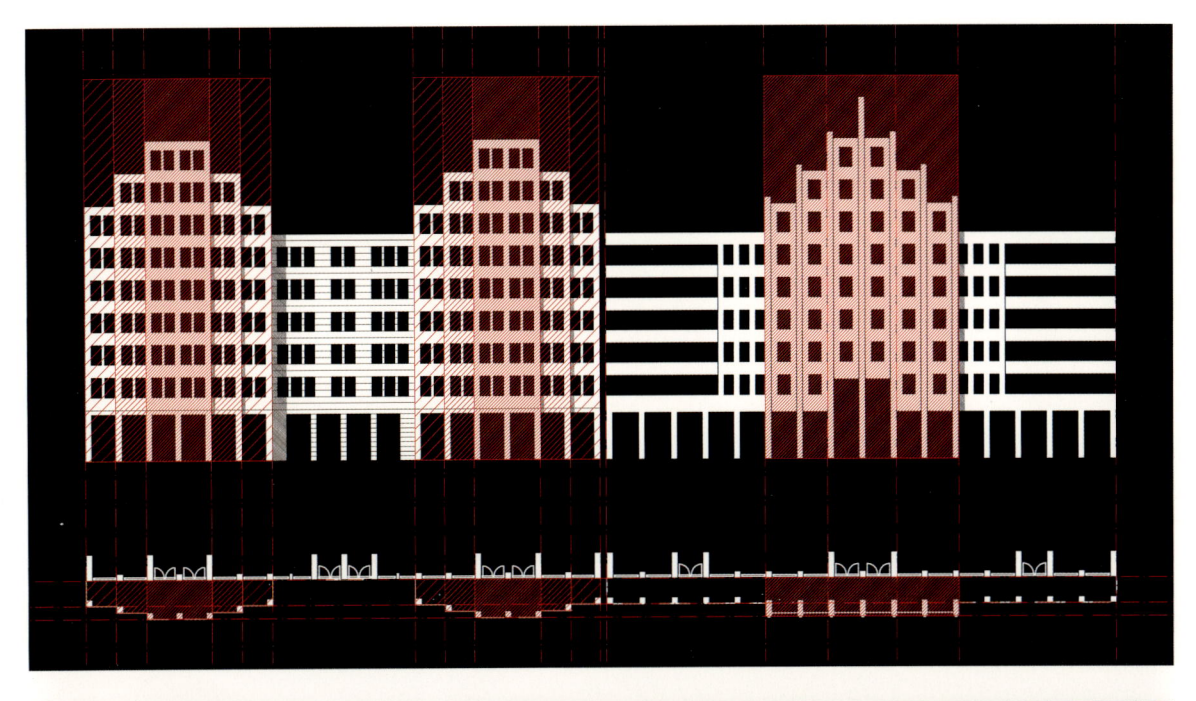

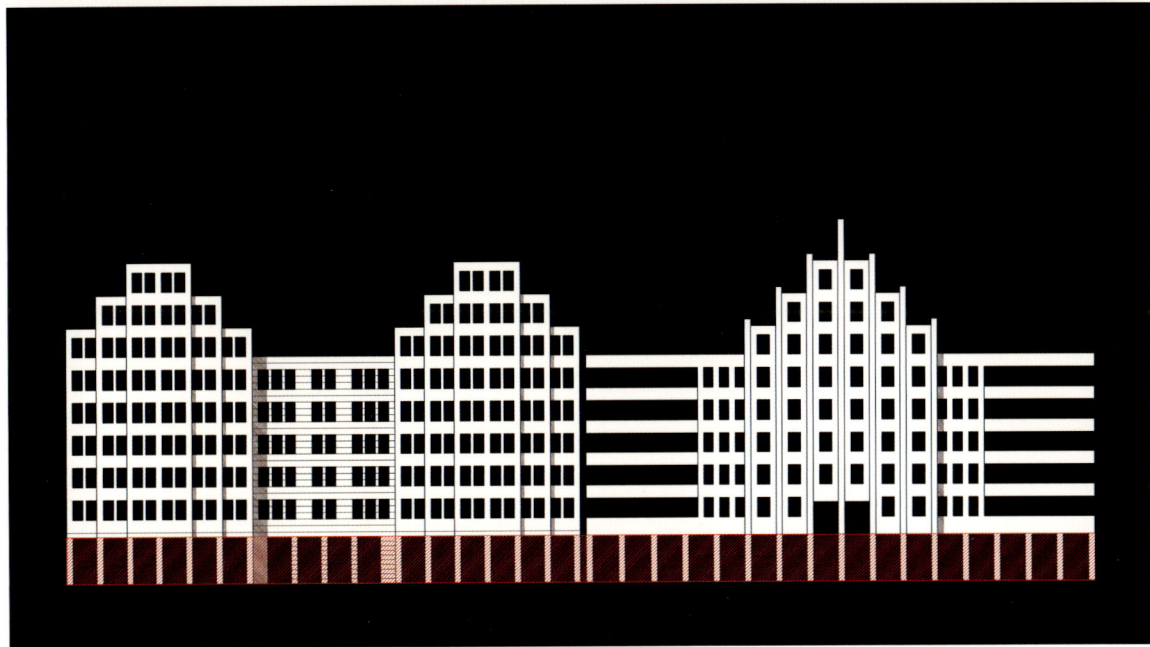

Oben: Vor- und Rücksprünge differenzieren die Fronten an der Straßenlinie.
Top: Projections and offsets add interest to the street façades.
Unten: Durchgängige Arkaden verzahnen den öffentlichen Raum mit den individuellen Gebäuden.
Bottom: Continuous arcades interlock the public space with the individual private structures.

Der neue Bund
The New Bund

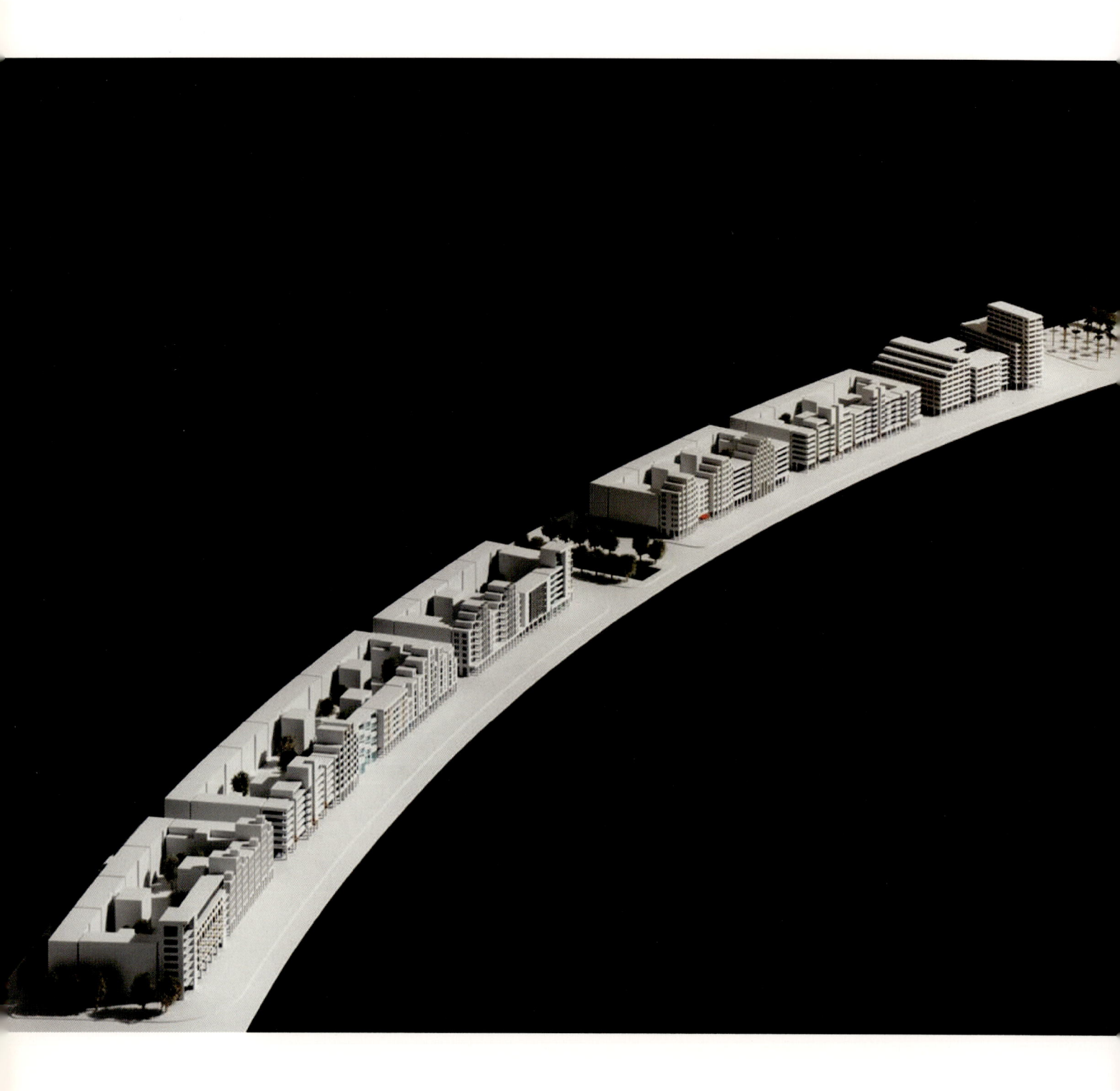

Bebauung des Bundes im Modell.
Model of the New Bund structures.

Lingang New City

Der neue Bund
The New Bund

Oben: Interpretation in der Fassadengestaltung.
Top: Interpretation of the façade design.

Der neue Bund
The New Bund

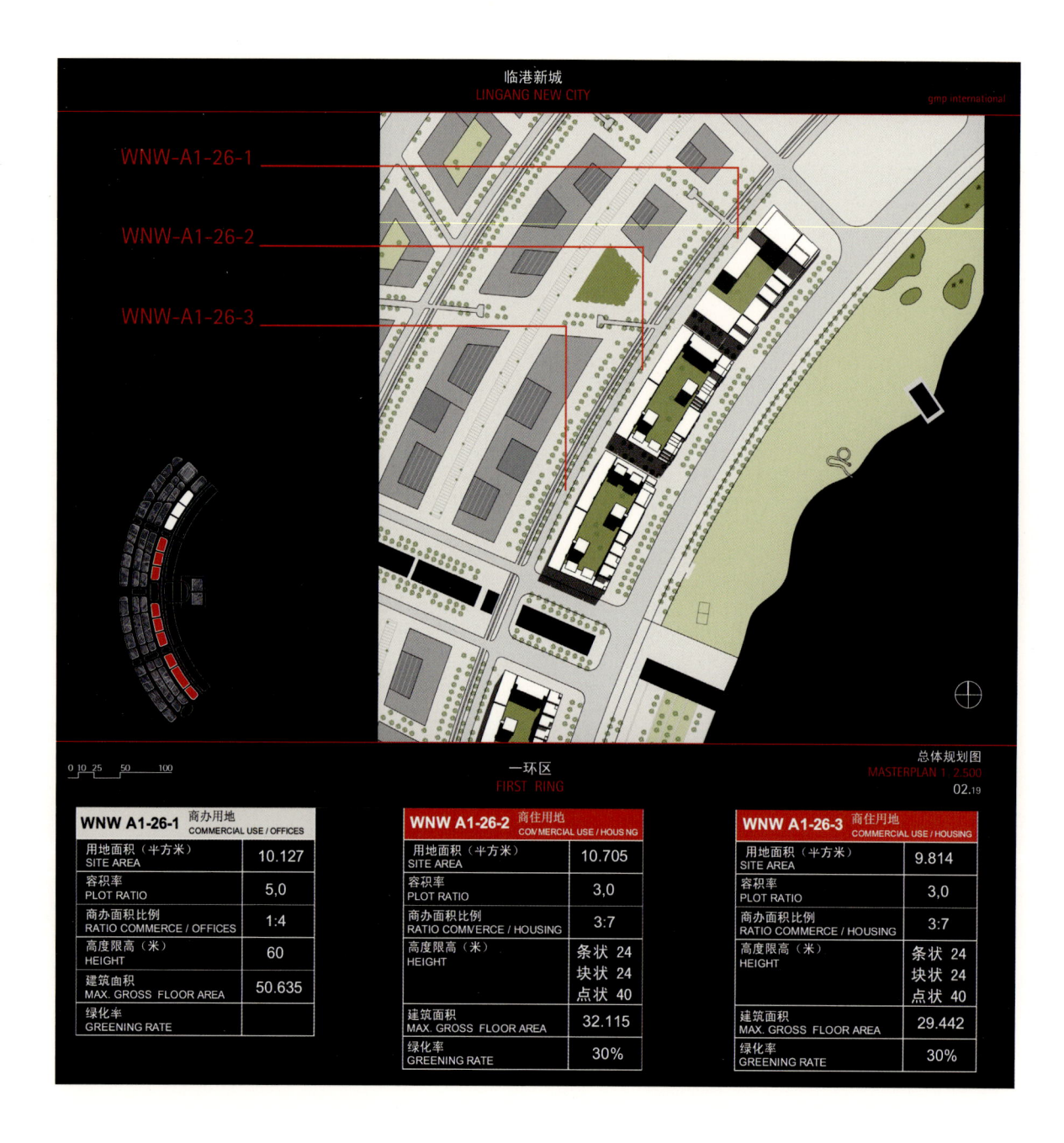

Nutzungausweisungen für einzelne Parzellen.
Planned uses of individual lots.

Bebauung des Bundes im Modell.
Model of the New Bund structures.

Der neue Bund
The New Bund

Oben: Schema.
Top: Diagramme.
Unten: Interpretation.
Bottom: Interpretation.

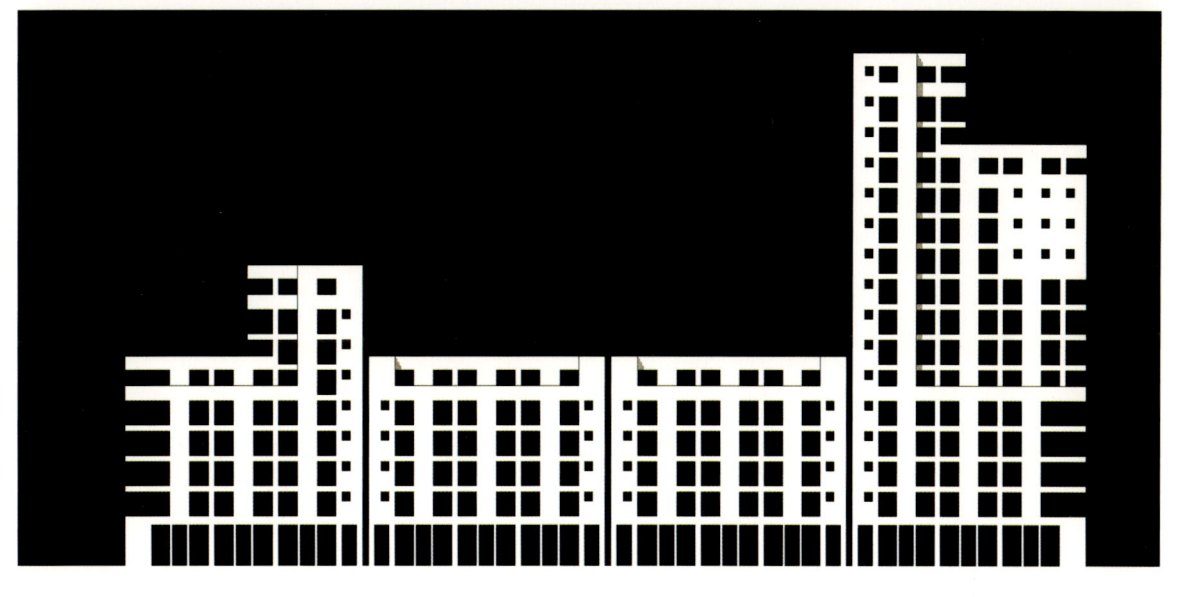

Oben: Interpretation des Schemas.
Top: Interpretation of the diagramme.
Unten: Strukturschema.
Bottom: Basic structural diagramme.

Der neue Bund
The New Bund

Beispielhafte Untergliederung
eines Blockes in Wohneinheiten.
Examplary block subdivided into
residential units.

Oben: Interpretation und Schema.
Top: Diagramme and interpretation.
Unten: Interpretation und Schema.
Bottom: Diagramme and interpretation.

Lingang New City

100

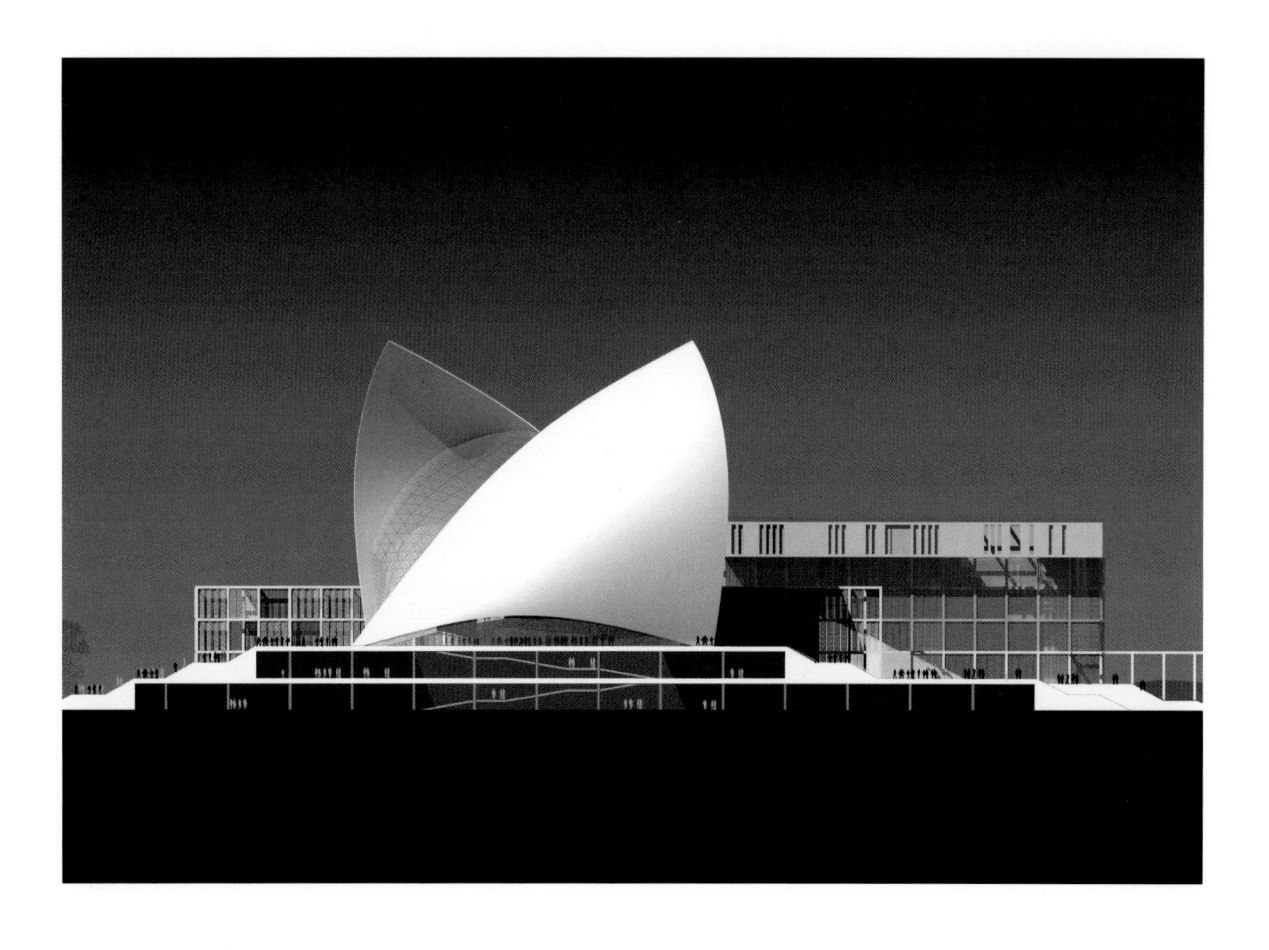

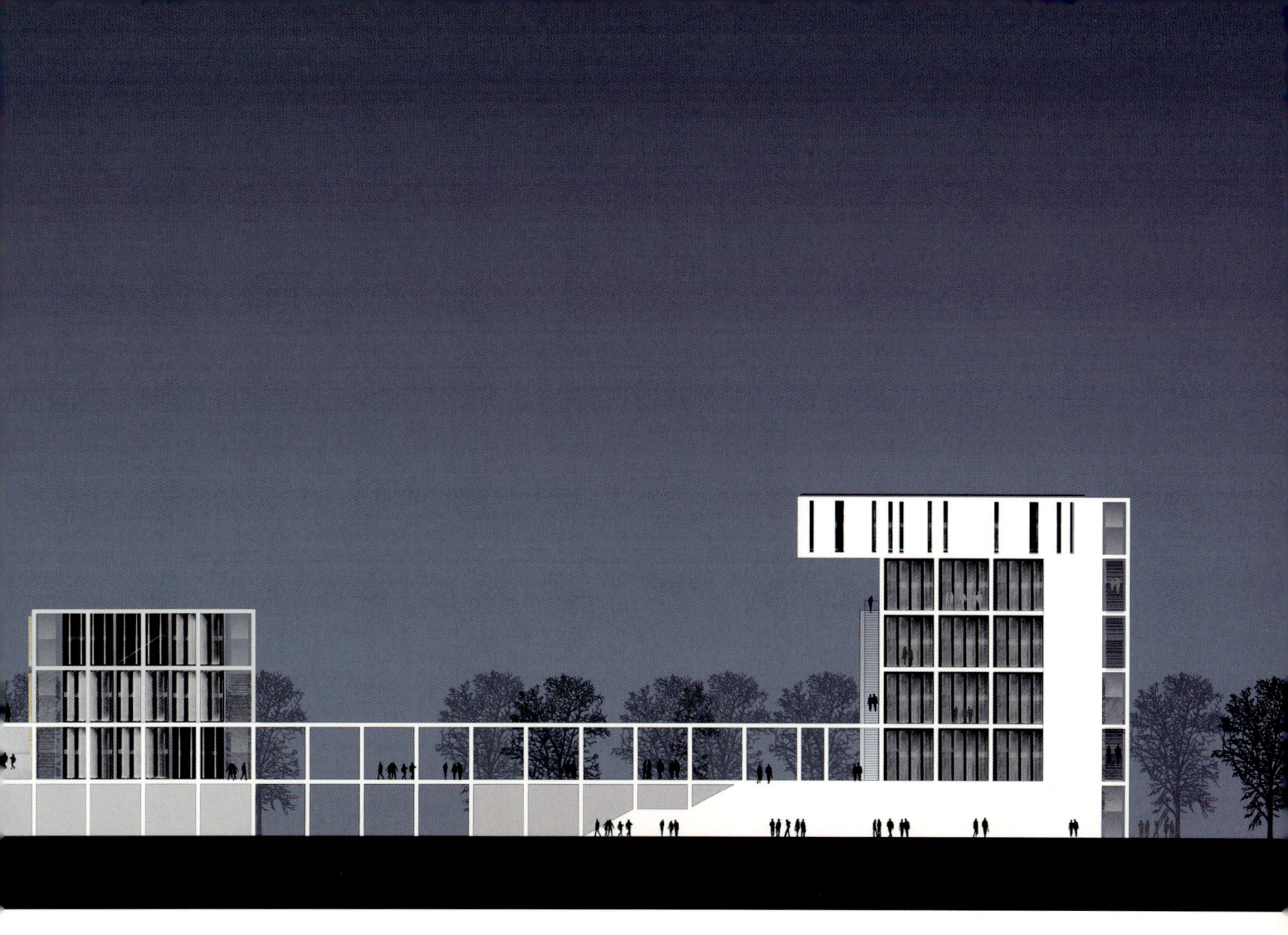

Schifffahrtsmuseum, Jugendzentrum und Bibliothek in Lingang New City

Die solitärhaften Baukörper des Schifffahrtsmuseums, des Jugendzentrums und der Bibliothek werden mit Hilfe einer einheitlichen Form- und Materialsprache zu einer homogenen Gesamtanlage zusammen geführt.
Arkaden, Stege, Brücken und Luftbalken bilden subtile Gestaltungsmittel, welche im Gesamtspiel von Licht und Schatten unter Einbindung von Wasser- und Grünflächen dem Komplex der drei unterschiedlichen Funktionen entwurflichen Zusammenhang verleihen.
Aus dieser formalen Gesamtgestalt setzt sich das mittig zwischen Bibliothek und Jugendzentrum gelegene

Maritime Museum, Youth Centre and Library in Lingang New City

The solitaire-type structures of the Maritime Museum, the Youth Centre and the Library are combined to form a homogenous overall complex with the help of the uniform use of shapes and materials.
Arcades, footbridges and open beams form subtle design elements that, in an overall play of light and shade and integrating the water and green areas, lend the complex of the three different functions a coherence of design.
Centrally placed between the Library and the Youth Centre, the Maritime Museum, with its expressive roof shape, stands out distinctly and independently against this formal overall construction. Two light roof shells,

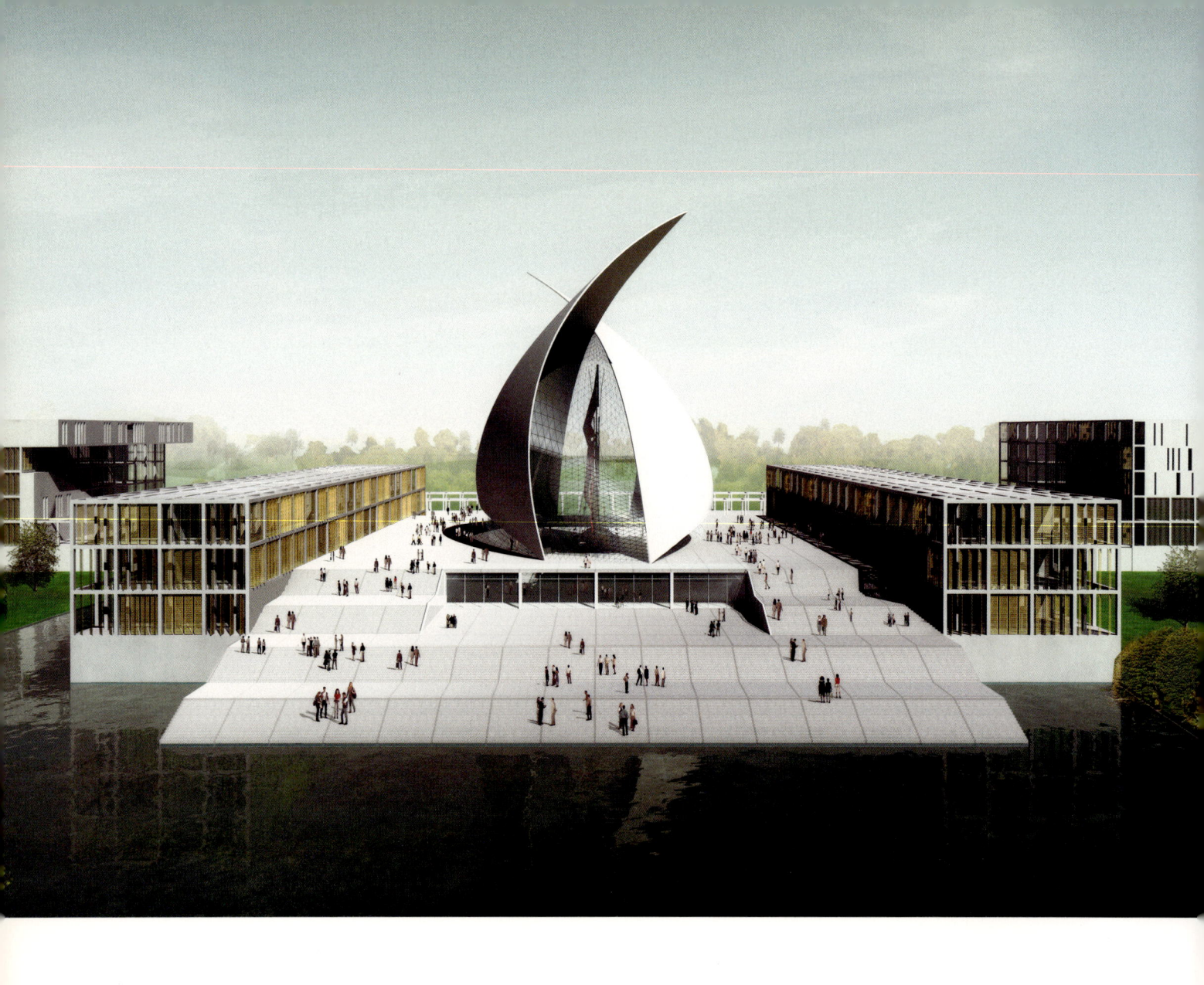

Schifffahrtsmuseum mit seiner expressiven Dachform deutlich und eigenständig ab. Zwei gegeneinander gesetzte leichte Dachschalen, welche im weitesten Sinn die maritime Form und Analogie eines „Segels" beim Betrachter hervorrufen, bilden das für die Gesamtfigur wichtige und identitätsbildende Leitbild für das Museum. In dem sich unter dieser Dachform spannenden hallenförmigen Luftraum sollen große, historische Schiffsexponate kulturgeschichtlich gewertet und dem Publikum zugänglich gemacht werden.

Die sich gegeneinander verschränkenden „Segelflächen" stehen frei auf einem Sockel, in dem sämtliche museumsbedingten Funktionen enthalten sind. Großzügige Freitreppen laden zum Verweilen ein und bilden einen unmittelbaren Bezug zu den landschaftlich gestalteten Freianlagen.

facing each other and overlapping, that in the broadest sense evoke in the observer the idea of a maritime shape and an analogy to a "sail", create the identity-forming landmark of the Museum that is so decisive for the overall character of the complex. The large, hall-like space below this roof construction is intended for the exhibition of large, ancient ships that have been assessed as being valuable to cultural history. Here they will be made accessible to the general public.

The entwined "sails" stand freely on a base in which all the functions of the Museum are accommodated. Spacious open staircases are inviting places to linger and bear an immediate relation to the landscaped open spaces.

The formal design elements of the publicly accessible pedestal that can be reached via a generously arranged

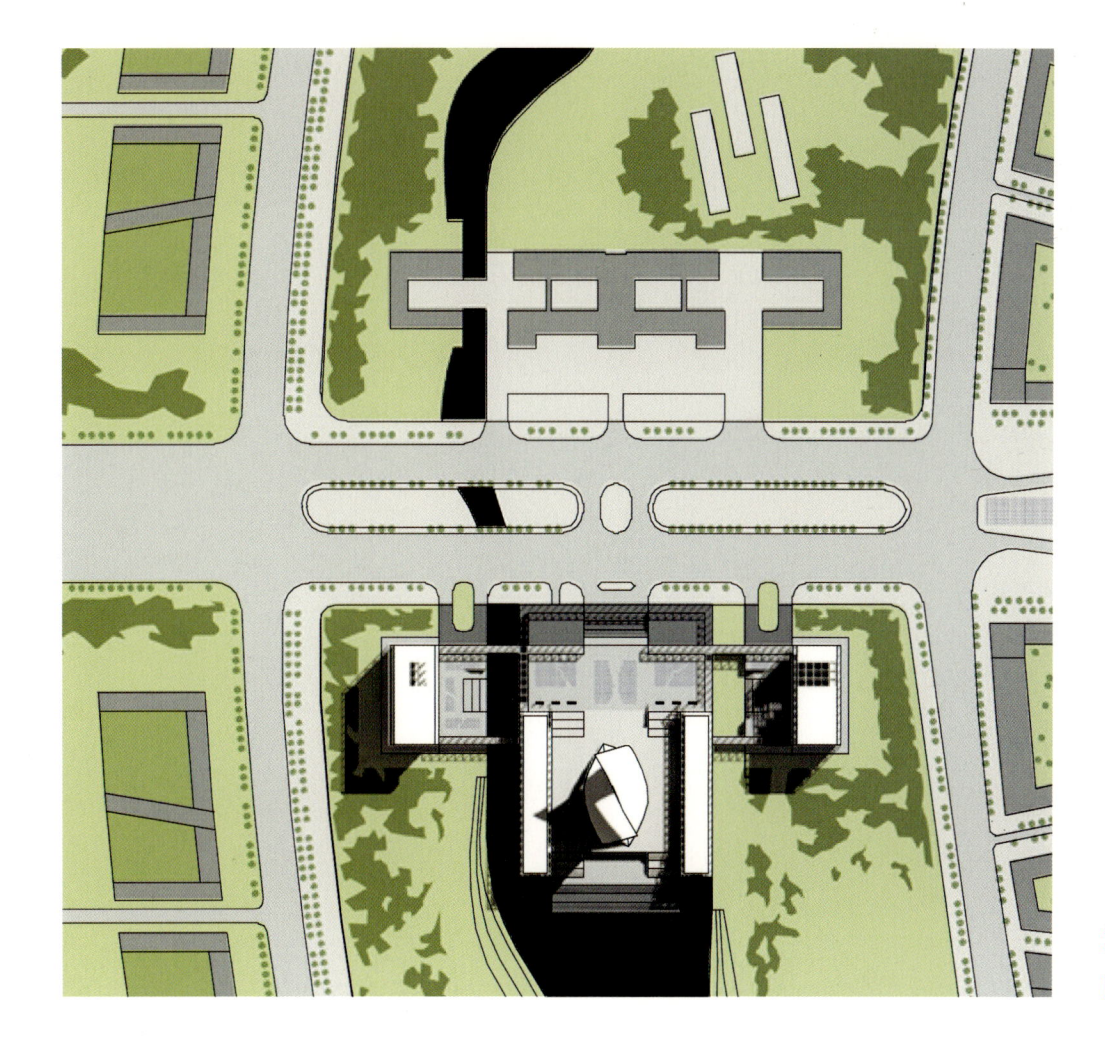

Schifffahrtsmuseum
Maritime Museum

Die formalen Entwurfselemente des frei zugänglichen Sockels, welcher über eine großzügige Freitreppe erschlossen wird, findet sich auch bei den zwei direkt benachbarten Gebäuden, Bibliothek und Jugendzentrum.
Diese beiden formal und entwurflich verwandten Baukörper stehen sich auf einer imaginären Achse gegenüber und flankieren somit das Schifffahrtsmuseum mit seiner leichten, weithin sichtbaren maritimen Dachform.

outside staircase can also be found in the two directly adjoining buildings, the Library and the Youth Centre. These two formal, structurally related building components stand on an imaginary axis directly opposite one another and therefore flank the Maritime Museum with its light marine roof construction that is visible from a great distance.

Shanghai Nanhui District Administrative Office Centre

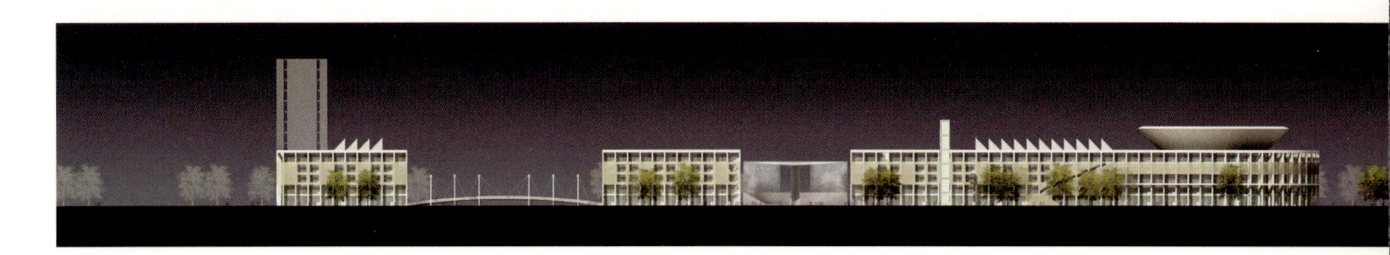

Lingang New City

Shanghai Nanhui District Administrative Office Centre

Die exponierte Lage des Grundstücks an einer der Haupteinfahrtsstraßen von Lingang New City fordert eine ebenso exponierte wie auch klare architektonische Komposition der einzelnen Haupt- und Nebengebäude des Office Center, die sich zu einem übergeordneten Ensemble gruppieren.

Der zentrale Platz der Anlage wird von einem großen quadratischen Dach überspannt, ein von diesem permanent herunterlaufender Wasservorhang definiert zusätzlich noch den Platz und sorgt für eine angenehme Kühlung und eine hohe Verweilqualität. Diesem Patio schließen sich im Osten und Westen der Anlage zwei mit Sheddächern

Shanghai Nanhui District Administrative Office Centre

The exposed position of the plot by one of the main access roads of Lingang New City demands a similarly exposed as well as distinct architectural composition of the individual main buildings and annexes of the Office Centre which will be grouped together to form a super-ordinate ensemble.

The central square in the complex is spanned by a large quadratic roof, a curtain of water permanently running down from this lends additional emphasis to the square and ensures pleasant cooling and a high incentive to linger here.

In the east and west of the complex two light-filled entrance halls covered with shed roofs adjoin this patio.

überspannte, lichtdurchflutete Eingangshallen an.
Im östlich gelegenen Hauptgebäude gelangt man über kaskadenartig angelegte Treppen in die zentrale Zone, die von einem bis zu 2.500 Personen fassenden Konferenzsaal abgeschlossen wird.
Im Westen der Anlage gruppieren sich die Nebengebäude um den vom Fluss durchbrochenen palmenbestandenen Innenhof.

In the main building on the east side a cascade-like staircase leads to the central zone that is crowned by a conference hall with capacity for up to 2,500 people.
On the western side of the complex the annexes are grouped around the inner courtyard with its palm trees and the river flowing through it.

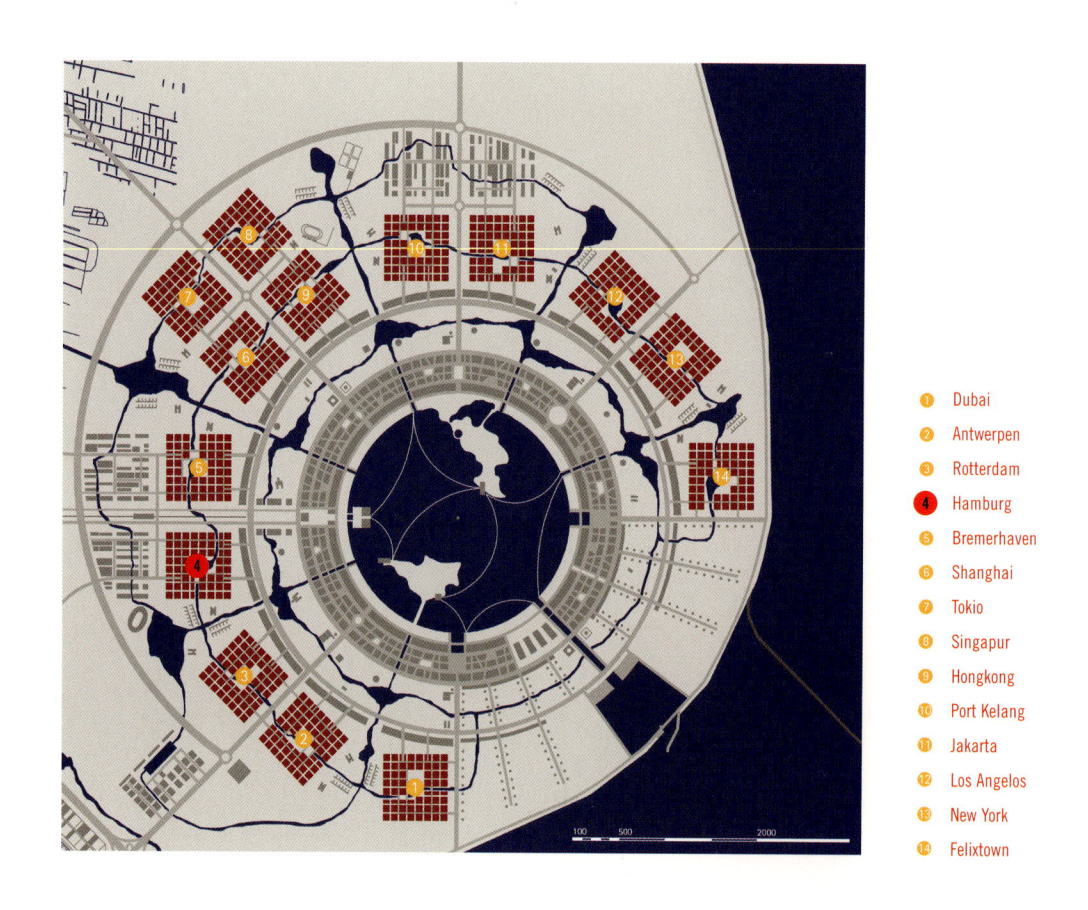

① Dubai
② Antwerpen
③ Rotterdam
④ Hamburg
⑤ Bremerhaven
⑥ Shanghai
⑦ Tokio
⑧ Singapur
⑨ Hongkong
⑩ Port Kelang
⑪ Jakarta
⑫ Los Angelos
⑬ New York
⑭ Felixtown

„Die beiden bedeutsamen Dinge in China sind eine unverwechselbare Identität und städtische Bedingungen, die den Begriff der Urbanität verdienen und ein städtisches, verknüpftes Leben ermöglichen – Arbeiten, Einkaufen, Wohnen!"

"The two important things in China are an unmistakable identity and urban conditions that are worthy of urbanity and allow urban, cohesive existence—working, shopping, living!"

Stadtinseln

Die 14 Wohnquartiere, die sich im dritten Ring von Lingang New City um das Zentrum herum gruppieren, sind als definierte, ausgewiesene Bereiche eingebettet in den gewachsenen Landschaftsraum der Provinz von Nanhui. Als autarke Kleinstzentren mit Geschäften, Dienstleistungen, medizinischer Grundversorgung, Kindergarten und Kinderkrippe bilden sie eigenständige Gemeinden. Während sie durch Einheitlichkeit in Größe, Raster, Grundmodul und einen vorgegebenen Materialkanon eine eindeutige Gruppe darstellen, so sind sie in der Gestaltung des öffentlichen Raumes differenziert. Plätze und städtische Parks werden durch internationale Hafenstädte, die als Paten fungieren, geprägt. Dies schafft den Spielraum für eine jeweils eigene Identität und Unverwechselbarkeit.

Urban Islands

The 14 residential quarters, arranged in the third ring around the centre, are embedded as defined, identifiable areas in the expanded countryside area of the Nanhui province. These self-sustaining mini-centres with shops, services, basic medical care, kindergartens and crèches form self-sufficient communities.
Whilst their common size, grid and basic module, as well as a pre-determined canon of materials, show that they are clearly part of a group, the design of the public spaces gives each of them a unique character. The squares and public parks are strongly influenced by international harbour cites which serve as models of inspiration, thus allowing scope for individuality and an unmistakable identity.

Stadtinseln
Urban Islands

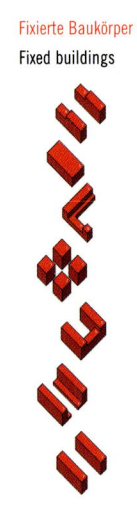

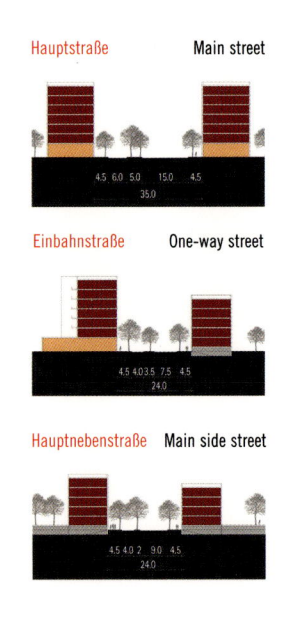

Fixierte Baukörper
Fixed buildings

Hauptstraße — Main street

Einbahnstraße — One-way street

Hauptnebenstraße — Main side street

110

Lingang New City

Gestaltungszone III: Stadtinseln III.1 Wohnhäuser

1.1 Baukörper

1.1.1 Typen: Zeilen- und Punkthäuser, um innere, begrünte Höfe angeordnete Bebauung, Modulbildung.

1.1.2 Geschossigkeit: Variation von 3-5 Geschossen, Ausnahmefall in Stadtkernnähe 7 Geschosse, Variation der Traufhöhe siehe Masterplan.

1.1.3 Sockelzonen: Ausbildung einer Sockelzone mit 1/2 Geschoss à 1,50 m, Nutzung als tiefergelegtes offenes Parkgeschoss im Souterrain.

1.1.4 Hauptgeschosse: 3-5 Hauptgeschosse à 3,00 m Geschosshöhe.

1.1.5 Traufhöhen: zulässige Traufhöhen +11,50 m (3 Geschosse), +14,50 m (4 Geschosse) und +17,50 m (5 Geschosse) ab Oberkante Gelände, in Ausnahmefällen zulässige Traufhöhe +23,50 m (7 Geschosse) ab Oberkante Gelände, Variation der Traufhöhe siehe Masterplan.

1.2. Proportionen

1.2.1 Module: Festlegung der Module auf 66,00 m x 66,00 m Achsmaß Grundstücksfläche im Regelfall. Ausnahmefälle: Städtebaulich begründet, siehe Masterplan.

1.2.2 Achsmaße und Raster: Raster 1,65 m, Achsmaß 8,25 m mit acht Wohneinheiten pro Etage; Raster 1,65 m, Achsmaß 6,60 m mit zehn Wohneinheiten pro Etage.

1.3. Fassaden

1.3.1 Gliederung der Fassaden: Lochfassade mit rechteckigen, stehenden Fensterformaten; vertikale Gliederung durch Betonung der Eingänge und Treppenhäuser; Rücksprünge, Überhöhungen, Erker und Loggien sind zulässig und gliedern die Fassade zusätzlich vertikal.

1.3.2 Fassadenmaterialien: Die Fassaden müssen als Ziegelfassade ausgebildet werden. In geringem Maß (ca. 20%) sind auch heller Naturstein mit stumpfer Oberfläche und Putz sowie Sichtbeton und Holz zulässig. Verspiegelte Verglasungen werden ausgeschlossen.

1.3.3 Farben: Farbspektrum zwischen hellem bis dunklem Gelb, Rot, Weiß und Grau, glasierte Ziegel als Ornament sind zulässig.

1.3.4 Fenster und Türen: rechteckige, stehende Formate, Fassadenöffnungsanteil 40%.

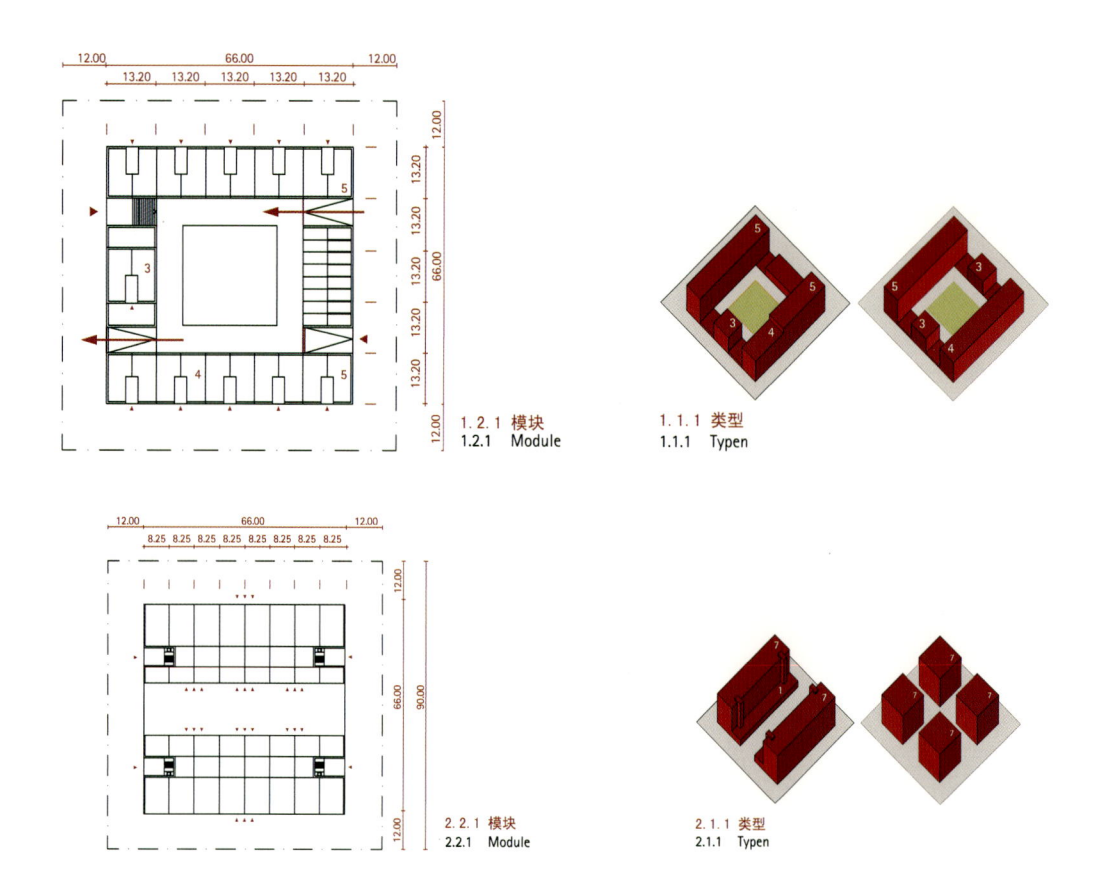

III.2 Wohn- und Geschäftshäuser und Parkhaus (Mischnutzungen)

2.1 Baukörper

2.1.1 Typen: Zeilen- und Punkthäuser in Fußgängerzone angeordnet, Modulbildung.

2.1.2 Geschossigkeit: 5-7 Geschosse, Variation der Traufhöhe siehe Masterplan.

2.1.3 Sockelzonen: Ausbildung einer Sockelzone mit einem Geschoss à 4,50 m als Gewerbefläche.

2.1.4 Hauptgeschosse: 4-6 Hauptgeschosse à 3,00 m Geschosshöhe, Wohn-, Gewerbe- oder Parkfläche.

2.1.5 Traufhöhen: zulässige Traufhöhen +17,50 m (5 Geschosse) und +23,50 m (7 Geschosse) ab Oberkante Gelände, Variation der Traufhöhe siehe Masterplan.

2.2. Proportionen

2.2.1 Module: Festlegung der Module auf 66,00 m x 66,00 m Achsmaß Grundstücksfläche. Öffentliche Durchwegung, Plätze, offene Passage siehe Masterplan sind einzuhalten.

2.2.2 Achsmaße und Raster: Raster 1.65 m, Achsmaß 8,25 m; Gewerbefläche: Unterteilung der Module frei nach Nutzungsbedarf (Anzahl der Achsen); Wohnfläche: 8 Wohneinheiten pro Etage.

2.3. Fassaden

2.3.1 Gliederung der Fassaden: Lochfassade mit rechteckigen, stehenden Fensterformaten; vertikale Gliederung durch Betonung der Eingänge und Treppenhäuser, z.B. Rücksprünge, Überhöhungen.

2.3.2 Fassadenmaterialien: Die Fassaden müssen als Ziegel- oder Putzfassade ausgebildet werden. In geringem Maß (ca. 20%) sind auch heller Naturstein mit stumpfer Oberfläche und Sichtbeton zulässig. Verspiegelte Verglasungen werden ausgeschlossen.

2.3.3 Farben: Farbspektrum zwischen hellem bis dunklem Gelb, Rot, Weiß und Grau, glasierte Ziegel als Ornament sind zulässig.

2.3.4 Fenster und Türen: rechteckige, stehende Formate, Fassadenöffnungsanteil 50 %.

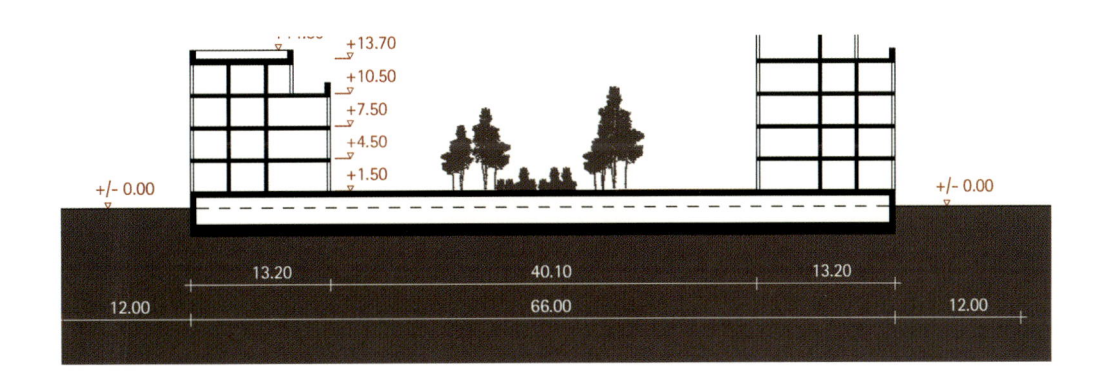

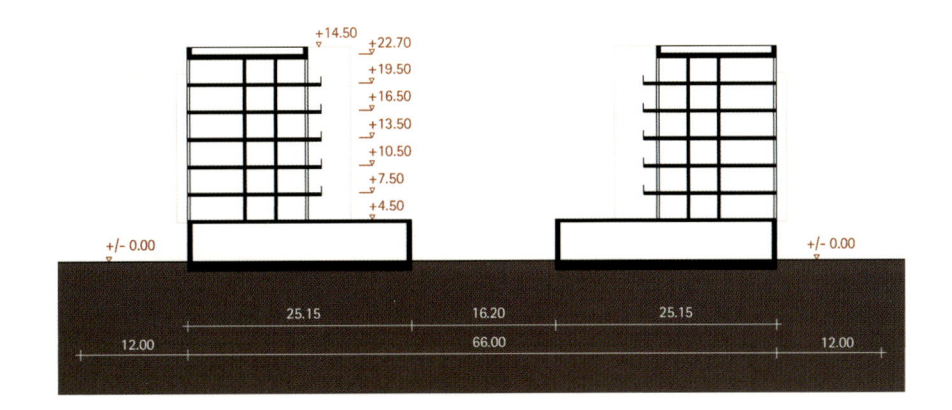

Deutsche Schule in Peking
German School, Beijing

Die deutsche Schule in Peking. Obgleich das Umfeld desolat wirkt, handelt es sich um eine der ersten Adressen in Peking. Links das Apartmenthaus, rechts die Schule.

The German School in Beijing. Although the surroundings seem to be in a desolate state, this location is one of the best addresses in Beijing. On the left the apartment block, on the right the school building.

Stadtbausteine **Urban Modules**

Wettbewerb 1998 – 1. Preis
Entwurf Meinhard v. Gerkan
mit Michael Biwer
Partner Klaus Staratzke
Projektleitung Sibylle Kramer, Michael Biwer
Mitarbeiter Knut Maass,
Ulrich Rösler, Michèle Watenphul,
Jörn Bohlmann, Rüdiger v. Helmolt, Diana Heinrich
Statik Weber-Poll, Hamburg
Bauherr
Bundesrepublik Deutschland, BBR
Bauzeit 1999 – 2000
BGF Schule 9.658 m²
Dienstwohnungen: 9.657 m²
BRI Schule 33.534 m³
Dienstwohnungen 30.923 m³

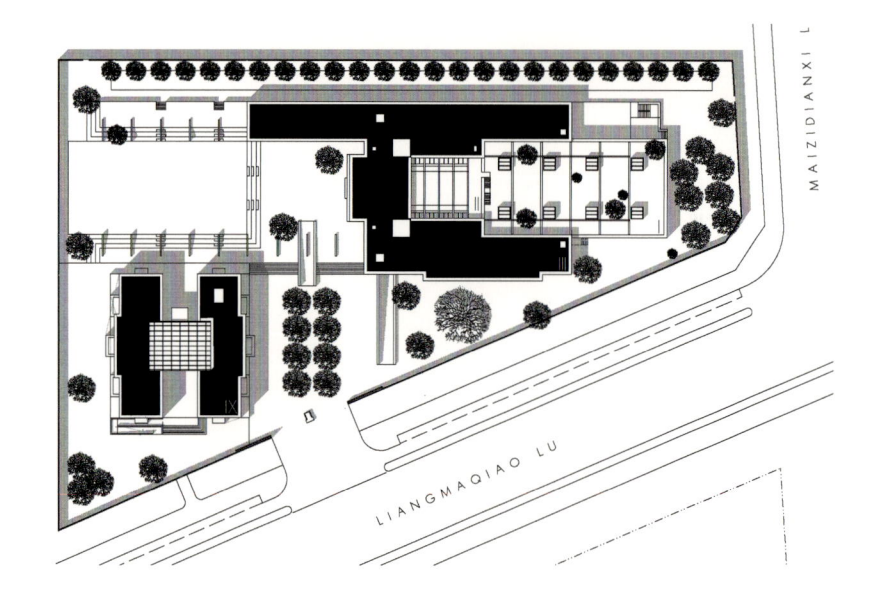

Deutsche Schule und Apartmenthaus in Peking

Das Grundstück liegt im 3. Diplomatenviertel der Stadt; die stark befahrene Straße Liangmaquiao-Lu und eine heterogene Umgebung prägen das Umfeld. Aus dieser Situation entwickelte sich die Idee einer auf sich bezogenen Baukörperdisposition, die über feste Raumkanten das Grundstück in definierte Freiräume teilt. Ein Wechselspiel aus Freiräumen, Abgrenzung und Öffnung entsteht, das die chinesische Bautradition der Gruppierung von Baukörpern aufgreift.

Das Ensemble wird aus einem horizontal geprägten Schulgebäude und, im Kontrast dazu, einem vertikalen Wohnkomplex gebildet. Beide Gebäude gliedern sich durch eine Teilung in Schichten, die als durchgängiges Strukturmerkmal einen übergeordneten Zusammenhang herstellen. Beim Schulgebäude flankieren zwei dreigeschossige Riegel die mittlere Schicht der Sondernutzungen.

Foyer, Aula und Sporthalle folgen in additiver Reihung aufeinander. Mobile Trennwände schaffen ein flexibles und großzügiges Raumkontinuum. Hier können auch außerschulische Veranstaltungen stattfinden.

Die mittlere Gebäudeschicht der Sondernutzungen hebt sich durch Bodenbeläge aus Parkett und Holzwandverkleidungen von den Lehrbereichen ab. Bei diesen stehen weiße Wände und Decken im Kontrast zu roten Bodenbelägen. Einbauelemente wie Türen, Zargen und Schränke sind aus auberginefarbenen Betoplantafeln gefertigt, die üblicherweise als Schalplatten für Ortbetonkonstruktionen dienen.

Eine einfache, übergeordnete Orientierung im Gebäude ist sowohl durch die Baukörpergliederung als auch durch die Trennung der Materialien nach Funktionen gegeben.

In den Obergeschossen schließen die Klassenflügel begrünte Dachgärten ein, die die Freifläche der Schule erweitern. Vor dem Lärm und den Emissionen der stark befahrenen Straße geschützt, eignet sich dieser Außenraum für Freiklassen, zur Freizeitgestaltung und als Lesegarten – eine grüne Enklave in der Stadt. Ebenerdig schließt in gleicher Flucht wie Foyer, Aula und Sporthalle das um einige Stufen abgesenkte Außenspielfeld der Schule an den Pausenhof an.

Das Wohngebäude orientiert sich mit der Eingangshalle zur Hauptstraße hin. Über eine offene Glashalle sind zwei parallel stehende, neungeschossige Riegel miteinander verbunden. Aus der wettergeschützten Eingangshalle

German School and Apartment House, Beijing

The site is located in the city's 3rd diplomats' district; the much used road Liangmaquiao-Lu and the heterogeneous neighbourhood characterize the surrounding area. The concept of a self-orientated building complex was developed from this situation, with strong spatial edges dividing the site into clearly defined open spaces. An interplay of open spaces, delimitation and openings is created, reflecting the Chinese tradition of the grouping of building structures.

The ensemble is formed by a horizontally emphasized school building and a contrasting vertical residential complex. Both buildings are ordered by division into layers which, as a superior structural characteristic, generate an overall continuity.

At the school building, two three-storeyed building parts flank the central layer for special uses.

Foyer, great hall and sports hall are allocated in an additive sequence. Mobile partition walls create a flexible and generous spatial continuum. In this area other than school events can take place.

Parquet flooring and wooden wall cladding contrast the central building layer for special uses with the teaching areas, where white walls and ceilings are contrasted with red floor surfaces. Fitted elements such as doors, framings and cupboards made of from aubergine-coloured concrete panels which usually serve as shutter boards of in-situ concrete constructions.

A clear, superordinate orientation in the building is provided by the order of the building units as well as the separation of materials according to functions. On the upper levels, classroom wings integrate landscaped roof terraces which enlarge the open space of the school. Protected from the noise and emissions of the much used road, this open space is suitable for open air classes, leisure use and as reading place – a green enclave in the city.

The entrance hall of the residential building is orientated towards the main road. An open glass hall connects two parallel, nine-storeyed building parts. Access to the apartments is possible from the weather protected entrance hall via detached staircases and lifts. In total the building contains 45 apartments orientated towards the east – four or six units per level with five different apartment types with between 65 and 210 m² of floor area.

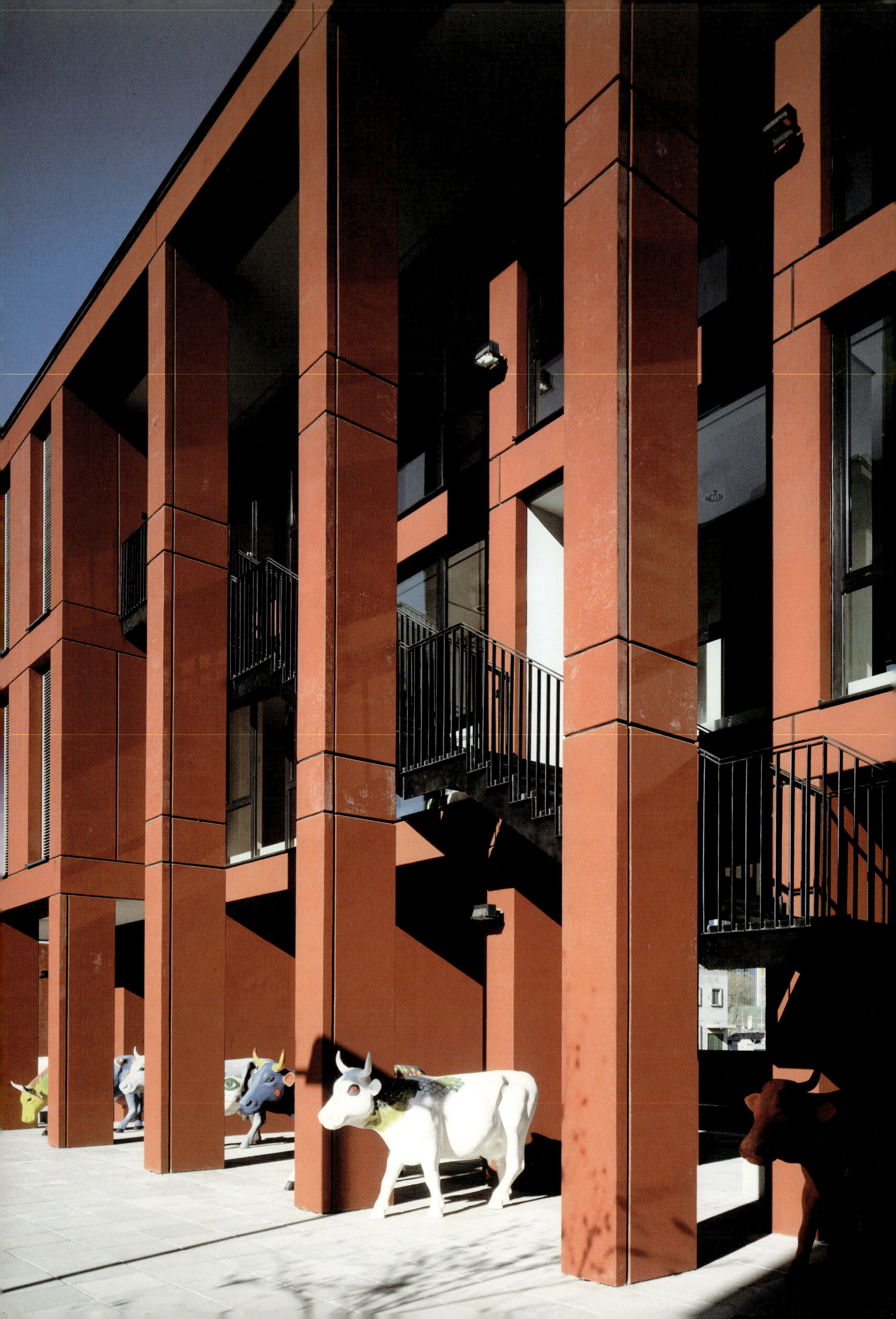

erfolgt die Erschließung der Wohnungen über eingestellte Treppenhäuser und Aufzüge. Insgesamt beinhaltet das Gebäude 45 ost-westorientierte Wohnungen – pro Geschoss vier oder sechs mit fünf verschiedenen Wohnungstypen und zwischen 65 und 210 m^2 Wohnfläche.

Die Wohnräume sind durch Wintergärten erweiterbar. Gliederung und Materialien für Fassade und Innenräume folgen den Überlegungen für das Schulgebäude. So wird das Farbkonzept der kaiserlichen Farben rot und gelb auch im Wohngebäude fortgesetzt. Vom Schulgebäude mit seiner roten Fassade aus Betonfertigteilen und den roten Bodenbelägen im Innenraum unterscheidet sich das Wohngebäude durch seine gelbe Betonfertigteil-Fassade sowie gelbe Bodenbeläge.

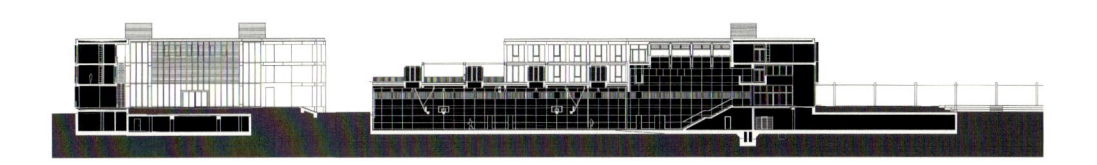

The living space can be increased with winter gardens. Division and materials for façade and interiors follow the considerations taken for the school building. Consequently the colour concept of the imperial red and yellow colours is repeated in the residential block. The school building with its red façade made of pre-fabricated concrete elements and red floorings in the interior is thus contrasted with the residential block with its yellow pre-fabricated concrete façade elements as well as yellow flooring.

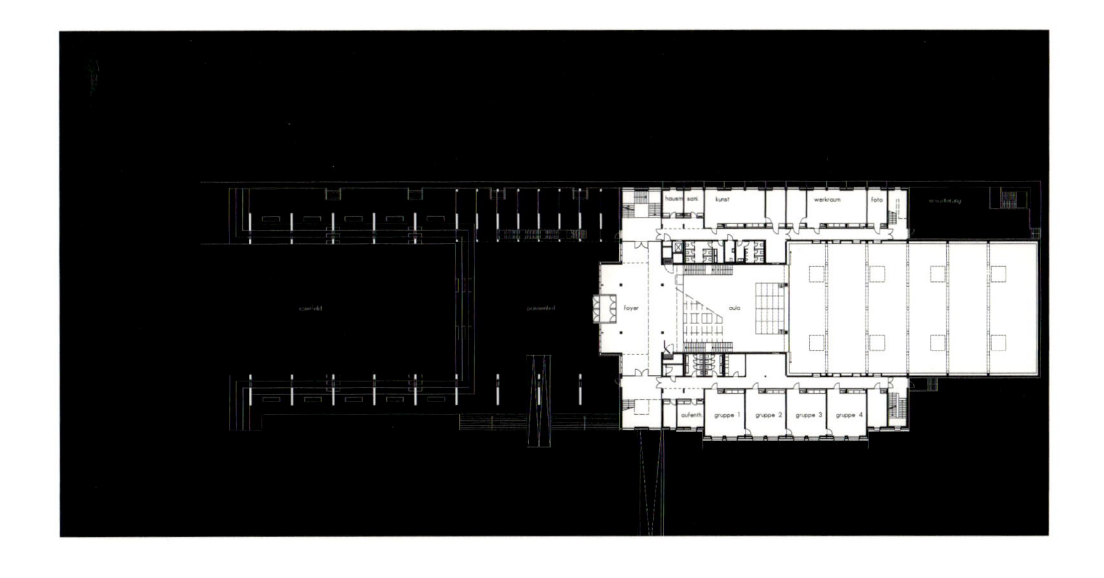

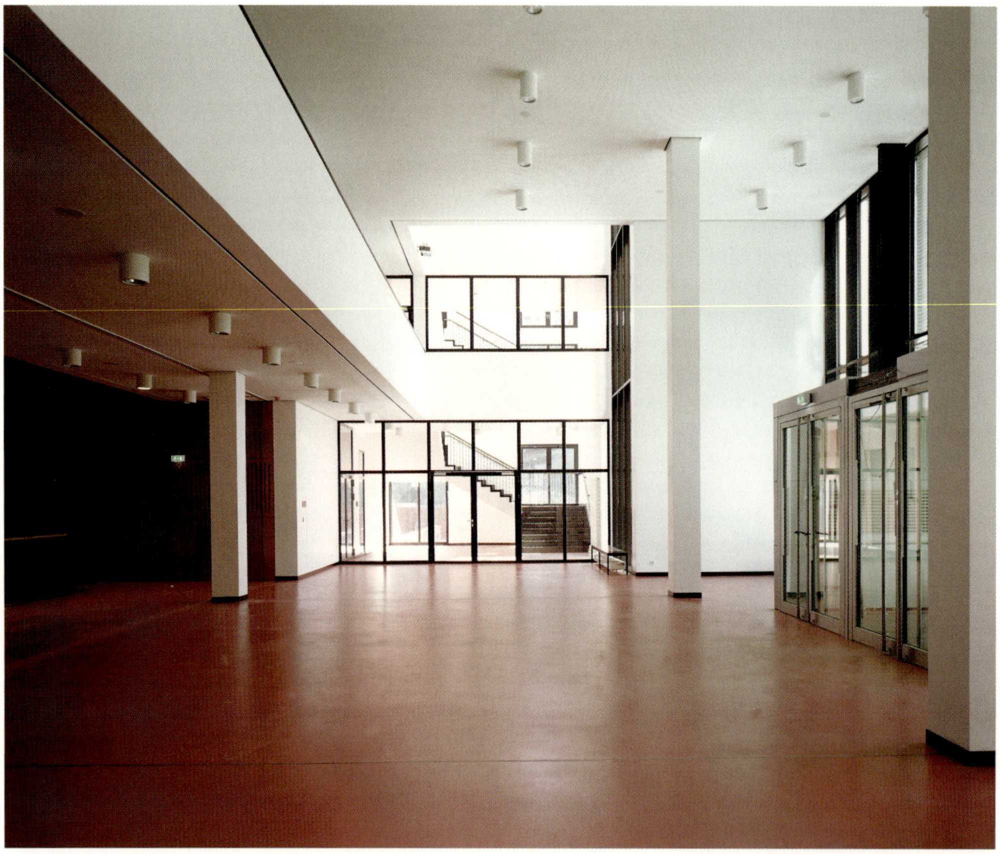

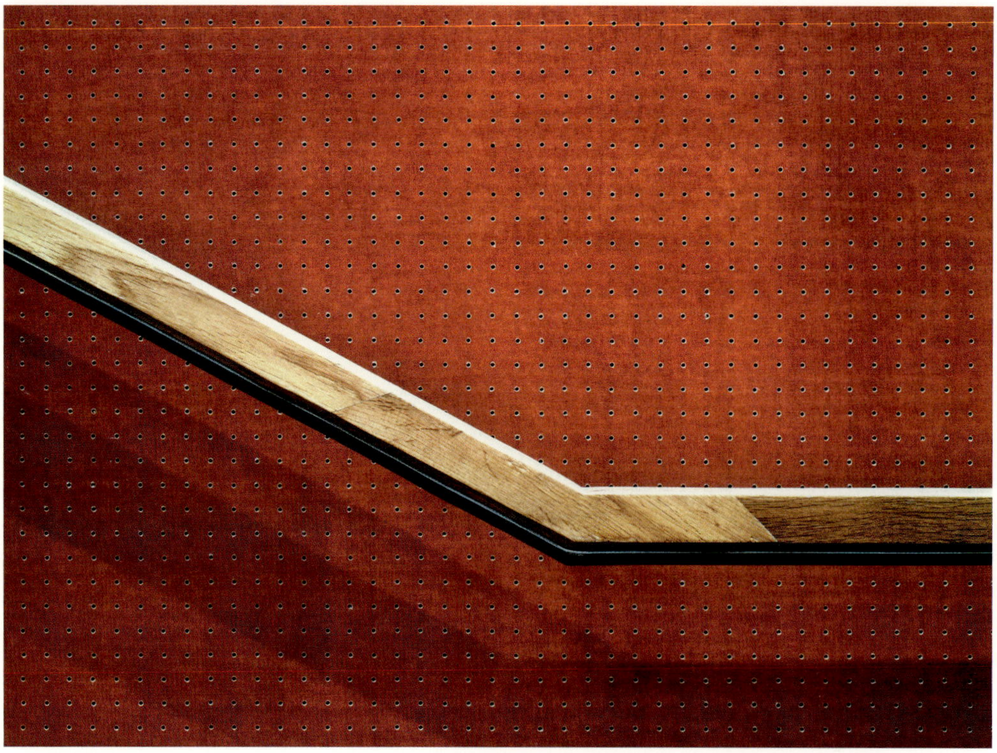

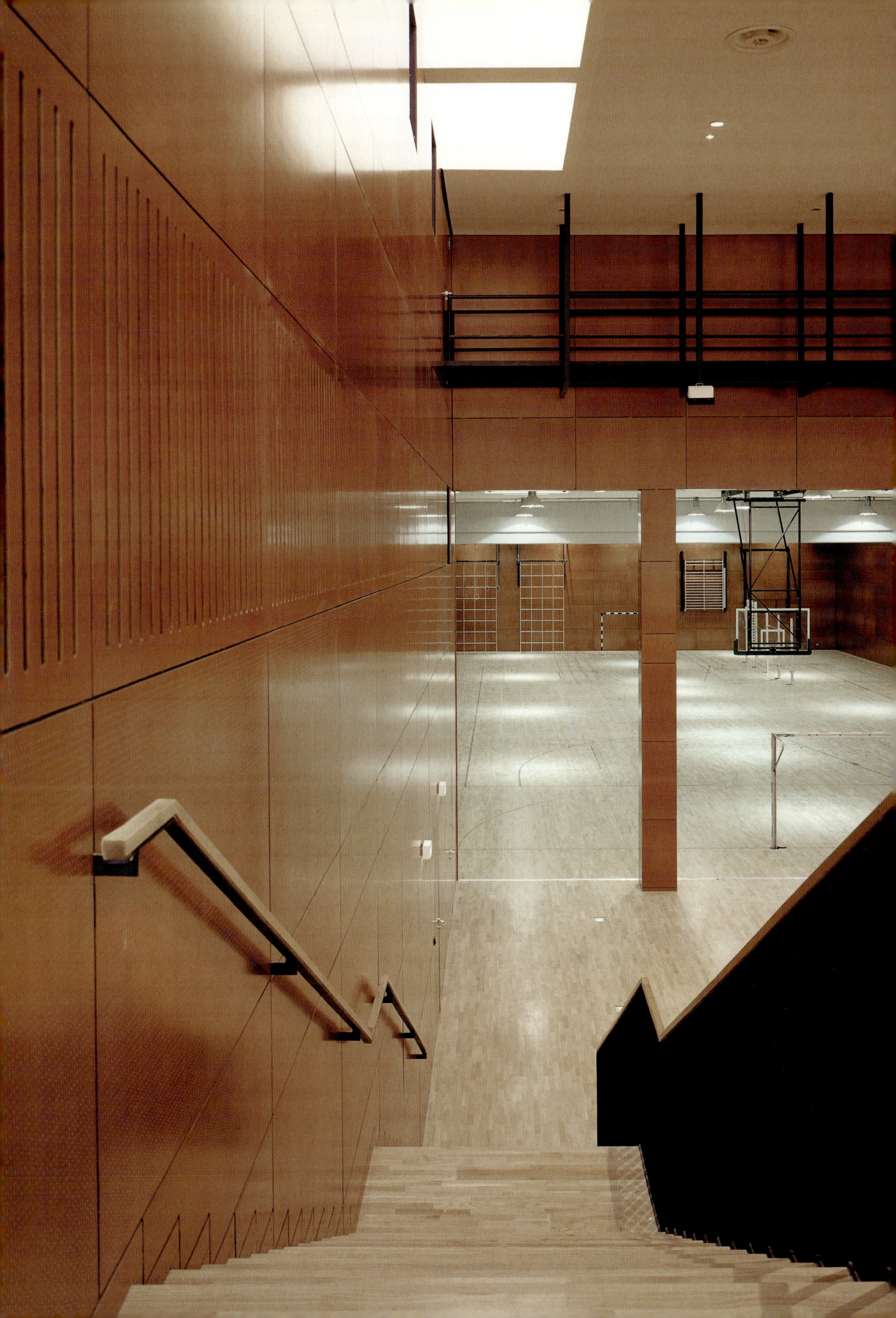

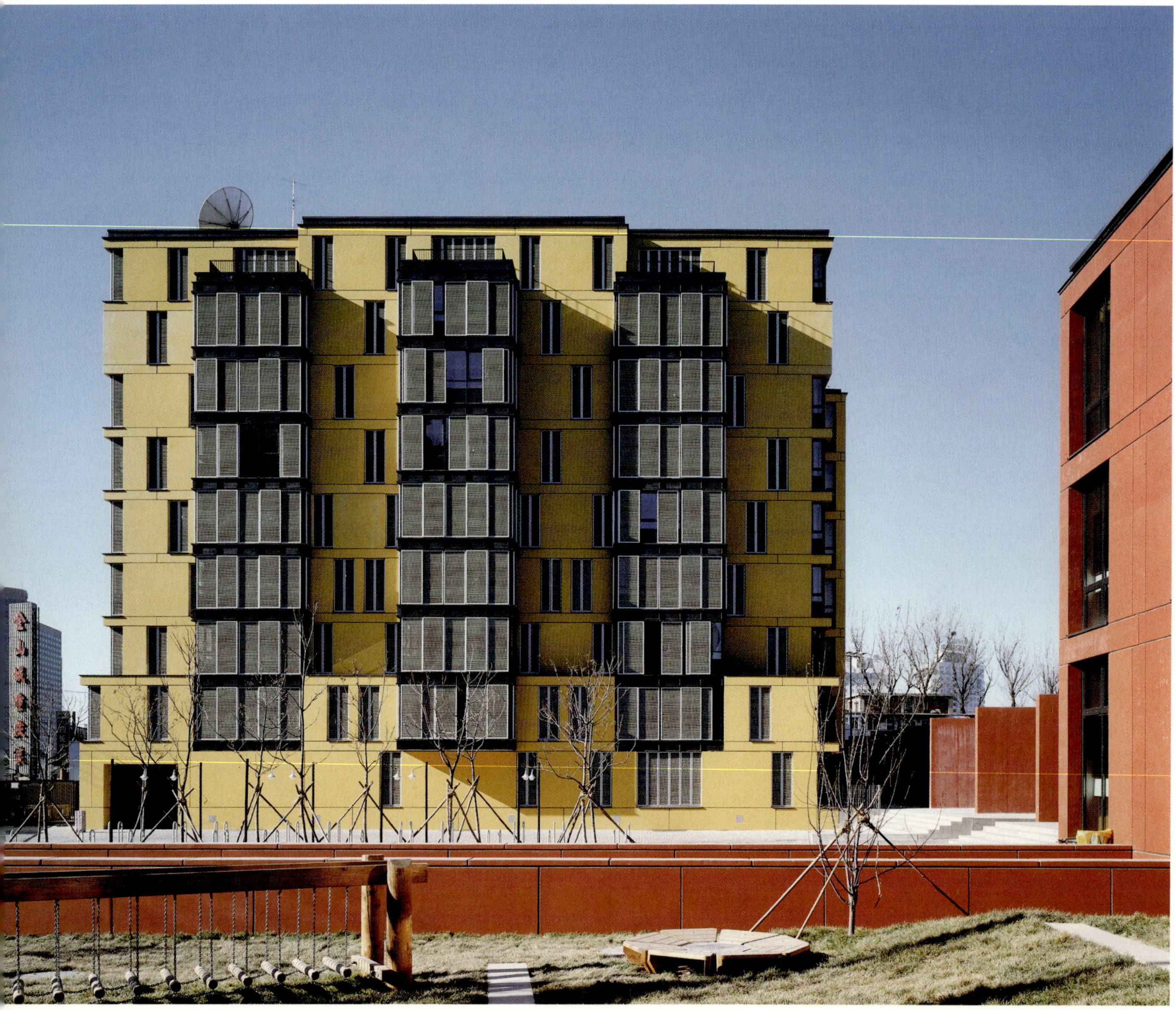

Stadtbausteine **Urban Modules**

Internationales Messe- und Kongresszentrum, Nanning
Nanning International Convention & Exhibition Centre

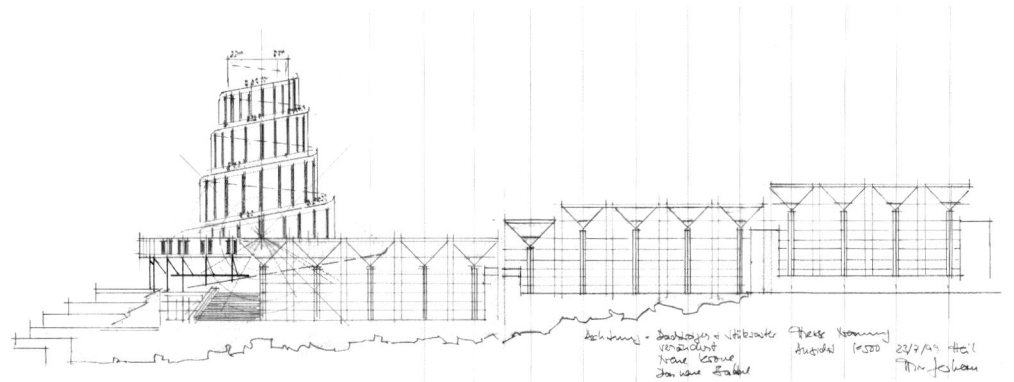

Stadtbausteine **Urban Modules**

125

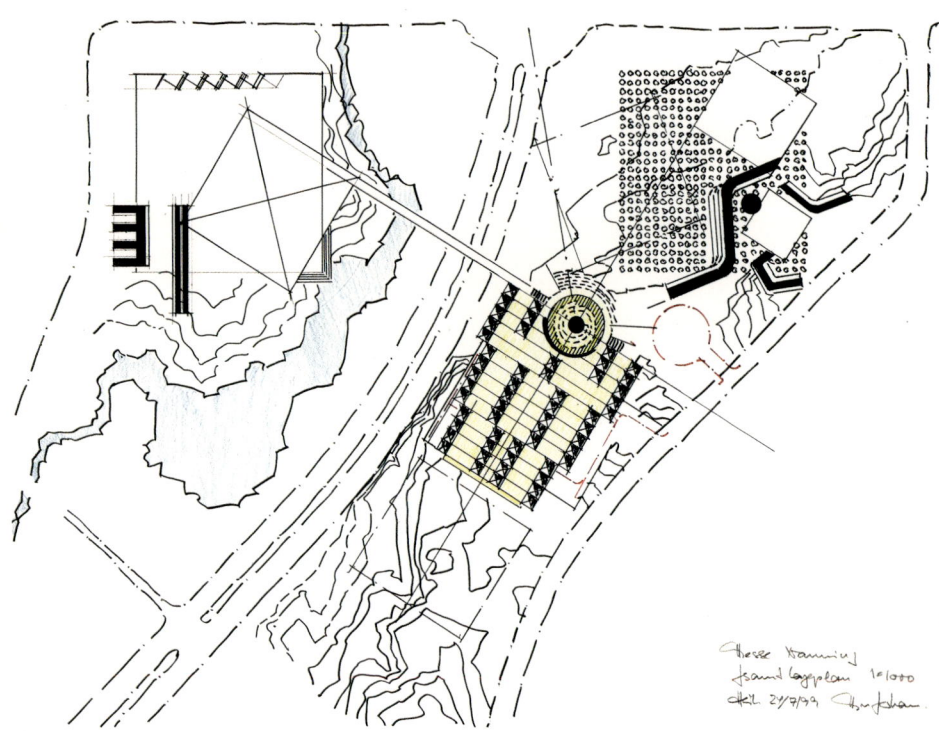

Internationaler Wettbewerb 1999 – 1. Preis
Entwurf Meinhard von Gerkan und Nikolaus Goetze
Projektleitung Dirk Heller, Karen Schroeder
Mitarbeiter Christoph Berle, Kai Siebke, Georg Traun, Friedhelm Chlosta, Meike Schmidt, Wencke Eissing-Poggenberg, Stefanie Schupp, Oliver Christ, Jochen Schwarz, Eckhard Send, Iris van Hülst, Thomas Eberhardt
Chinesisches Partnerbüro Guangxi Architectural Comprehensive Design & Research Institute, Nanning
Statik Schlaich Bergermann und Partner
Haustechnik HL-Technik
Landschaftsplanung Breimann + Bruun
Bauherr Nanning International Convention & Exhibition Co., Ltd.
Bauzeit 1999–2003
BGF ca. 90.000 m²
BRI ca. 1.200.000 m³
Erweiterung der Messe um 6 Hallen mit insgesamt noch einmal 40.000 m² bis Juni 2005.

Internationales Messe- und Kongresszentrum, Nanning

Das am Hang gelegene Grundstück mit einer Höhendifferenz von 45 m befindet sich am Rand von Nanning inmitten eines die Stadt umgebenden Grüngürtels.

Eine multifunktionale Halle bildet mit ihrem gefalteten Kuppeltragwerk mit einer Gesamthöhe von 70 m und einem Durchmesser von 48 m den Kopf der Messeanlage und ragt als Landmarke über die Silhouette der Stadt hinaus. Ihre Dachkonstruktion besteht aus einem filigranen Stahltragwerk, das beidseitig mit einer transluzenten Membran bespannt ist. Die kreisrunde Halle kann aufgrund ihrer zentralen Lage auch getrennt vom Ausstellungs- und Konferenzbetrieb genutzt werden. Als Rotunde bietet sie in idealer Weise Platz für Ausstellungen, große Konferenzen, Theateraufführungen, Konzerte und Eröffnungszeremonien.

Unterhalb der Halle befindet sich das ebenfalls separat nutzbare Kongresszentrum mit fünf Sälen und einem angrenzenden Restaurant.

Die Ausstellungshallen schließen an die Rotunde an und sind von beiden Seiten eines zweigeschossigen Foyers begehbar. Die neun Hallen des ersten Bauabschnitts, die jeweils über zwei Ausstellungsebenen verfügen, können auf beiden Ebenen zu Gruppen zusammengeschlossen werden, so dass Veranstaltungen unterschiedlichster Größe möglich sind. Die Größe der Hallen variiert zwischen 2.100 und 3.200 m², ergänzt um eine Halle mit einer Fläche von 5.000 m². Alle Hallen werden über zwei Seiten mit Tageslicht versorgt und können bei Bedarf verdunkelt werden. Ein Natursteinsockel bildet das optische Fundament; während der Veranstaltungen kann er als Freiterrasse und Ausstellungsfläche genutzt werden. Stahlbetonstützen, die vor den aufragenden Natursteinsockeln stehen erstrecken sich über die volle Höhe der beiden Hallenebenen und tragen das signifikante Dach, das durch die Einschnitte der Kerne, in denen sich die haustechnischen Anlagen befinden, rhythmisch gegliedert wird.

Natürliche Materialien und Oberflächen mit den ihnen eigenen haptischen und ästhetischen Qualitäten bestimmen die Erscheinung des Messe- und Kongresszentrums. Außen wie auch im Innenraum überwiegen Naturstein, Glas und Beton, Farben wurden nur sparsam und zur Akzentuierung besonderer Funktionen eingesetzt.

Im Jahr 2005 wurde die zweite Bauphase mit weiteren sechs Hallen in südlicher Richtung und einem Verwaltungsgebäude abgeschlossen.

Nanning International Convention & Exhibition Centre

The site on a slope with a height difference of 45 m is located on the outskirts of Nanning within the green belt surrounding the city.

A multi-functional hall with a folded domical roof, 70 m high and 48 m in diameter, forms the head of the exhibition complex and rises above the city silhouette as a landmark. The roof is conceived as a filigree load-bearing steel structure, which is on both sides covered with a translucent membrane. Due to its central location, the circular hall can be used separately from the exhibition and conference operations. As a rotunda it provides an ideal space for exhibitions, large conventions, theatre plays, concerts and opening ceremonies.

The convention centre comprising five halls and an adjoining restaurant is located below the hall und can be used separately.

The exhibition halls adjoining the rotunda are accessible from both sides of a two-storeyed foyer. The nine halls realized during the first construction phase, all of them designed with two exhibition levels, can be interlinked on both levels as groups, providing for a variety of events. The dimension of the halls varies between 2,100 m² and 3,200 m², supplemented by one hall with a floor area of 5,000 m². The halls are naturally lit on two sides and can be blacked out when required.

A stone plinth forms the visual foundation; during events it can be used as an open-air terrace and exhibition area. Reinforced concrete columns, positioned in front of the ascending stone socle, stretch across the complete height of both hall levels and support the distinct roof, which is rhythmically structured by the recesses of the cores accommodating the technical plant and services.

Natural materials and surfaces with their inherent haptic and aesthetic qualities characterize the appearance of the exhibition and convention centre. Externally and internally, stone, glass and concrete are the predominantly used materials; colours were scarcely used and only applied for the accentuation of special functions.

In 2005, the second construction phase comprising another six halls located to the south and an administration building was completed.

In the river valley at the foot of the exhibition centre the building was realigned with an open-air theatre. The

128

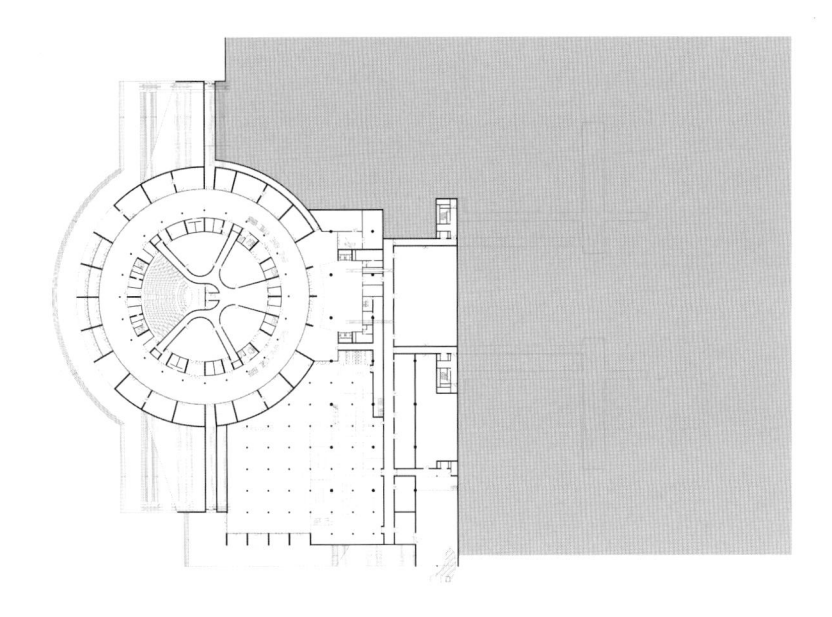

Im Flusstal am Fuße der Messe wurde der Bau durch ein open-air Theater arrondiert. Das ovale Theater mit ca. 35.000 Plätzen ist in einen Hang eingebettet und öffnet sich in Richtung Messe. Diese bildet den Hintergrund für das jährlich stattfindende Nanning Folksong Festival.

oval theatre with approximately 35,000 seats is embedded into a slope and opens up towards the exhibition centre which forms the backdrop for the annual Nanning Folksong Festival.

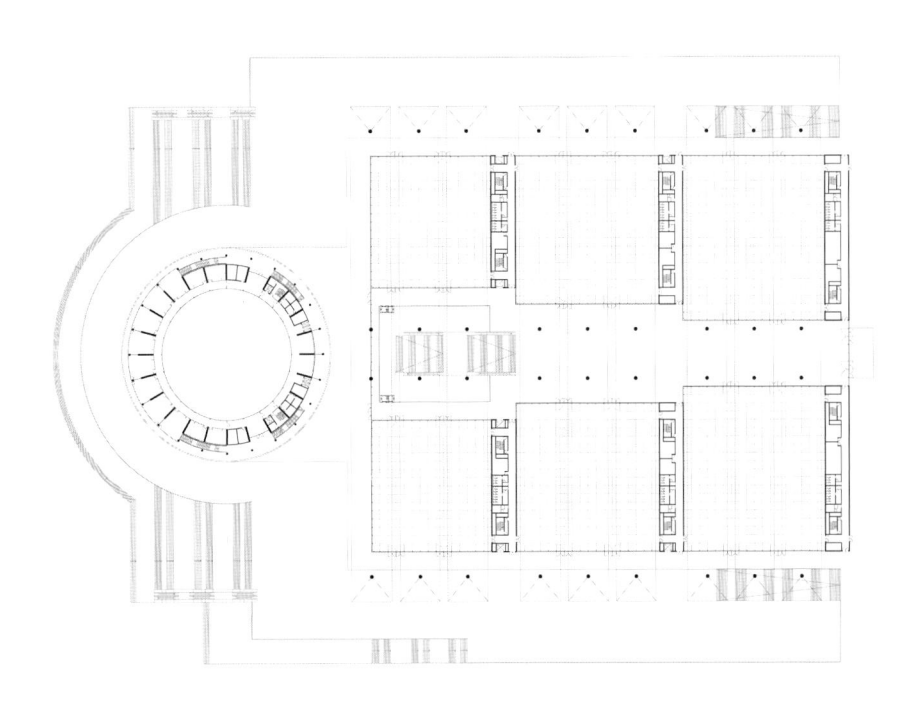

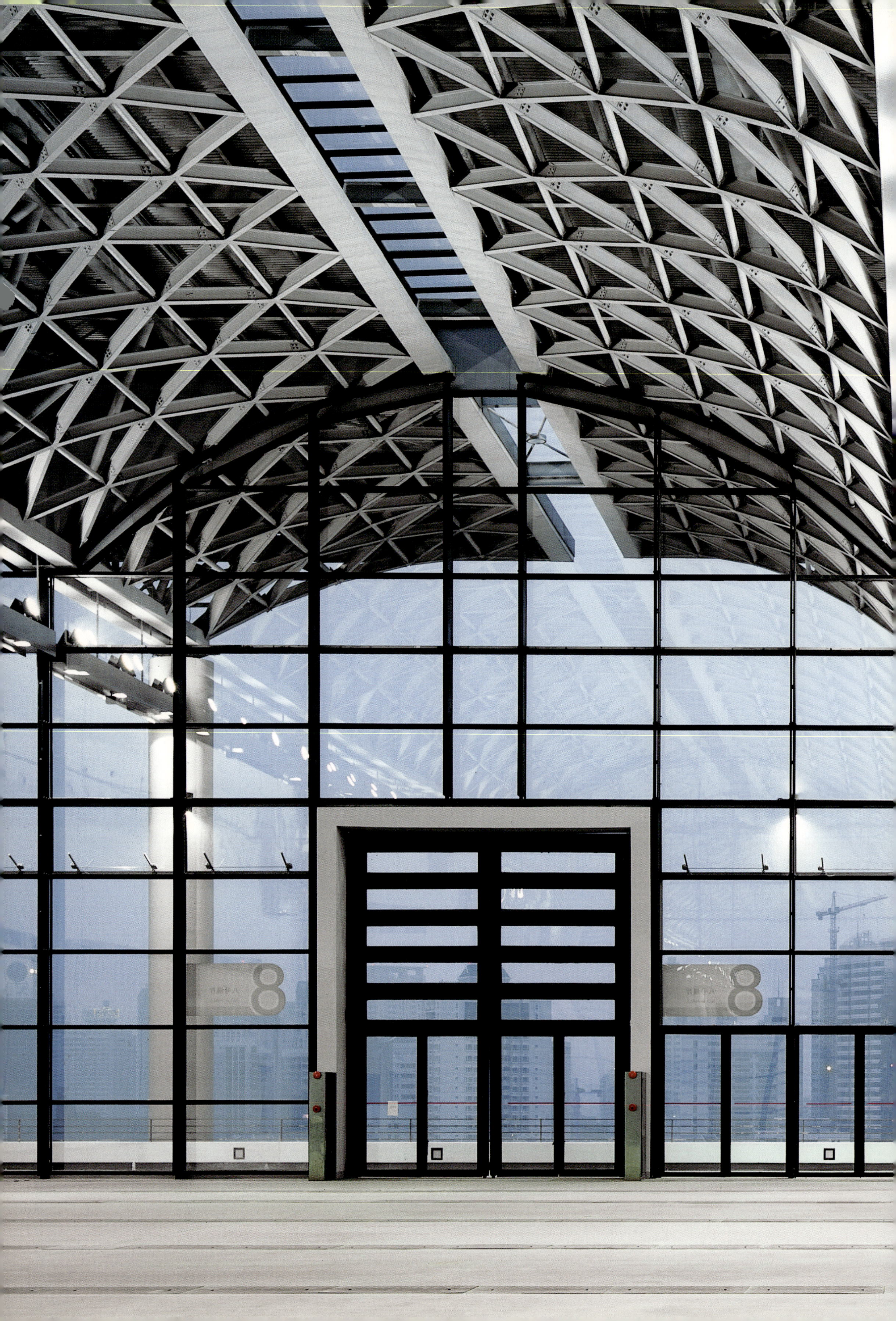
8
8

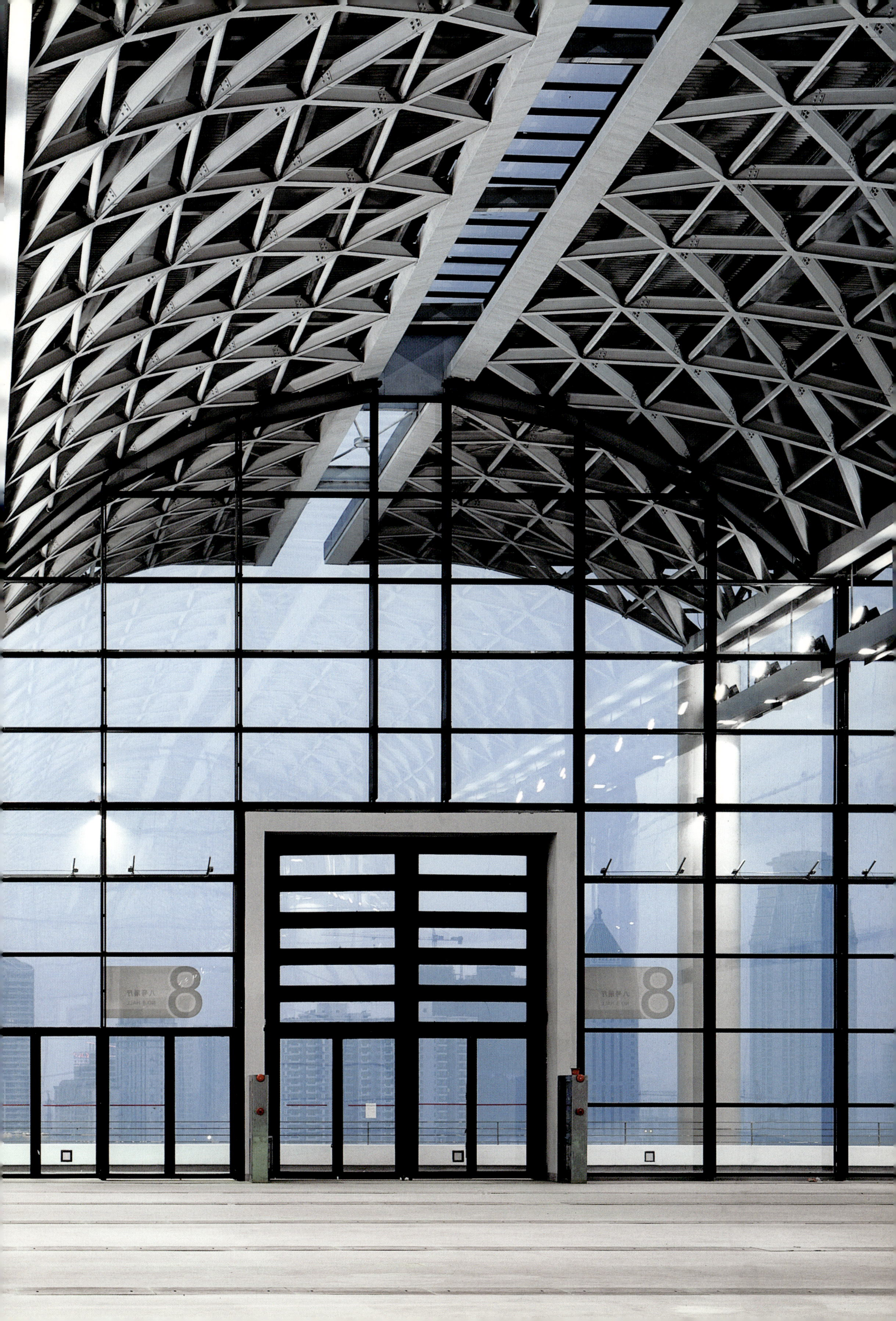
8
8

Kongress- und Messezentrum, Shenzhen
Shenzhen Convention & Exhibition Centre

Stadtbausteine **Urban Modules**

展览中心

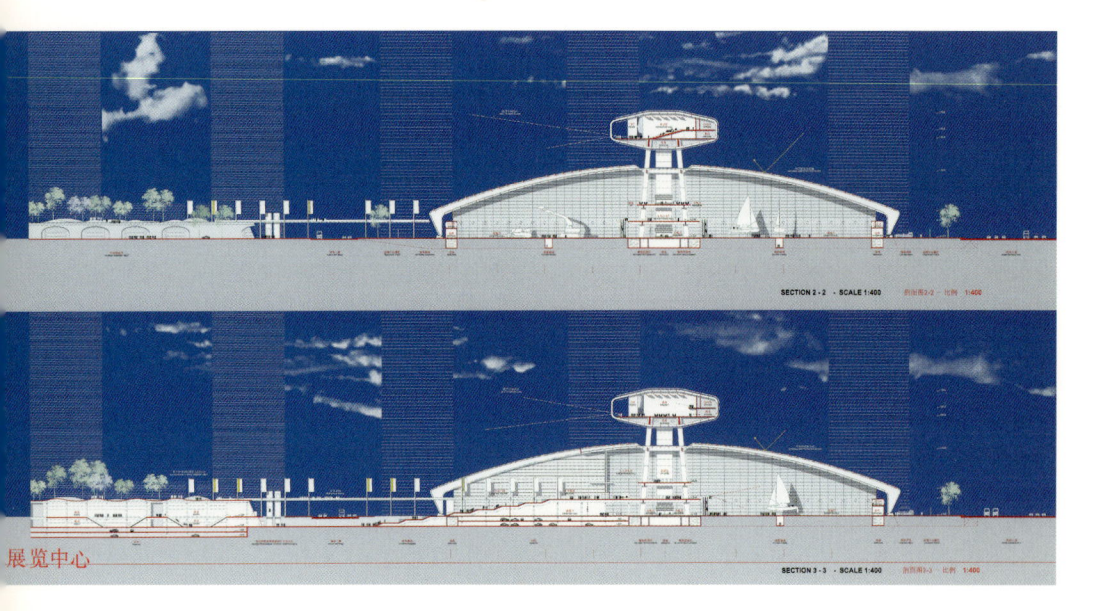

Realisierungswettbewerb 2001 – 1. Preis
Entwurf Volkwin Marg mit Marc Ziemons
Partner Nikolaus Goetze
Projektleitung Marc Ziemons, Thomas Schuster
Mitarbeiter Entwurf Karen Seekamp, Dirk Balser, Sven Greiser, Martin Marschner, Moritz Hoffmann-Becking, Yingdi Wang, Wei Wu
Mitarbeiter Ausführung Susanne Winter, Dirk Balser, Carsten Plog, Katja Zoschke, Karen Seekamp, Yingdi Wang, Wei Wu, Martina Klostermann, Iris van Hüst, Flori Wagner, Tina Stahnke, Marina Hoffmann, Heike Kugele, Otto Dorn, Jeanny Rieger
Chinesisches Partnerbüro China Northeast Architectural Design Institute, Shenzhen
Statik Schlaich Bergermann und Partner, Stuttgart
Haustechnik HL-Technik, Hamburg
Landschaftsplanung Breimann + Bruun, Hamburg
Bauherr Shenzhen Convention & Exhibition Center
Bauzeit 2002–2004/2005
BGF 256.000 m²

Kongress- und Messezentrum, Shenzhen

Das Bauprogramm der neuen Messeanlage inmitten der jungen Stadt Shenzhen erfordert in besonderem Maße eine Synthese von Städtebau, Architektur und Konstruktion zu einer ganzheitlichen Struktur mit urbaner Kompaktheit. Die gesamte Ausstellungsfläche befindet sich auf einer Ebene mit einem rechteckigen Grundriss von ca. 280 m x 540 m. Die erhöhte Eingangs- und Besucherplattform auf einer Höhe von 7,50 m über dem Ausstellungs- und Straßenniveau erlaubt die separate Erschließung einzelner Hallen oder zusammengefasster Hallenkomplexe. Dieses durch die Höhenlage völlig von der Ausstellerlogistik getrennte Erschließungssystem in der Mittelachse der Hallen erlaubt eine beliebige Zuordnung von Hallenabgängen und verschafft den Besuchern einen leichten Überblick über das Ausstellungsgeschehen.

Entlang dieser Mittelzone sind in Abständen von 30 m große, stählerne A-förmige Stützbock-Konstruktionen angeordnet. Sie ragen fast 60 m in die Höhe und stemmen das 360 m lange, 60 m breite und 20 m hohe Kongressgebäude um mehr als 15 m über die eigentliche Hallenkonstruktion. Die A-Stützböcke sind rahmenartig versteift und untereinander zur Stabilisierung verbunden.

Das röhrenförmige Kongressgebäude schwebt über den Ausstellungshallen und kann je nach Wunsch separat, in halber Größe oder in Kombination mit den Ausstellungen betrieben werden.

Das SZCEC erinnert mit über 540 m Länge an den berühmten Kristallpalast der Weltausstellung in London von 1851 und überbietet die Länge der großen Glashalle der Messe Leipzig von 1996 um das Doppelte.

Das gläserne Gewölbe über den neun Ausstellungshallen erscheint bei Tageslicht wie eine filigrane Skulptur, nachts strahlt es wie ein Kristall. Die Fontänen und Wasserkaskaden des Eingangsplatzes sind ebenfalls erleuchtet und das Kongresszentrum wird von unten farbig angestrahlt. Es bildet als langer, horizontaler Baukörper einen Gegensatz zur stets vertikalen Ästhetik der vielen Hochhäuser, die das Messezentrum beidseitig einfassen.

Shenzhen Convention & Exhibition Centre

The building program of the new exhibition centre in the young city of Shenzhen requires a considerate synthesis of urban planning, architecture and construction, thereby achieving an integral structure with an urban density.

The total exhibition area is located on one level with a rectangular floorplan of approximately 280 m by 540 m. The elevated entrance and visitor platform is located 7.50 m above exhibition and street level and allows separate access to individual halls or combined hall complexes. Due to its elevated position the circulation system in the central axis of the halls is completely separated from the logistic systems of the exhibitors. Consequently this allows an optional allocation of access to the exhibition areas below and provides a clear orientation regarding the complete exhibition proceedings for all visitors.

Along this central zone large, A-shaped steel trestle structures are positioned at intervals of 30 m. These rise to almost 60 m and elevate the 360 m long, 60 m wide and 20 m high congress building to a height of more than 15 m above the actual hall structure. The A-shaped trestles have a frame-like stiffening and are interconnected to produce mutual stabilization.

The tube-shaped congress building hovers above the exhibition halls and can, according to the respective demands, be operated as a separate unit, with fifty per cent of its capacity or in combination with the exhibition area.

The SZCEC with its length of more than 540 m reminds of the famous Crystal Palace of the London World Exhibition in 1852 and surpasses the large glass hall of the Leipzig Exhibition Centre built in 1996 with double the length.

The glass vault covering the nine exhibition halls appears in daylight like a delicate sculpture, at night it radiates like a crystal. The fountains and water cascades of the entrance square are also illuminated and the congress centre receives a coloured illumination from below. The long, horizontal structure forms a contrast to the predominantly vertical aesthetic of the numerous high-rise towers which frame the exhibition centre on both sides.

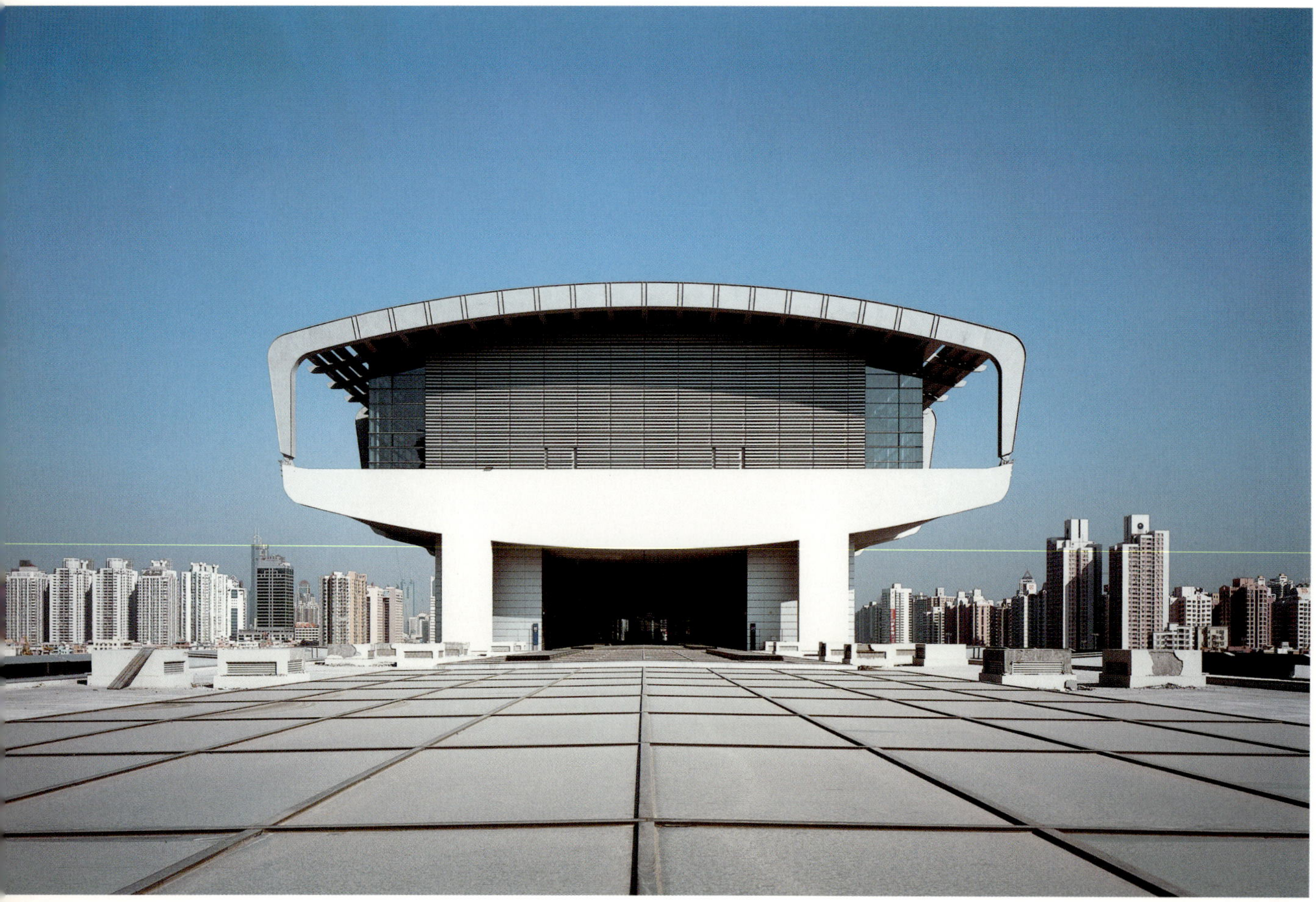

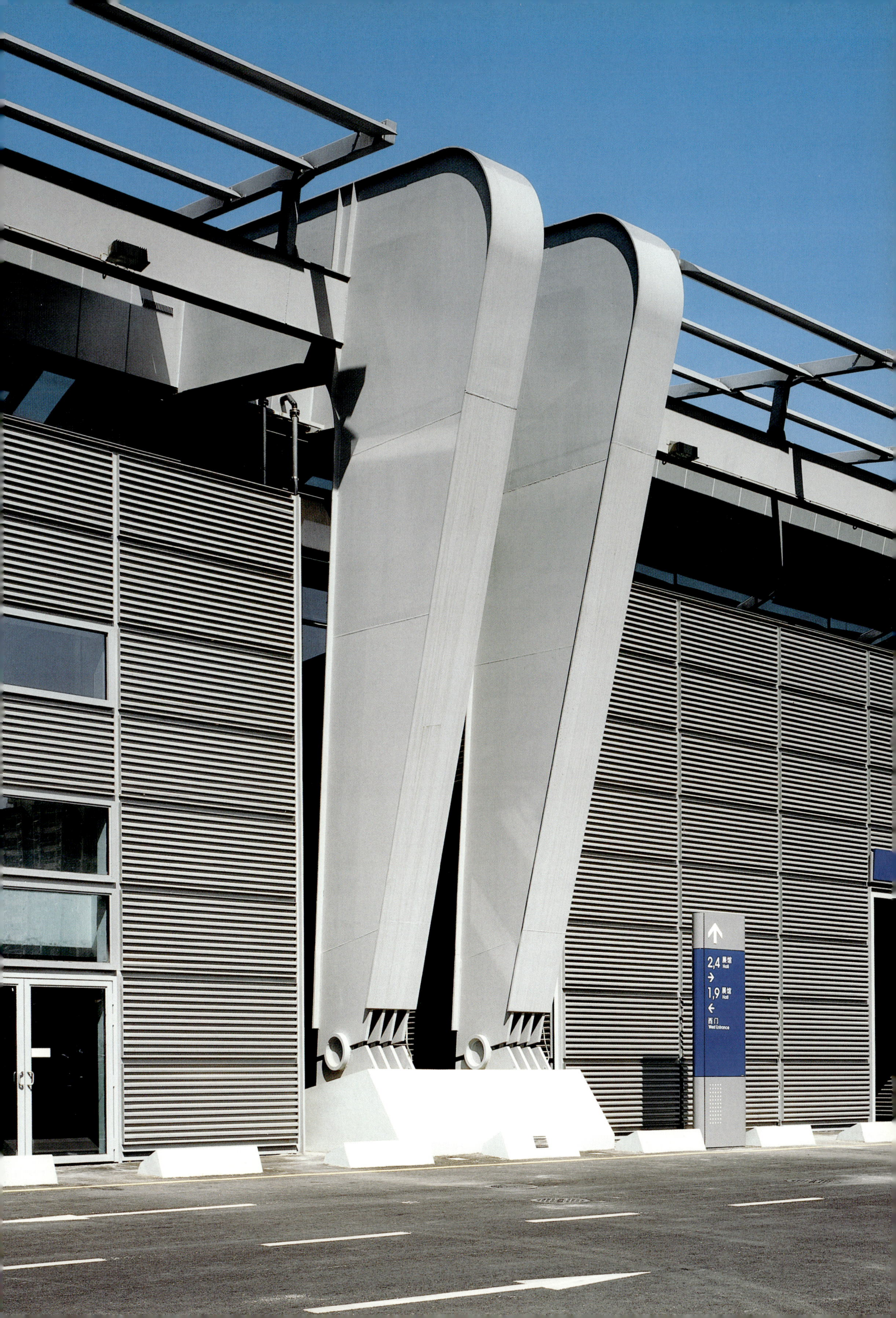
2,4 展馆 Hall
1,9 展馆 Hall
西门 West Entrance

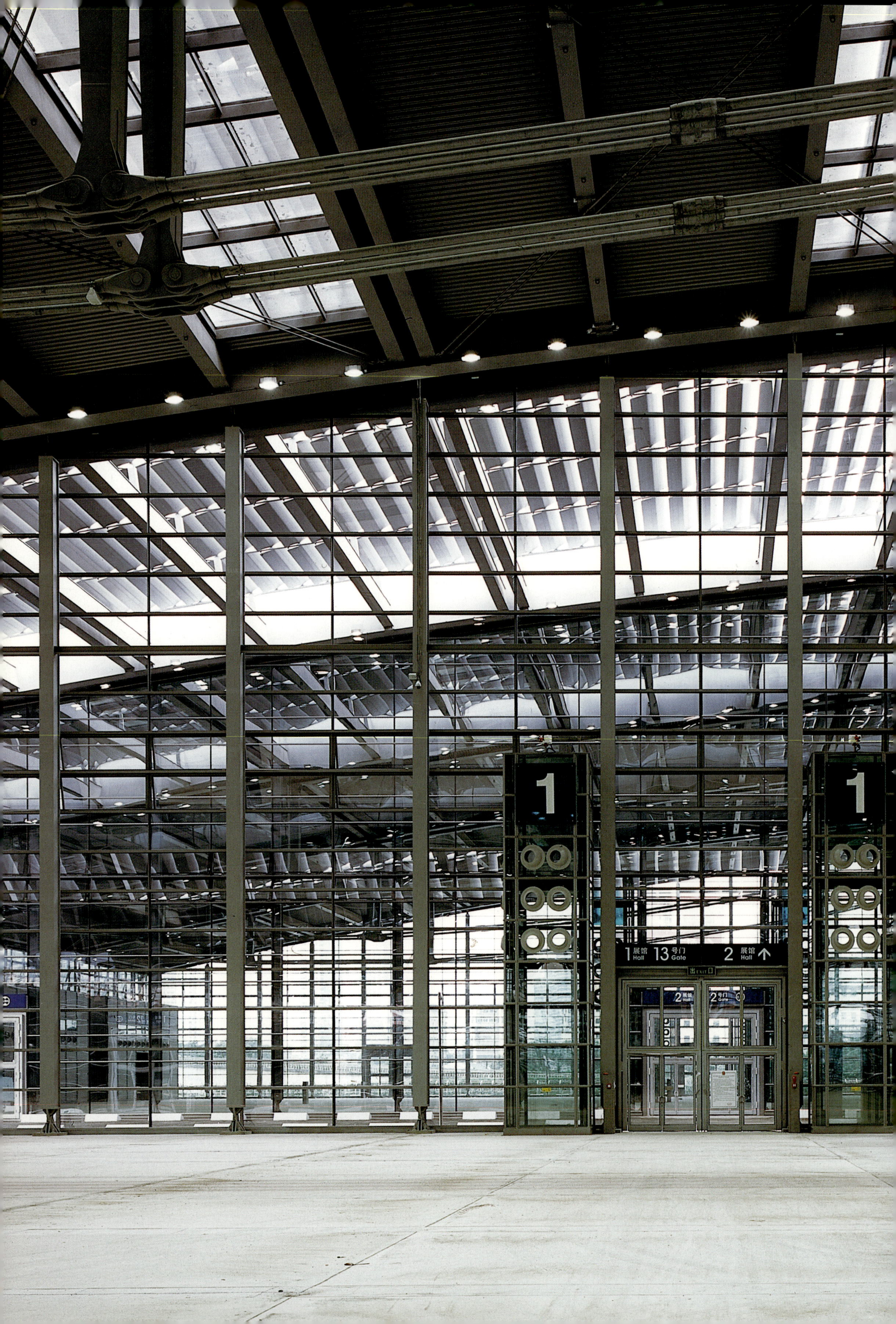
1
1 展馆 Hall
13 号门 Gate
2 展馆 Hall
1

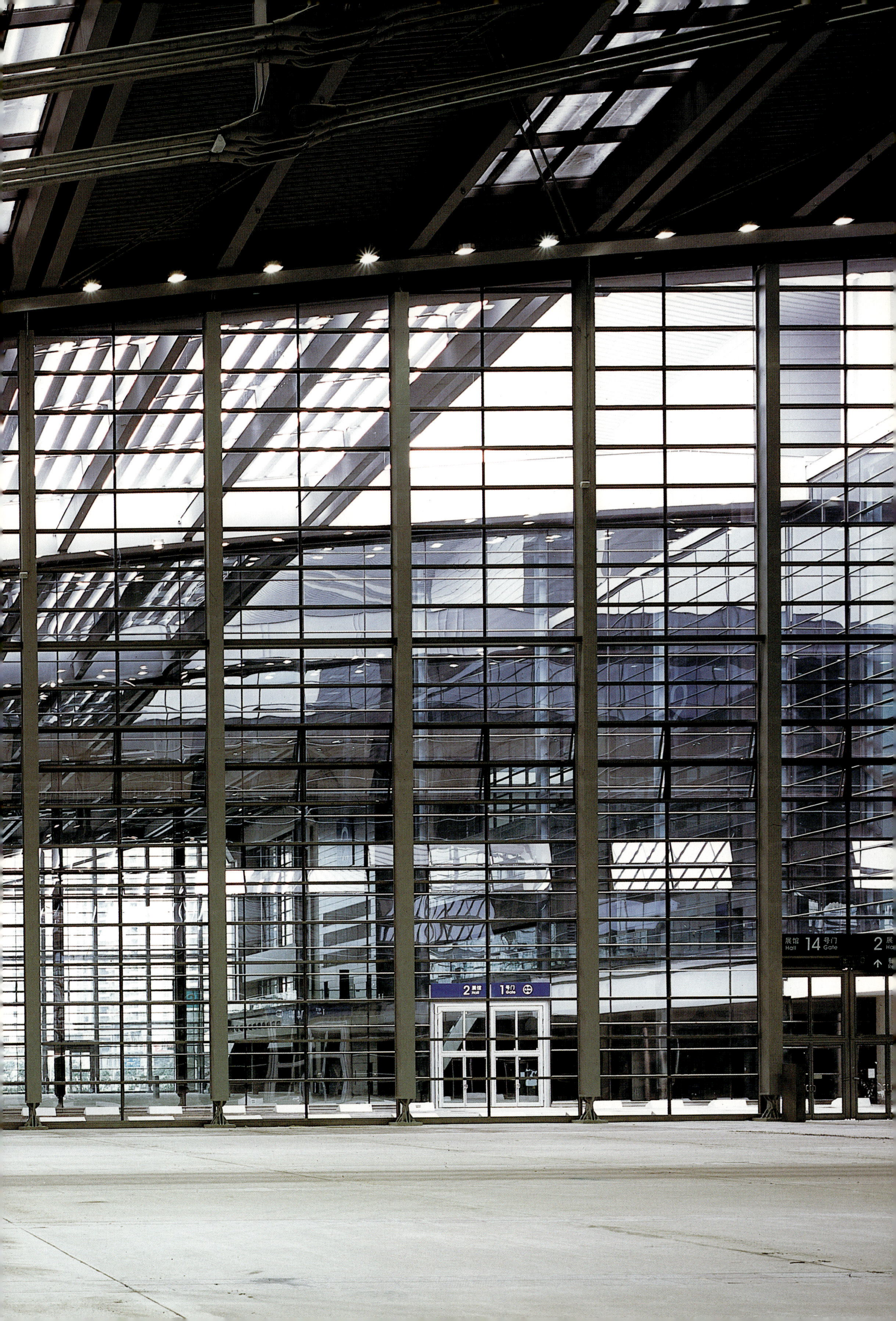
2 展馆 Hall
1 号门 Gate
展馆 Hall 14 号门 Gate

Shanghai-Pudong Museum
Museum, Shanghai-Pudong

Stadtbausteine **Urban Modules**

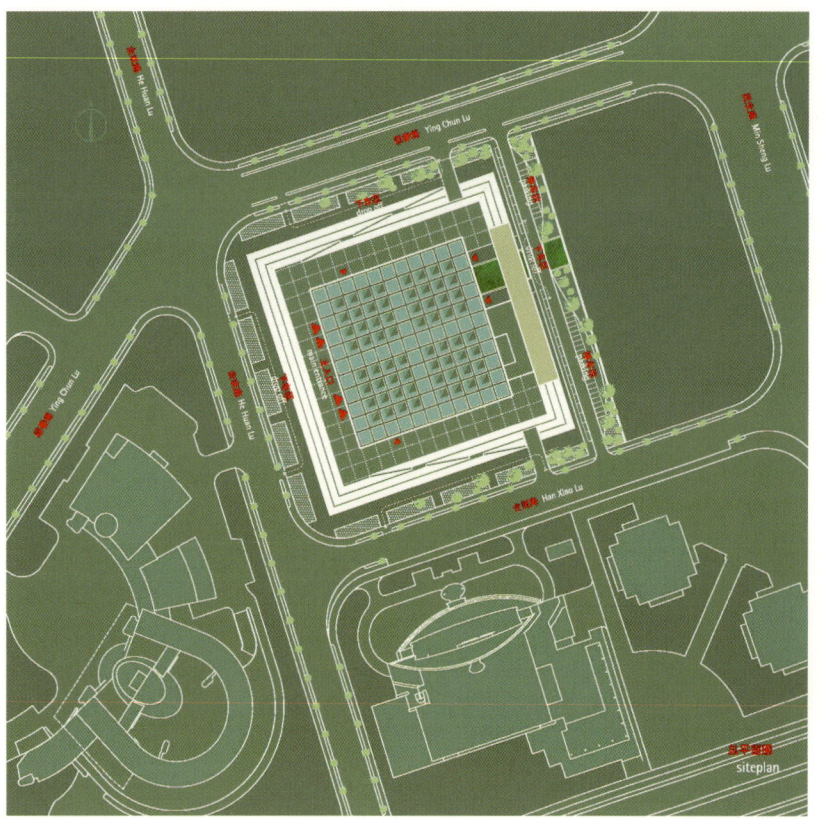

Wettbewerb 2002 – 1. Preis
Entwurf Meinhard von Gerkan
Partner Nikolaus Goetze
Projektmanager Dirk Heller, Karen Schroeder
Projektteam Christoph Berle, Wencke Eissing, Georg Traun, Friedhelm Chlosta, Kai Siebke, Meike Schmidt, Wei Wu, Holger Wermers, Birgit Föllmer, Hinrich Müller, Udo Meyer, Thomas Eberhardt
Chinesisches Partnerbüro SIADR, Shanghai Institute of Architectural Design & Research Co., Ltd.
Bauherr City of Shanghai, New District Pudong
BGF 41,000 m²
BRI 250,000 m²
Bauzeit 2003–2005

Shanghai-Pudong Museum

Das Museum Shanghai-Pudong zählt zu den wichtigsten städtischen Projekten des neuen Distrikts. Gegenüber der historisch gewachsenen Kernstadt von Shanghai entsteht derzeit auf der anderen Flussseite ein neues „Manhattan": der Stadtteil Shanghai-Pudong mit dem zur Zeit höchsten Büro- und Hotelgebäude Chinas.

Das neue Shanghai-Pudong Museum soll die Geschichte dieses Stadtbezirks und seine Entwicklung umfassend dokumentieren und archivieren. Gleichzeitig sollen moderne, multifunktionale und offene Ausstellungsflächen entstehen, die die Öffentlichkeit mit einer ständigen Ausstellung und mit Sonderausstellungen zu ausgewählten Themen über die Stadtgeschichte und Stadtentwicklung informieren.

Der Sockel, als eines der wichtigsten architektonischen Elemente des Museums, hebt das Hauptgebäude mit den Ausstellungshallen vom Niveau der umgebenden Straßen ab und unterstreicht die zentrale Bedeutung des Komplexes. Einfachheit und Reduktion der Materialien bestimmen den klaren Kubus.

Die Gebäudekomposition setzt sich aus drei Elementen zusammen: dem quadratischen Hauptgebäude mit zentralen Funktionen, einem deutlich breiteren, 4 m hohen Sockel mit umlaufenden Treppen, der die Archive beherbergt und einem Gebäuderiegel an der östlichen Seite mit Räumen für die Verwaltung.

Die Fassade des oberen, geschlossenen Teils des Hauptgebäudes dient nicht nur als Wetterschutz sondern auch als Kommunikationsfläche. Sie setzt sich aus zwei parallelen Fassadenebenen zusammen, wobei die äußere aus Glas besteht und die innere Fassade aus raumhohen, geschlossenen Wandpaneelen. Diese Elemente sind entlang ihrer Längsachse drehbar und können – entsprechend den jeweiligen Anforderungen des Ausstellungskonzeptes – geschlossen oder geöffnet werden, sodass Sichtbeziehungen von innen nach außen und umgekehrt entstehen.

Die äußere Fassade fungiert als Medium zwischen Museum und Öffentlichkeit: Die transparente Glashaut wird mit aufgerasterten Bildern aus dem Bestand des Archivs bedruckt, die aus der Entfernung gesehen wiederum ein Großbild ergeben. An exponierten Stellen sollen auf semi-transparentem Glas mittels im Fassadenzwischenraum angeordneter Projektoren Bilder, Filme oder Text projiziert werden.

Museum, Shanghai-Pudong

The Museum in Shanghai-Pudong is one of the most important urban projects in this new district. Opposite the historically grown city centre of Shanghai a new "Manhattan" comes into being on the other side of the river: The district Shanghai-Pudong with the highest office- and hotel building at present in China.

The new Museum in Shanghai-Pudong is meant to document and archive the district's history and development comprehensively. Simultaneously modern, multifunctional and open exhibition spaces are developed to inform the public with a permanent exhibition and special exhibitions about the city's history and development.

The base as one of the main architectural features of the museum elevates the main building with the exhibition halls above the level of the surrounding streets and emphasizes the central importance of the complex. Simplicity and reduction of the materials dominate the clear cube.

Three elements form the building complex: the square-shaped main building with central functions, a much broader, 4 metres high base with surrounding stairs which accommodates the archives and a bar-shaped building on the eastern side for the administration.

The façade of the upper, closed part of the main building not only serves as weather protection but also as a communication surface. It is made of two parallel façade-layers. The outer layer consists of glass and the inner one of room-high closed wall panels. These elements can be rotated along their longitudinal axis and can be opened or closed, according to the particular requirements of the exhibition concept, so that views from the inside to the outside and vice versa are created.

The outer façade serves as a medium between museum and public: the transparent glass skin displays the content of the archive in small patterned pictures, which form a big picture when seen from a distance. In some exposed spaces pictures, movies or texts will be projected onto semi-transparent glass by video projectors mounted in wall recesses.

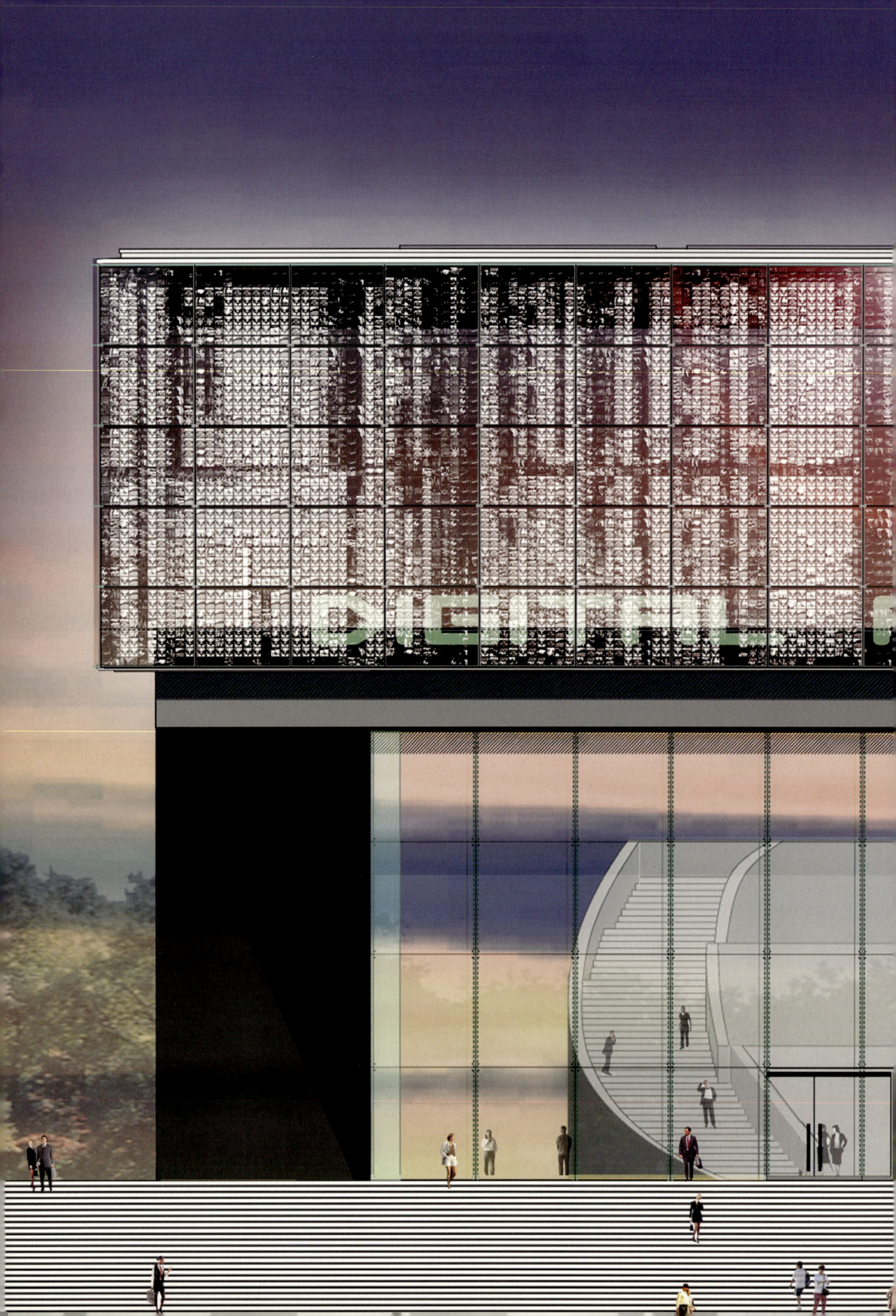
DIGITAL

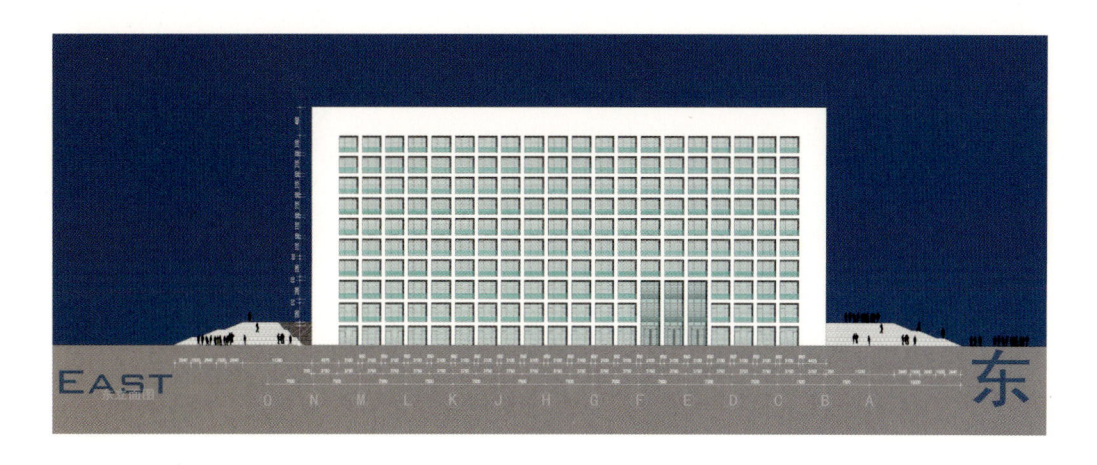

EAST 东

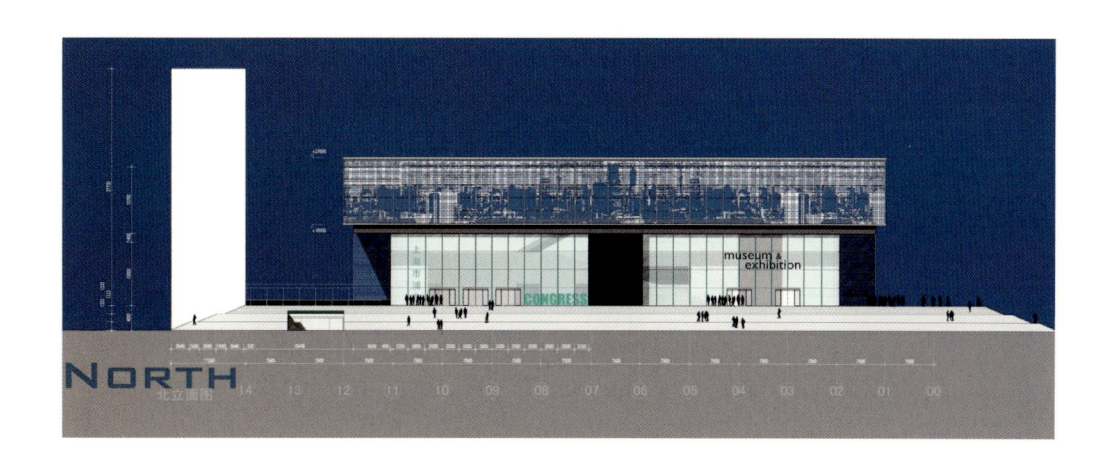

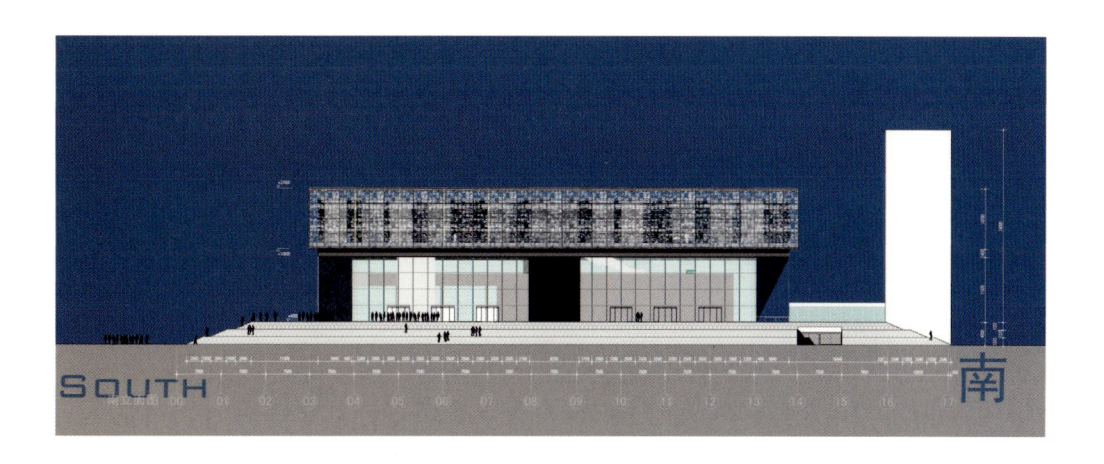

NORTH 北

WEST 西

SOUTH 南

Stadtbausteine **Urban Modules**

145

Sportzentrum mit Stadion und Schwimmhalle, Foshan
Sports Centre with Stadium and Indoor Swimming Pool, Foshan

Stadtbausteine **Urban Modules**

147

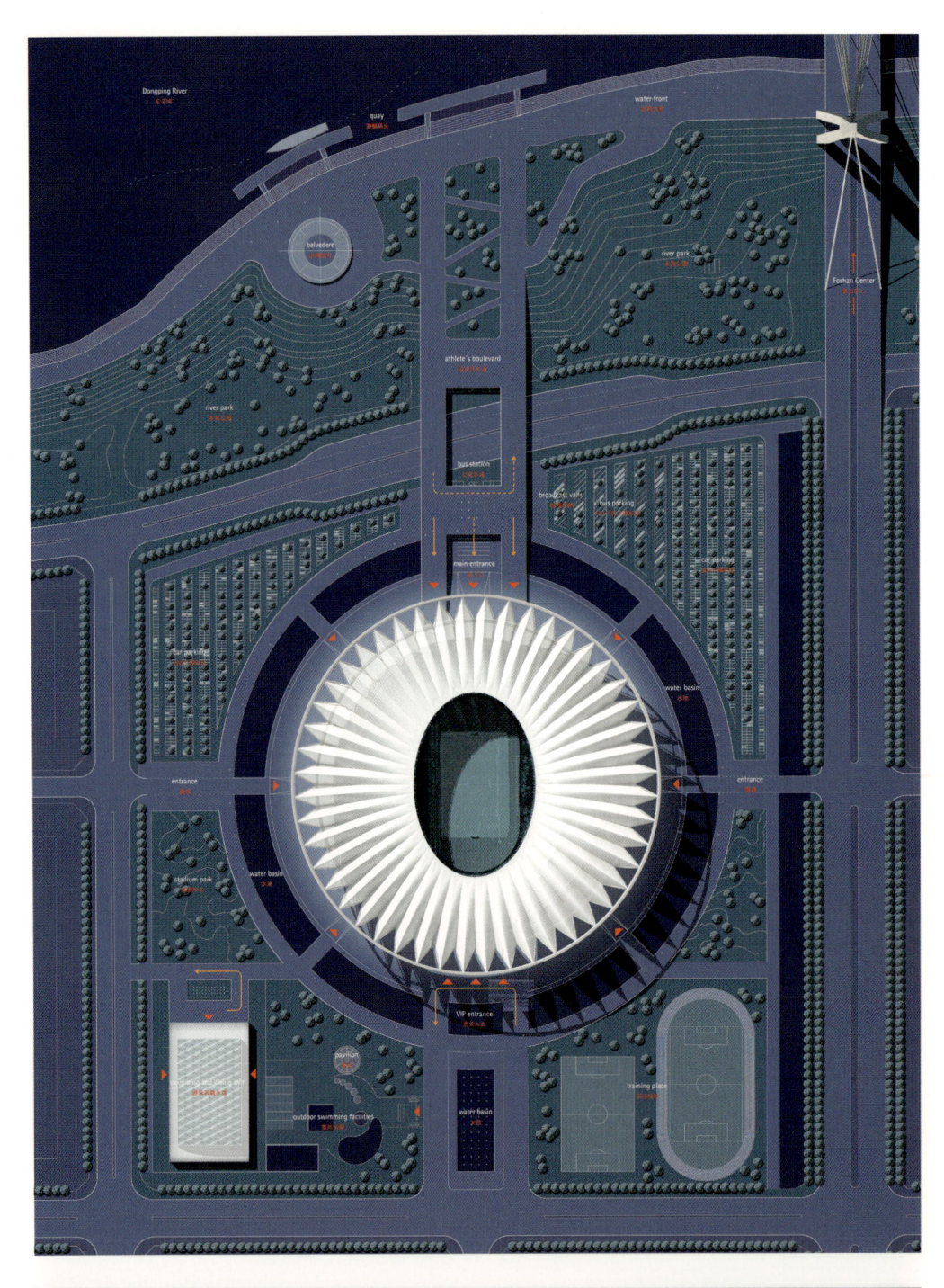

Wettbewerb 2003 – 2. Preis
und Beauftragung
Entwurf Volkwin Marg
mit Marek Nowak
Partner Nikolaus Goetze
Projektleitung Christian Hoffmann
Mitarbeiter Entwurf
Christoph Helbich, Mario Rojas
Toledo, Michael König, Sven Greiser,
Sebastian Hilke, Mark Jackschat
Mitarbeiter Ausführung
Michael Haase, Stefan Menke,
Franz Lensing, Björn Füchtenkord,
Sven Greiser, Silke Flaßnöcker, Ebi
Tang, Jennifer Kielas
Statik Schlaich Bergermann
und Partner, Stuttgart
Bauherr Foshan Construction
Bureau/Foshan Sports Bureau
Bauzeit 2004–2006
Sitzplätze Stadion: ca. 36.000
Sitzplätze Schwimmhalle: 2.800

Sportzentrum mit Stadion und Schwimmhalle, Foshan

Im Rahmen der 12. Guangdong Provinzfestspiele 2006 wird sich Foshan mit einem neuen Sportpark einer breiten Öffentlichkeit als moderne und aufstrebende Stadt präsentieren. Ein Multifunktionsstadion und eine Schwimmhalle bieten internationalen Wettkampfstandard, während weitere Trainings- und Freizeitsportanlagen auch den Besuchern zur Verfügung stehen.

Das kreisrunde Stadion überragt mit seinem riesigen, weißen Membrandach den Sportpark und gleicht – gelegen auf einem begrünten Hügel und umgeben von einem ringförmigen Wasserbecken – einer Lotusblüte im See.

Die Speichenradkonstruktion des Stadiondaches mit der gefalteten Membranabdeckung misst 350 m im Durchmesser und überdeckt sowohl die Tribünen als auch die äußeren Umgänge. Über dem Spielfeld kann das Dach je nach Bedarf geöffnet oder geschlossen werden. Mit einer großen Geste verbindet es die Stadionschüssel mit dem umge-benden Park und wird mit seiner Unverwechselbarkeit zum Symbol der Spiele 2006 werden.

Das Dach der Schwimmhalle ist ebenfalls mit einer leichten, transluzenten Membran gedeckt. Die Halle selbst ist in das Gelände eingelassen und stellt die städtebauliche Dominanz des Stadions nicht infrage; das Dach nimmt jedoch die grundlegende Entwurfsidee auf und lässt beide Gebäude als architektonisches Ensemble erscheinen.

Sports Centre with Stadium and Indoor Swimming Pool, Foshan

On the occasion of the 12th Guangdong Province Sports Meeting 2006 Foshan will present itself to the public as a modern and growing city. A multipurpose stadium and an indoor swimming pool will fulfill all the requirements of international sports competitions, while training and leisure sports facilities offer a large variety of activities to the visitors.

The circular stadium dominates the silhouette of the sports park with its huge, white membrane roof. Situated on a green hill and surrounded by a circular ring of water it looks like a lotus blossom in a lake.

The stadium's spokes-wheel roof construction with the folded membrane covering measures 350 m in diameter and covers not just the stands but the outside concourses as well. Above the field the roof can be opened and closed according to demand. With a grand and generous gesture it links the stadium bowl to the surrounding park and will turn into a symbol of the games of 2006.

The roof of the indoor pool is as well covered by a lightweight and translucent membrane roof. Embedded in the landscape it does not question the urban domination of the stadium, but its roof structure takes up the very architectural design idea, creating the strong and lasting impression of the two buildings as an architectural ensemble.

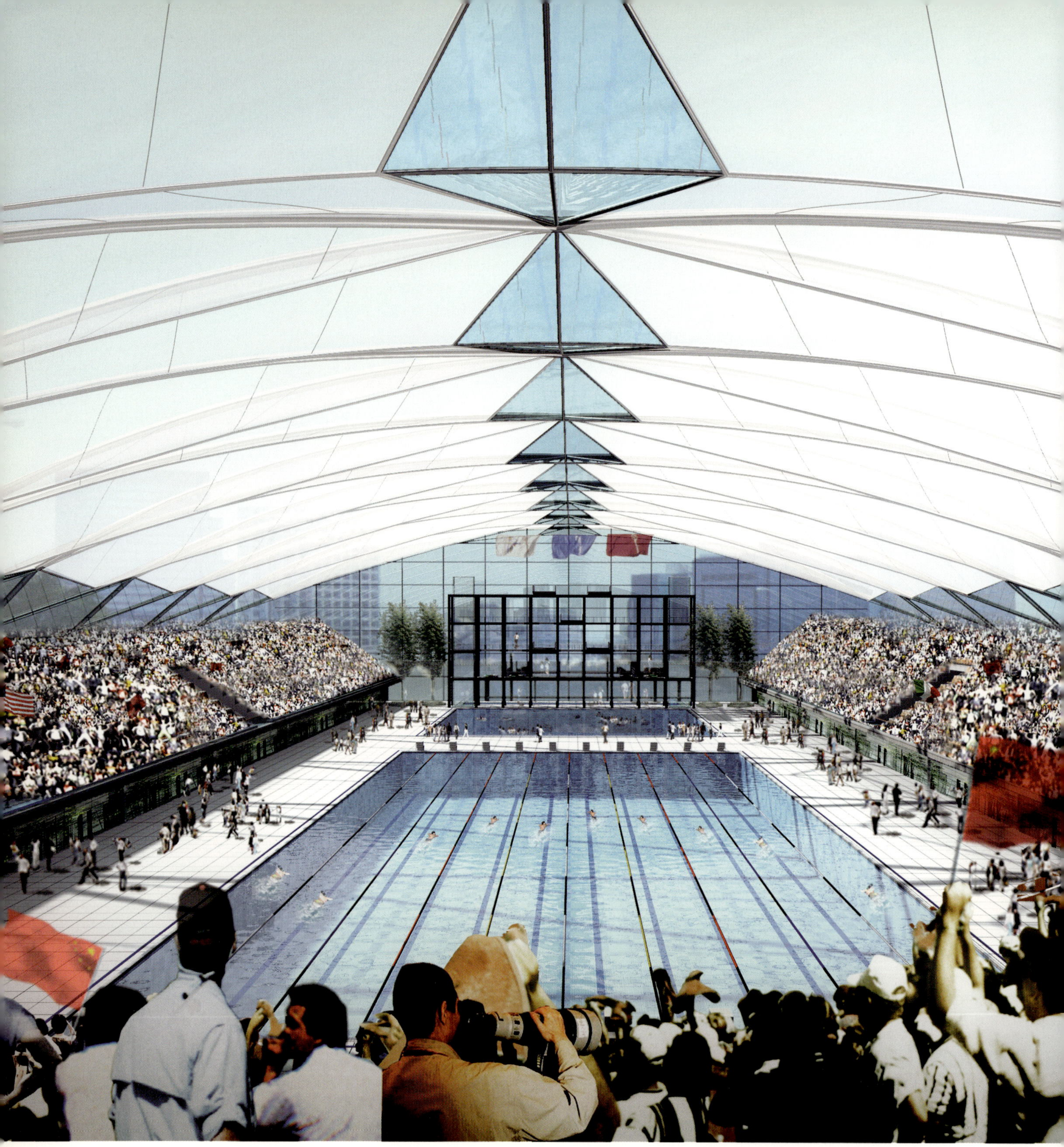

Stadtbausteine **Urban Modules**

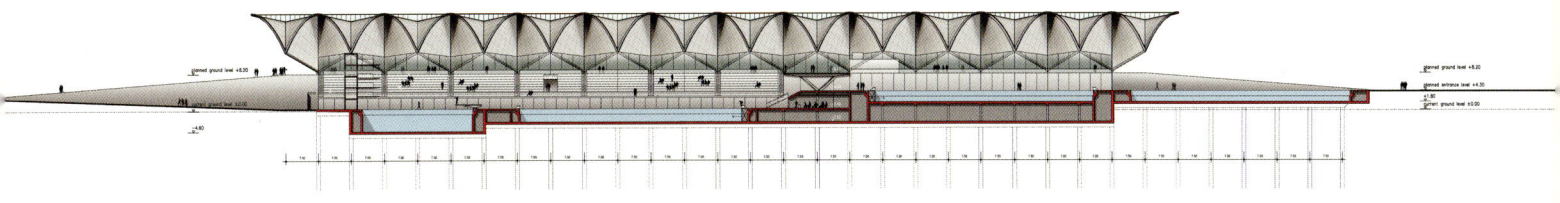

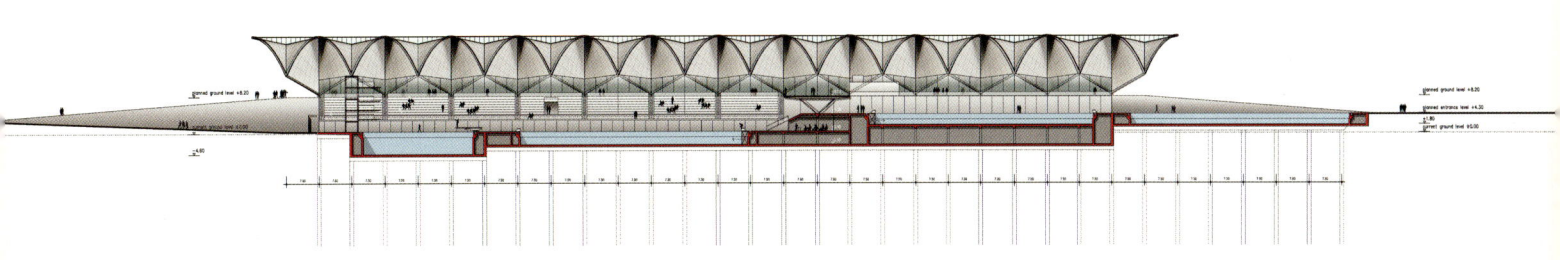

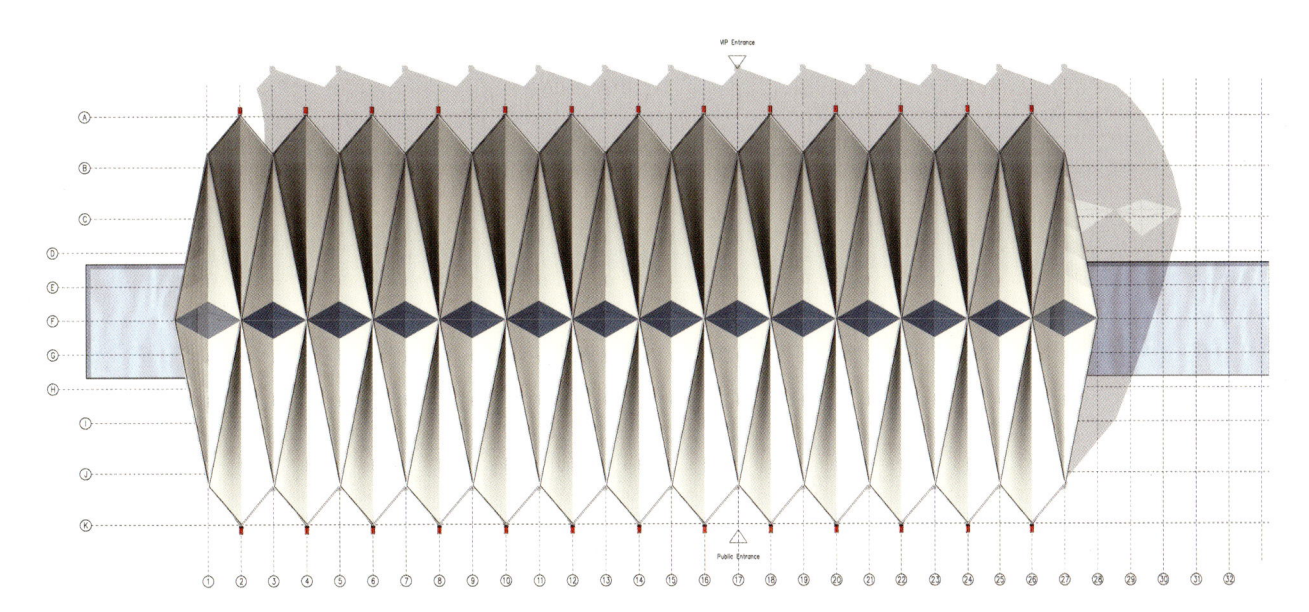

151

Grand Theatre, Chongqing
Grand Theatre, Chongqing

Stadtbausteine **Urban Modules**

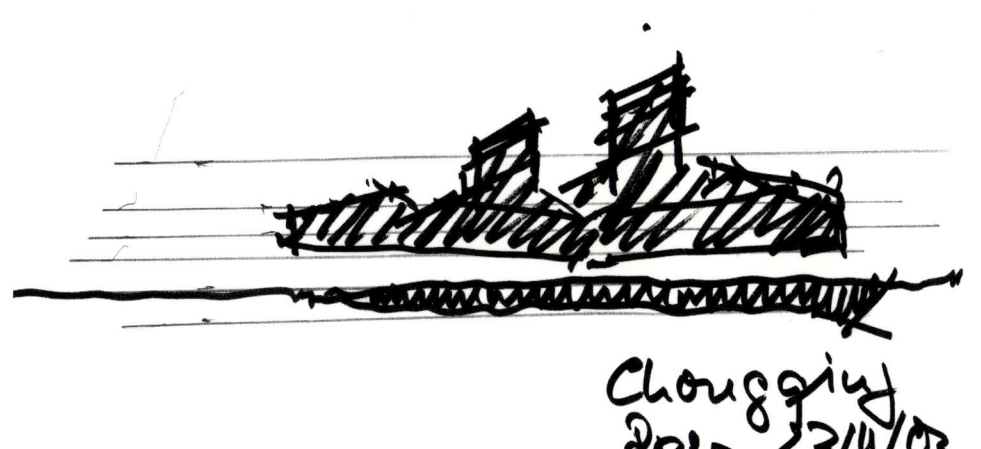

Wettbewerb 2004 – 1. Preis
Entwurf Meinhard von Gerkan mit Klaus Lenz
Partner Nikolaus Goetze
Projektleitung Volkmar Sievers
Mitarbeiter Entwurf Heiko Thiess, Monika van Vught, Robert Friedrichs, Matthias Ismael, Tobias Jortzick, Dominik Reh, Christian Dahle, Julia Gronbach
Mitarbeiter Ausführung Knut Maass, Kerstin Steinfatt, Jan Stolte, Nils Dethlefs
Bauherr Chongqing Urban Construction Investment
Bauzeit 2005–2007
BGF 70.000 m²

Grand Theatre, Chongqing

Eine großartige Theaterinszenierung zu besuchen bedeutet einen feierlichen Anlass, dem Alltagsleben entrückt zu sein.
Mit seiner Nähe zum Wasser schwebt das Grand Theatre über dem Fluss Jangtse. Surreale Lichtreflexe und Spiegelungen erzeugen poetische Kompositionen aus Realität und Fiktion, wie die Illusionswelt einer Theaterinszenierung.
Eine steinerne Sockelplattform bildet die Basis für die gläserne Skulptur, Grund- und Aufriss folgen trotz scheinbar willkürlicher Expressivität und maritimen Analogien streng den funktionalen Anforderungen.
Zwei Konzertsäle mit ihren zugeordneten Foyers liegen auf der Längsachse, gleichsam auf der „Kiellinie" eines Schiffes, und bilden so am Bug und Heck die Eingangsbereiche aus.
Mittig, also „mittschiffs", zu diesen beiden Eingangsbereichen liegt die Exhibition Hall, die somit alle Foyerflächen des Theaters miteinander verbindet. Dadurch können verschiedene Aufführungen und Veranstaltungen gleichzeitig durchgeführt werden.

Grand Theatre, Chongqing

Attending a magnificent theatrical performance means to celebrate, to escape from everyday life.
With its close proximity to the water, the Grand Theatre seems to hover above the River Yangtze. Surreal reflections of light create a poetic composition of reality and fiction, like the illusionary world of the theatre.
A stone platform supports the glass sculpture; the ground plan and elevation are subject to strict functional requirements despite their seemingly arbitrary expressiveness and maritime analogy.
Two concert halls with their respective foyers are situated in the longitudinal axis, similar to the "keel line" of a ship, thus forming entrance areas at the bow and the stern.
In the centre, in other words "midship" of these entrance areas, is the exhibition hall, which joins all the theatre foyers together. All kinds of performances and events can take place simultaneously, independent of one another.

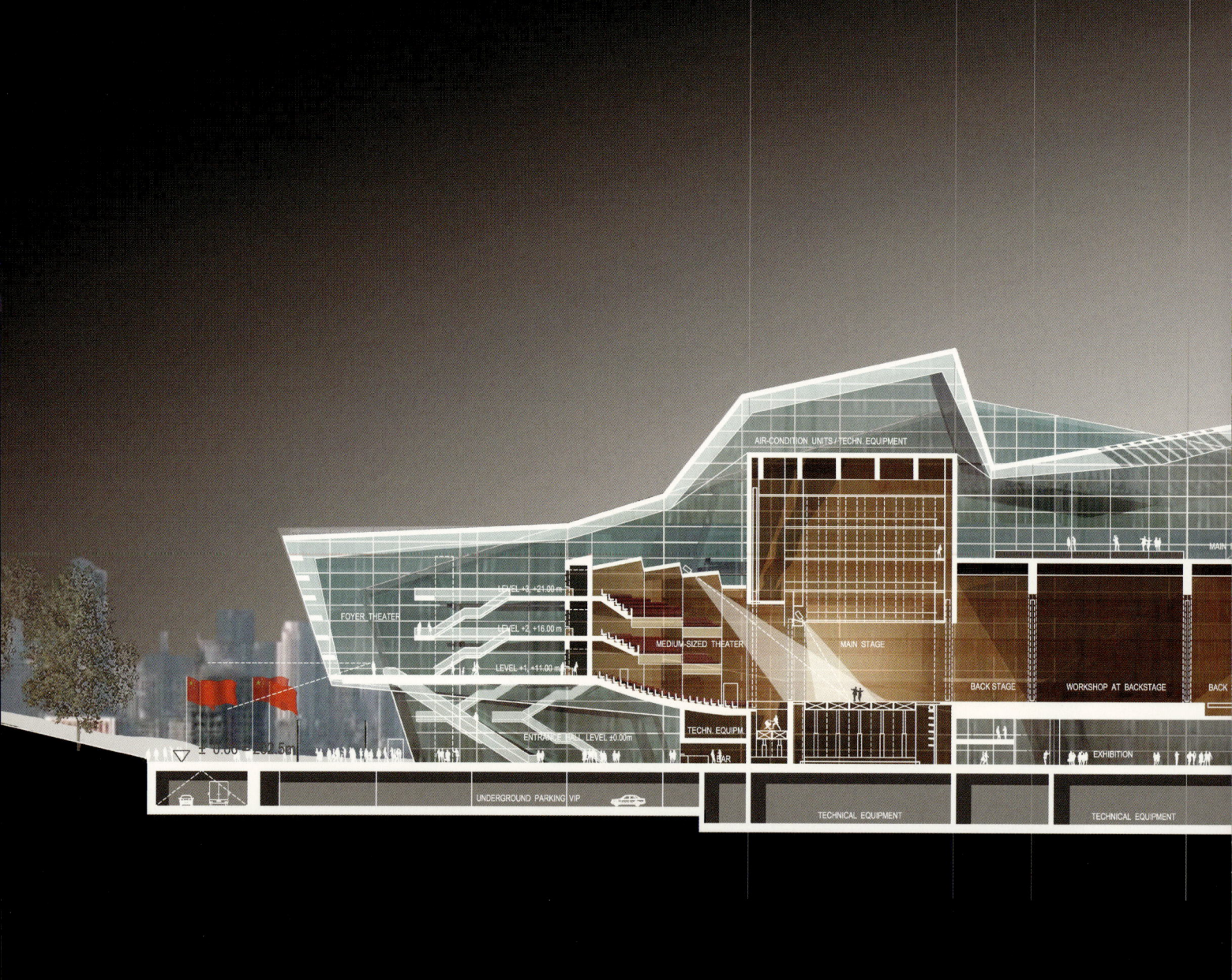

Grand Theatre, Chongqing
Grand Theatre, Chongqing

Stadtbausteine **Urban Modules**

Chinesisches Nationalmuseum, Peking
National Museum of China, Beijing

158

Stadtbausteine **Urban Modules**

屋顶
ROOF

26.5M 基本陈列
26.5M GENERAL DISPLAY

捐赠品展厅
DONATION EXHIBITION

电子影院
礼堂
学术报告厅
DIGITAL CINEMA
CEREMONY HALL
ACADEMIC REPORTING HALL

6.0M 大厅
6.0M GRAND FORUM

学术研究
ACADEMIC RESEARCH

国际交流展区
INTERNATIONAL
EXCHANGE
EXHIBITION

地铁
SUBWAY

行政管理
ADMINISTRATION

-2.5M 专题陈列
-2.5M SPECIAL DISPLAY

国际展区
INTERNATIONAL
EXHIBITION

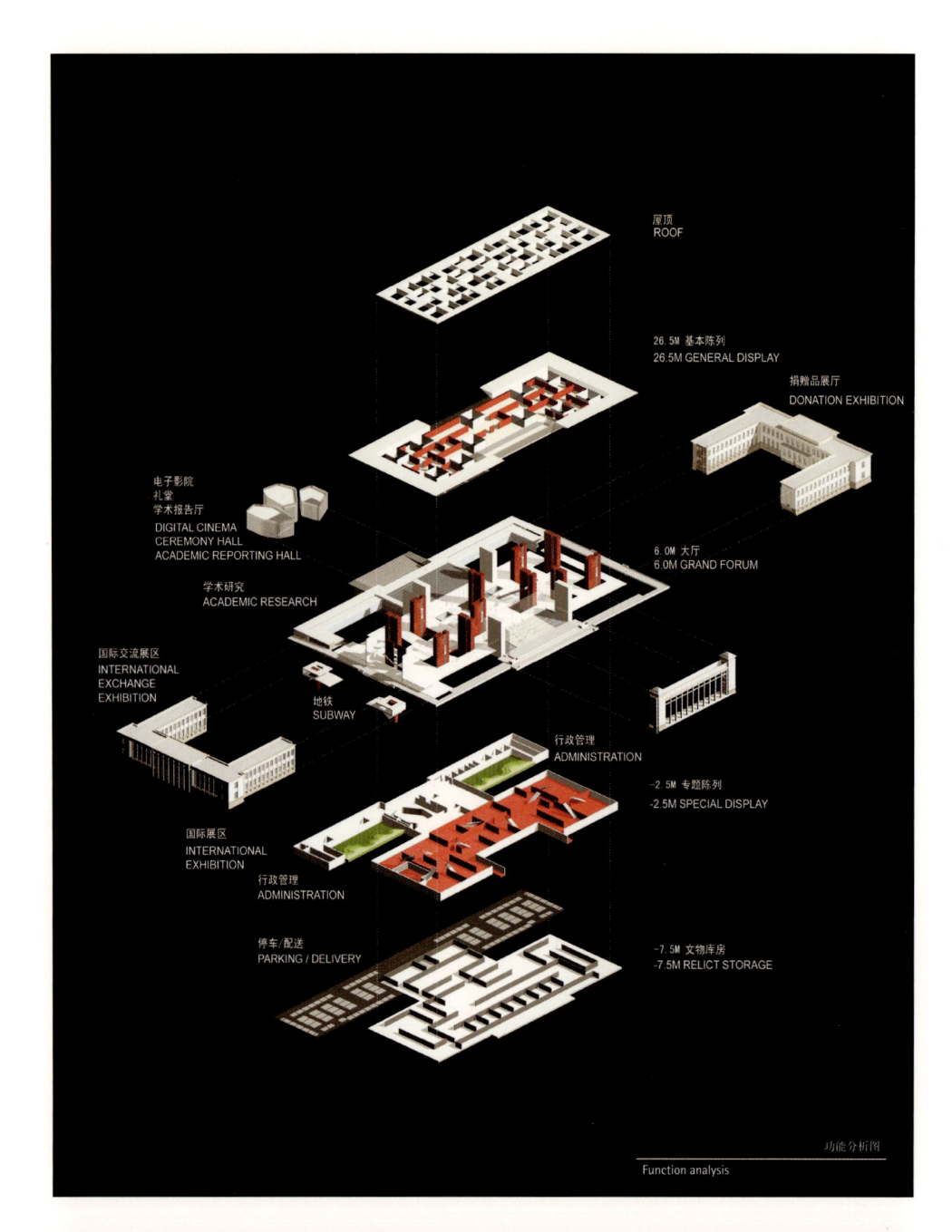

行政管理
ADMINISTRATION

停车/配送
PARKING / DELIVERY

-7.5M 文物库房
-7.5M RELICT STORAGE

功能分析图
Function analysis

Wettbewerb 2004 – 1. Preis
Entwurf Meinhard von Gerkan
mit Stephan Schütz
Mitarbeiter Entwurf Stephan Rewolle, Doris Schäffler, Gregor Hoheisel, Katrin Kanus, Ralf Sieber, Du Peng, Chunsong Dong
Bauherr The National Museum of China
BGF 170.000 m²
Bauzeit 2005–2007

Chinesisches Nationalmuseum, Peking

Das Chinesische Nationalmuseum ist die Vereinigung des vormaligen Chinese History Museum und des Chinese Revolutionary Museum und somit Schaufenster der Geschichte und Kunst einer der ältesten Kulturen der Menschheit.

Der Neubau des Museums liegt in der kulturellen und politischen Mitte Chinas, dem Platz des Himmlischen Friedens gegenüber der Verbotenen Stadt und der Großen Halle des Volkes.

Schwerpunkt der Entwurfsaufgabe ist die sensible Integration eines 170.000 m² großen Neubaus in das weltbekannte Platzensemble unter Mitnutzung einiger Teile des bestehenden Museums.

Der bestehende Bau zeigt Großzügigkeit und Würde durch seine gebäudehohen Kolonnaden, gleichzeitig fehlt es ihm jedoch an Offenheit und Transparenz im Inneren, da es durch das zentrale Eingangsgebäude blockiert ist.

Der Entwurf sieht vor, die vereinigten Museumsbauten durch ein Dach zu symbolisieren, das den öffentlichen Raum bedeckt und damit Wetterschutz für die Menschen bietet, die auf dem Vorplatz stehen.

Die Dachtraufe liegt in einer Höhe von 34,50 m, so dass die Große Halle des Volkes und das Chinesische Nationalmuseum in Höhe und Proportion ausbalanciert sind. Die geradlinige Silhouette des Daches versucht nicht, der Gebäudeerscheinung eine expressive oder sensationelle Geste hinzuzufügen.

Es soll sich der Proportion des Platzes anpassen und den Dialog mit der Großen Halle des Volkes betonen.

National Museum of China, Beijing

The National Museum of China is the union of the former Chinese History Museum and the Chinese Revolutionary Museum, and thus the showcase of the history and culture of one of the eldest cultures of mankind.

The new building is situated at the cultural and political centre of China, the Square of Heavenly Peace, opposite the Forbidden Town and the Great Hall of the People.

Focal point of the design is the sensitive integration of the 170.000 m² large new building in this world famous square ensemble using several parts of the existing museum.

The current building reflects generosity and dignity through the building-high colonnades but at the same time it lacks openness and transparency inside because it is blocked by the central entrance building.

The comprehensive museum is symbolized by a roof volume which covers the public space and provides protection from the elements.

The eaves of the roof are at a height of 34.50 m so that the Great Hall of the People and the National Museum of China are balanced in height and proportion. The straight silhouette of the roofing does not pretend to add an expressive and sensational architectural gesture to the appearance of the building. It intends to adjust the proportion of the square as well as to focus on the dialogue relationship with the Great Hall of the People.

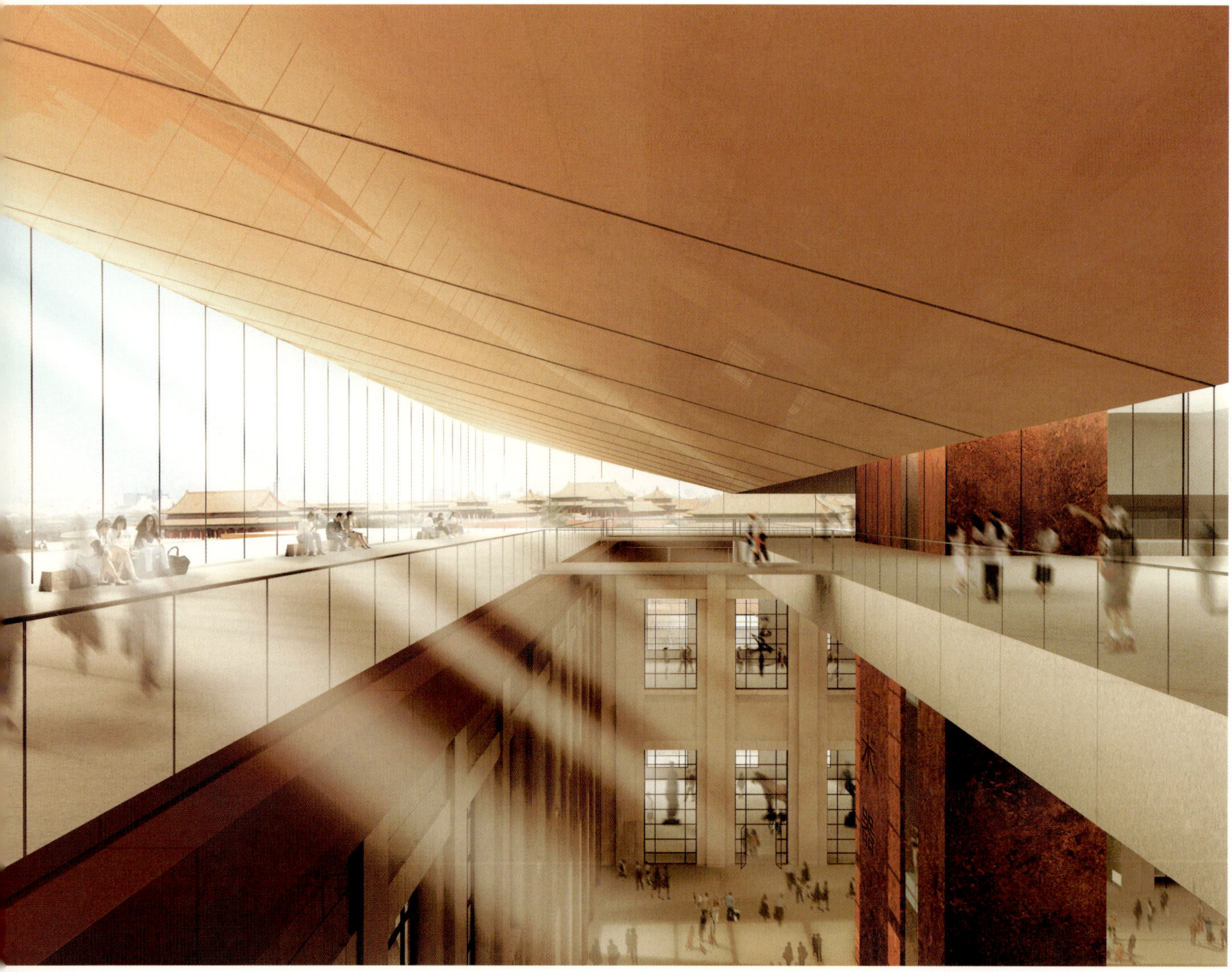

Stadtbausteine **Urban Modules**

Christliche Kirche, Peking
Christian Church, Beijing

Stadtbausteine **Urban Modules**

165

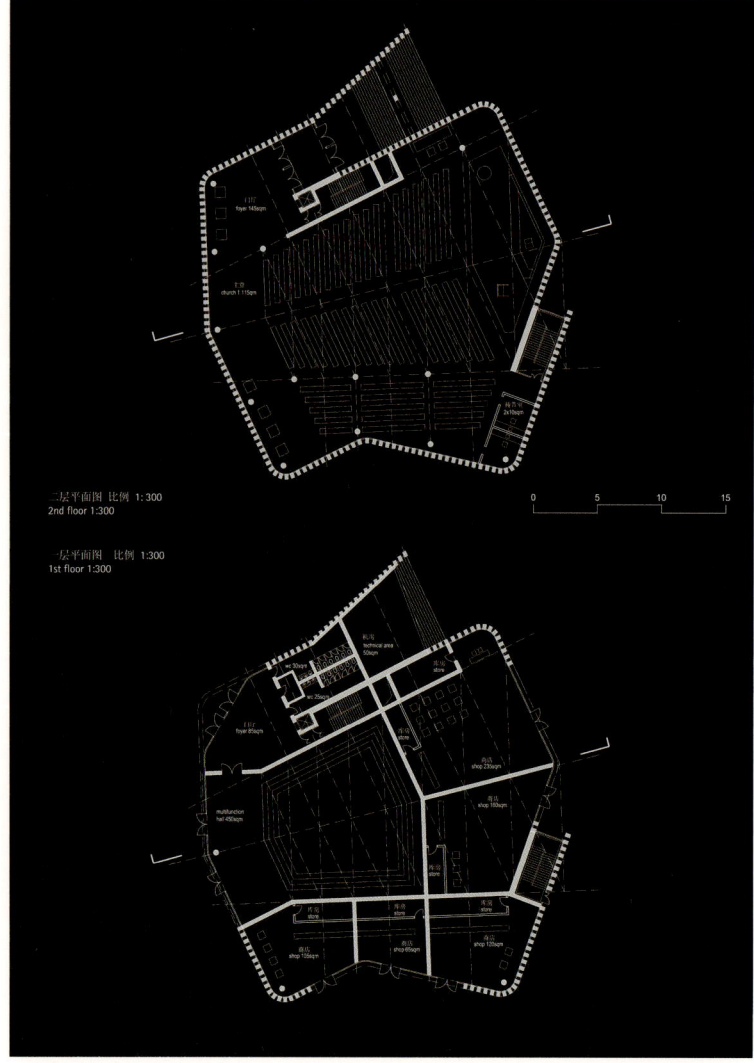

Wettbewerb 2004 – 1. Preis
Entwurf Meinhard von Gerkan
Projekt Partner Stephan Schütz
Mitarbeiter Stephan Rewolle, Gero Heimann, Katrin Kanus, Ralf Sieber, Xia Lin, Gregor Hoheisel
Bauherr China Zongguancun Culture Development Co., Ltd.
BGF 4.000 m²
Bauzeit 2005–2006
Baukosten 3,5 Mio Euro

Christliche Kirche, Peking

Eine chinesische Art von „Triple P": Public-Private-Partnership zeichnet diesen Entwurf für die größte christliche Kirche Chinas aus – einerseits durch seine kommerzielle Nutzungsfläche im Erdgeschoss und andererseits durch sein markantes Fassadenstabwerk.

Übergeordnetes Leitziel ist, den Baukörper durch seine geschwungene Form von den umliegenden kommerziell genutzten Gebäuden ästhetisch zu unterscheiden, um seine besondere Nutzung als Kirche zu betonen.

Über eine großzügige, portalartige Öffnung gelangen die Kirchenbesucher auf einer Freitreppe in die Hauptkirche im 1. Obergeschoss. Hier angekommen wenden sie sich nach Osten, wo der Altar steht. Durch den Wechsel von Öffnungen und geschlossenen Flächen vermittelt das Stabwerk der Fassade auch im Innern eine besondere, der sakralen Nutzung des Raums angemessene Lichtstimmung.

Das Fassadenstabwerk verleiht dem Gebäude eine einheitliche Gebäudehülle und wirkt so dem Eindruck eines heterogenen Baukörpers bewusst entgegengewirkt.

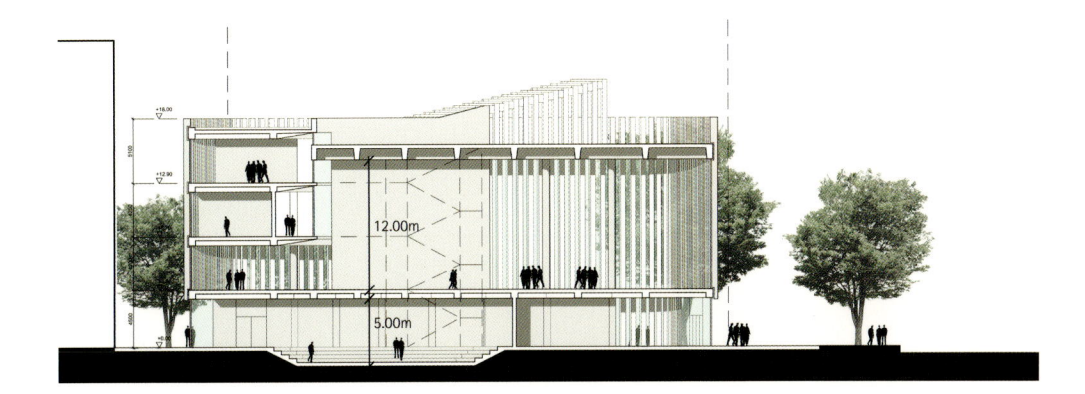

Christian Church, Beijing

A Chinese version of "Triple P": A public-private-partnership characterises this design for the largest Christian church in China. It comprises a ground floor for commercial use and a distinctive façade.

The primary aim of this design concept is the aesthetic differentiation of the building with its curved form from the surrounding commercially used buildings in order to emphasize its special function as a church.

The visitors enter the main church located on the first floor via a generous, portal-like opening and a flight of stairs. Arriving in this location they turn to the east, where the altar is positioned. The interplay of openings and solid areas in the façade's structure generates a special interior lighting atmosphere that is appropriate to the sacral use.

The façade structure provides a uniform building envelope and deliberately avoids giving the impression of a heterogeneous building.

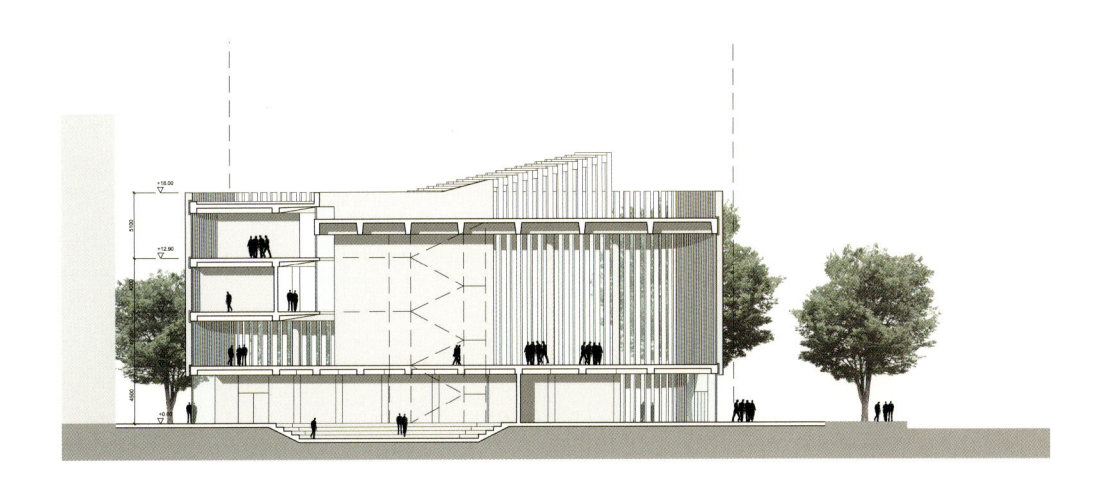

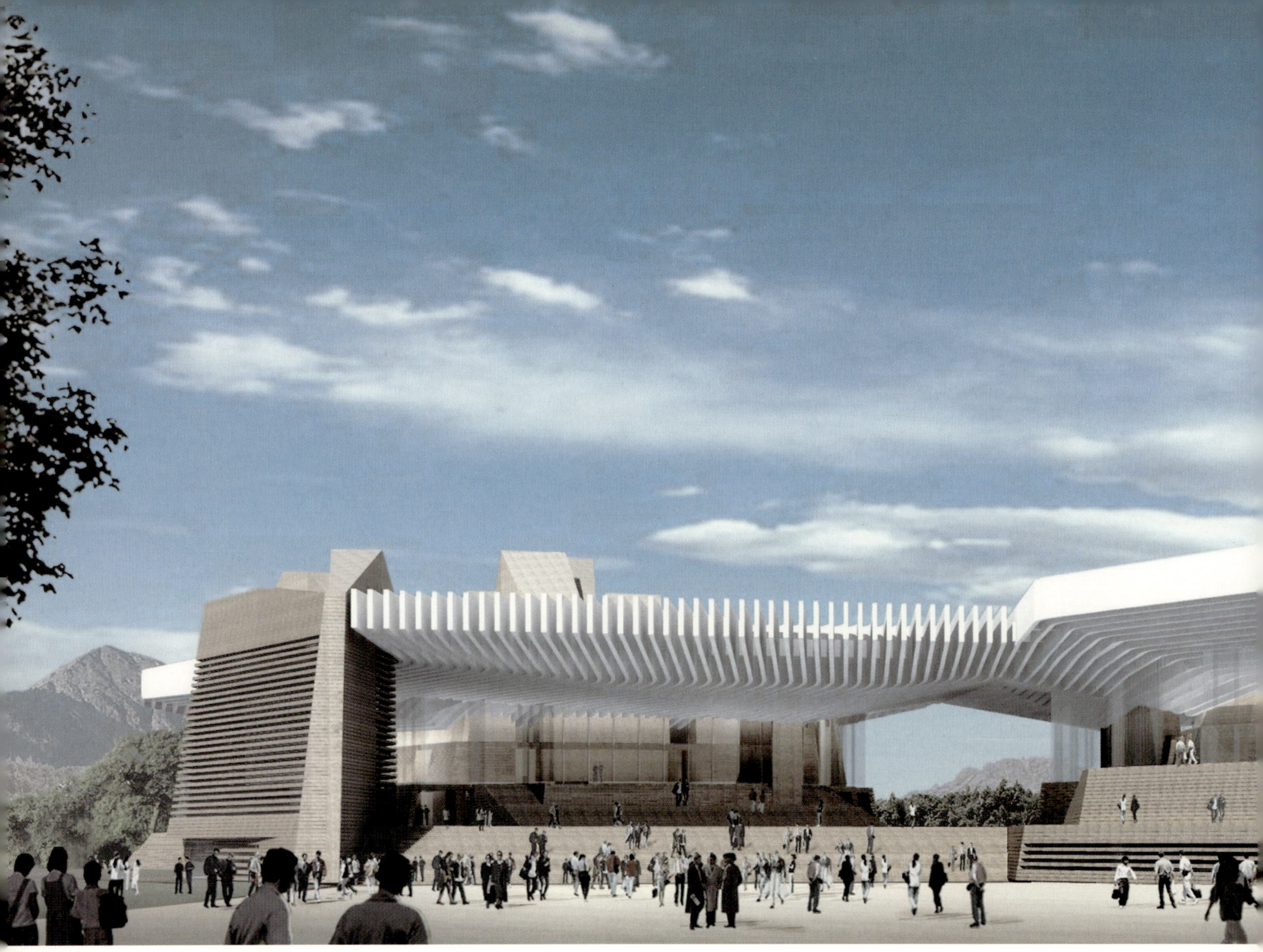

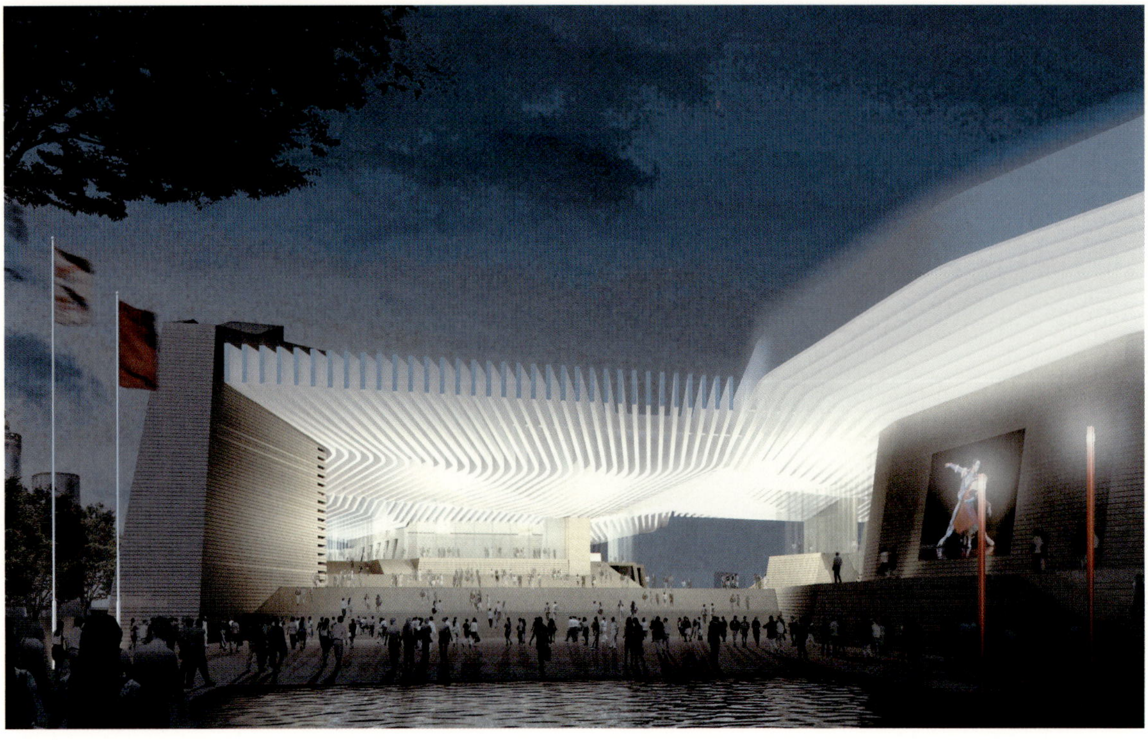

Grand Theater, Qingdao
Grand Theatre, Qingdao

Wettbewerb 2004 – 1. Preis
Entwurf Meinhard von Gerkan and Stephan Schuetz
Mitarbeiter Nicolas Pomränke, Clemens Kampermann, Sophie v. Mansberg, Xia Lin, Li Ling, Stephan Rewolle, Ralph Sieber, Giuseppina Orto
Bauherr Qingdao Conson Industrial Corporation
BGF 60.000 m²
Bauzeit 2005–2007

Grand Theater, Qingdao

Mit seiner höchsten Erhebung von 1.134 m über dem Meeresspiegel ist das Laoshangebirge das landschaftlich reizvollste und aus diesem Grund das bekannteste Gebirgsmassiv entlang der chinesischen Ostküste. Aufgrund der einzigartigen Lage des Massivs direkt am Meer sind die Berge des Laoshan oftmals in Wolken gehüllt, die der Landschaft eine mystische Atmosphäre verleihen.

Berge und Wolken: Es ist das Ziel des Entwurfes, Landschaft und Naturgewalten in die Sprache der Architektur zu übertragen. Wie ein Gebirgsmassiv erhebt sich das Gebäude aus der Landschaft, während ein schwebendes wolkengleiches Dach die Baukörper umgibt. Auf diese Weise entsteht ein einzigartiges Ensemble aus dem Bezug zum Genius Loci. Wie ein Gebirgsplateau erhebt sich eine öffentliche Terrasse aus dem umgebenden Park und lässt eine großzügige Platzfläche entstehen, die sich gleichermaßen zum Meer im Süd-Westen und zu den Bergen im Nordosten orientiert. Durch die Anhebung der Terrasse auf +4,50 m und durch eine leichte Verdrehung zur zentralen Parkachse entstehen attraktive Blickbeziehungen in die umgebende Landschaft. Die bergartigen Baukörper beinhalten die hauptsächlichen Funktionsbereiche des Theaters: 1. das Opernhaus, 2. die Konzert- und Multifunktionshalle, 3. das Medienzentrum, 4. das Hotel.

Das Wolkendach setzt dieses Naturschauspiel der wolkendurchzogenen Berggipfel in ein einzigartiges Architekturbild um, welches dem Entwurf Wiedererkennbarkeit und Identität verleiht: Schwere und Massivität der „Berge" auf der einen Seite, Leichtigkeit und Eleganz der „Wolke" auf der anderen Seite treten in einen spannenden Dialog.

Grand Theatre, Qingdao

With its highest peak rising 1,134 m above the sea level Mount Laoshan as well as the surrounding peaks are situated in the southeastern Shandong peninsula. Due to the unique climatic situation, the Laoshan mountains are very often wrapped in clouds which lend a particularly mystic atmosphere to the scenery.

Mountains and clouds: The aim of the design is to transform the landscape and the power of nature into architectural language. Like a mountain plateau, an open terrace rises up from the park and forms a generous public square, which is orientated to the sea in the southwest and to the mountains in the northeast. The terrace forms an open space underneath the cloud-like floating roof. By raising the plateau by 4.5 m and turning it slightly to the sea and to the Laoshan Mountains, a clear visual relation to the most scenic spots of Laoshan is produced. From the platform the major parts of the Grand Theatre rise like granite rocks, which is the local stone: 1. the opera house in the north, 2. the concert and multifunctional hall in the south, 3. the media centre in the west, 4. the artists' reception and training centre in the east.

Analogously to the predominant weather situation in the Laoshan Mountains, the roof of the Grand Theatre appears like a cloud drifting along the mountainlike volumes of individual buildings. That way a most poetic architectural image is created which makes the buildings recognizable all over the world. The expressive and massive rocks of the architectural landscape and the light and elegant cloudlike roof form an exciting architectural dialogue.

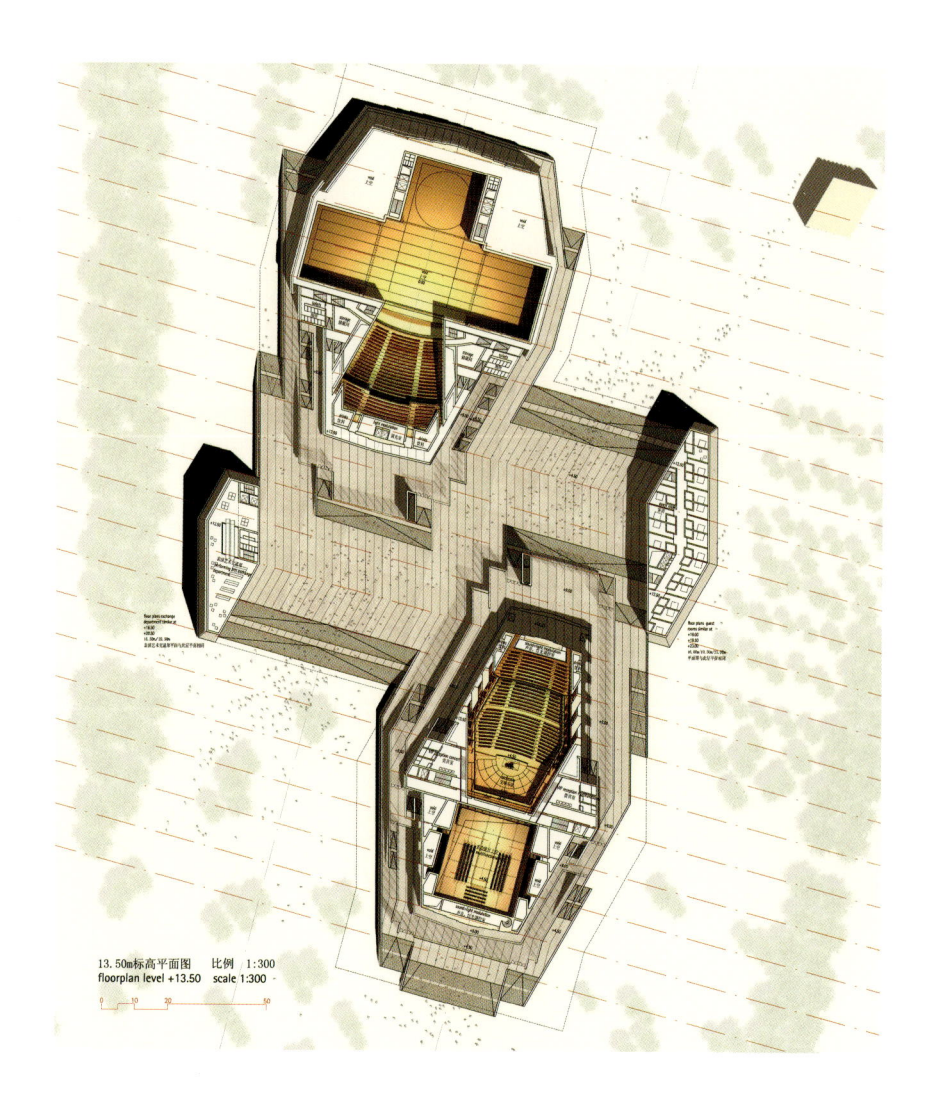

13.50m标高平面图　比例　1:300
floorplan level +13.50　scale 1:300

Stadtbausteine **Urban Modules**

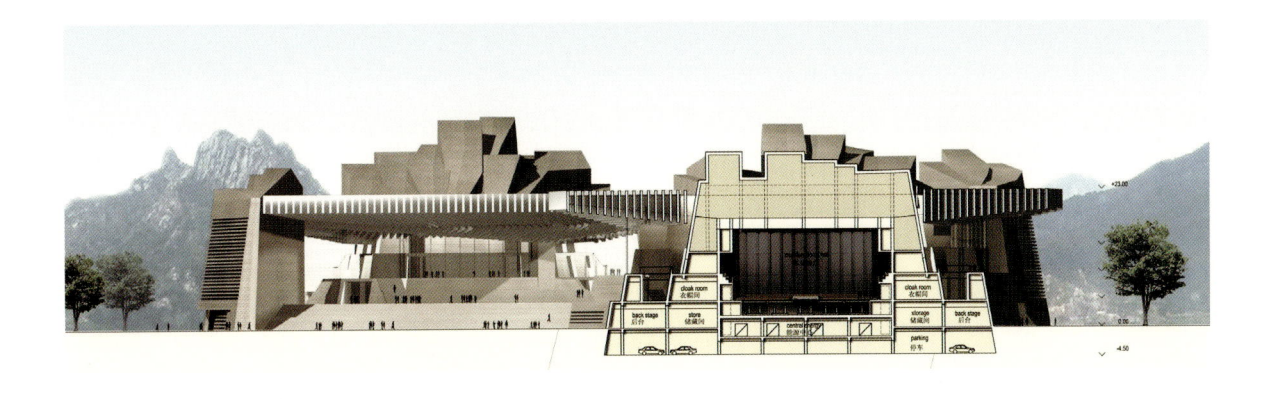

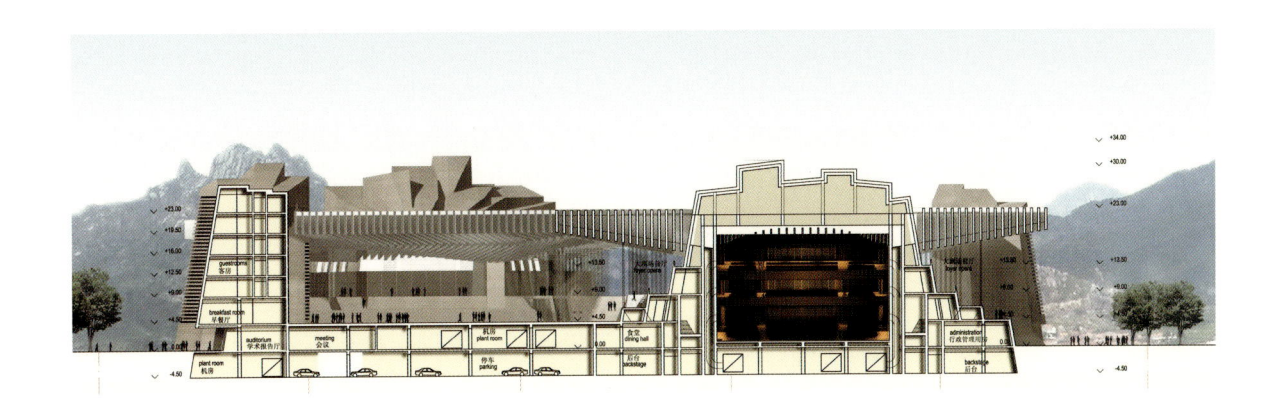

173

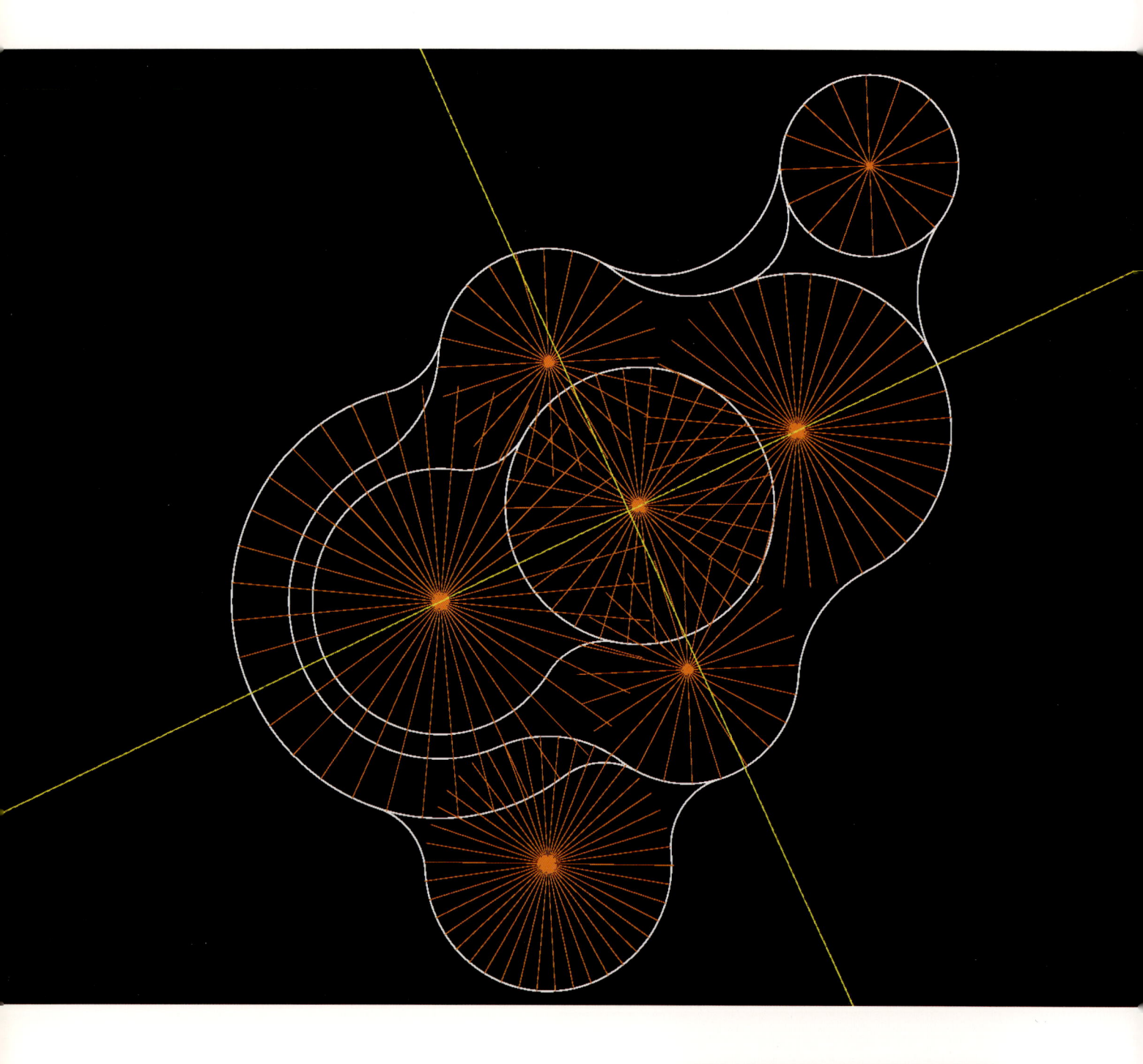

Guotai Theater, Chongqing
Guotai Theatre, Chongqing

174

Stadtbausteine **Urban Modules**

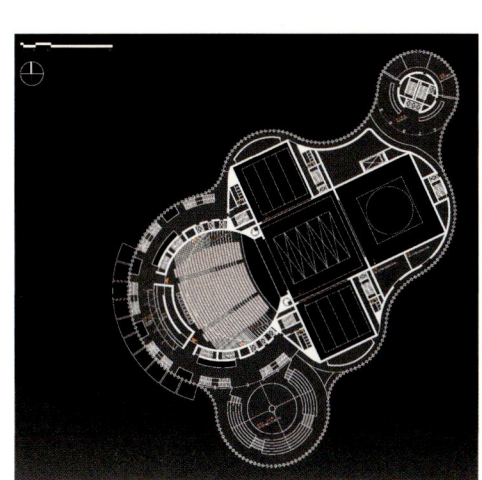

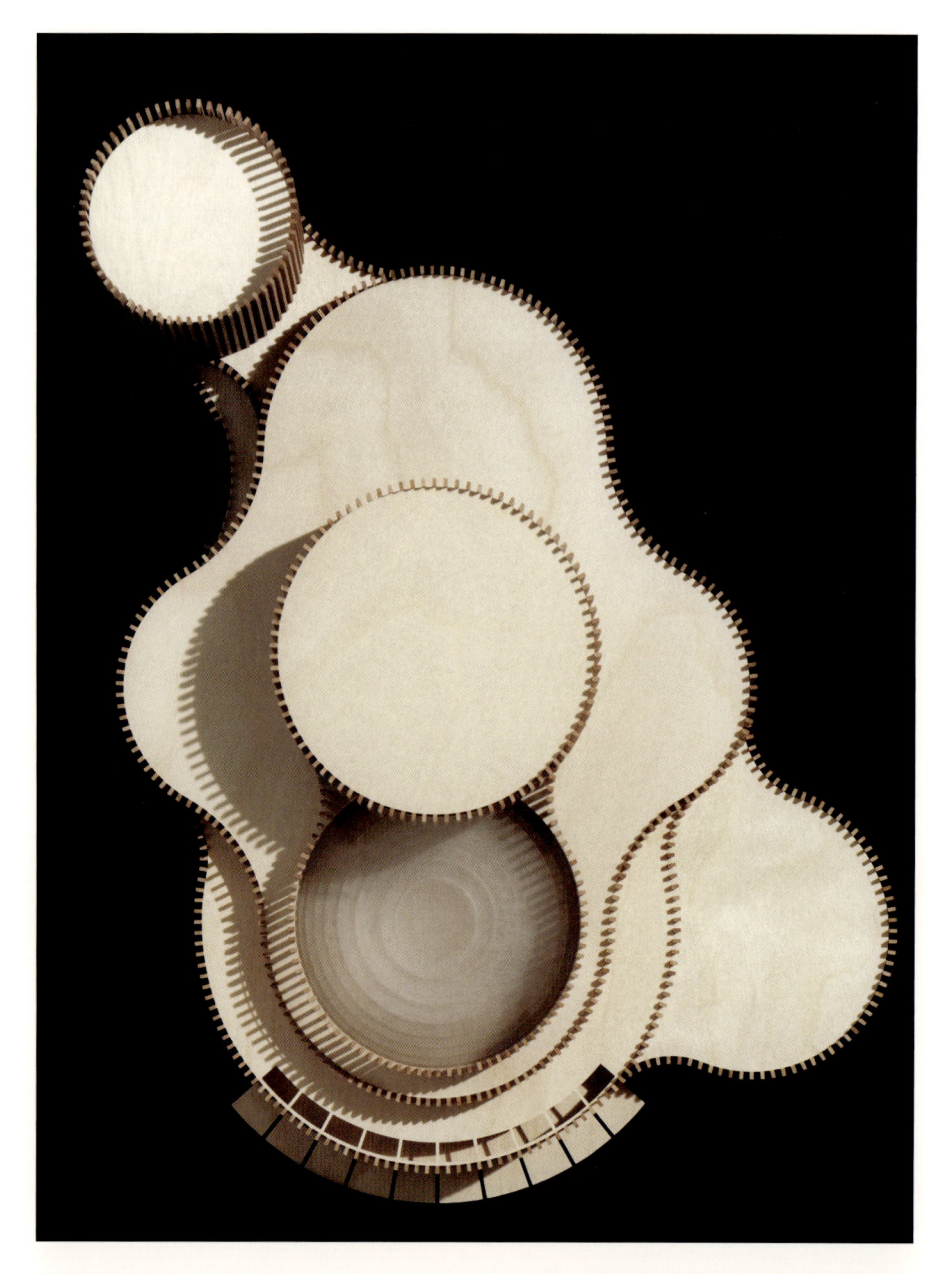

Wettbewerb 2005
Entwurf Meinhard von Gerkan mit Volkmar Sievers
Partner Nikolaus Goetze
Mitarbeiter Andrea Moritz, Sabrina Fienemann, Thilo Günther, Rouven Oberdiek
Bauherr Chongqing Real Estate Group
BGF 44.000 m²

Guotai Theater, Chongqing

Das neue Guotai-Theater von Chongqing erhält seine Identität aus den charakteristischen formalästhetischen Eigenschaften von der Natur, den Wolken und den Uferlandschaften des Jangtse-Flusses.

Das Guotai Theater ist kein Gebäude mit üblicher Fassade aus traditionell proportionierten Wand- und Fensterflächen. Das von innen nach außen dringende Licht, die Reflexion von Sonne, Wolken und Wasser auf den vielschichtig geneigten und gebrochenen Glasflächen lassen den Baukörper in immer wieder neuen, geheimnisvoll mystischen Lichtstimmungen erscheinen und erstrahlen.

Vertikale Lisenen gliedern die Kreiselemente und geben dem Theater seine besondere Ausdruckskraft. Die Lisenen wechseln sich mit offenen, gläsernen Fassaden ab, sodass ein lebhaftes Wechselspiel zwischen Innen und Außen, Transparenz und Dichte, Einblick und Ausblick entsteht.

Eine expressive Skulptur aus ineinander verschränkten Zylindern, die sich zueinander versetzen und verschieben, erzeugt in Aufsicht und Seitenansicht die metaphorische Darstellung von Wolken.

Die Skulptur des Baukörpers folgt trotz scheinbar willkürlicher Expressivität und maritimen Analogien streng den funktionalen Anforderungen. Jeder Funktion ist entsprechend der Größe und Lage im Gebäude ein separater Baukörper als Zylinder zugeordnet.

Die Gebäudehülle der neuen Hochhäuser des Theaters entwickelt sich über drei Schritte: strenge Kreisgeometrie der einzelnen Funktionsbereiche – Überlagerung der Kreisgeometrien miteinander – Verschmelzung der Kreise in Analogie zu Formationen von Flüssen, Inseln und Seen.

Das Theater steht auf einem Sockel, welcher die Besucher über geschwungene Treppen bis auf die Höhe der Eingangsebene des Foyers führt. Hieraus entwickelt sich formal auch der Brückenübergang weiter, der hinab zum Ufer des Jangtse-Flusses führt.

Die Foyers sind durchgehend in einer elegant wirkenden, hellen Gestaltung entworfen, während der Theatersaal konträr gestaltet ist: hier dominieren warme Farben. Warmes Kirschholz an den Wänden und Decken und rote Samtsitze bestimmen den Charakter des Saales. Die Konzertsaalgeometrie folgt den bewährten und traditionellen Formen mit einem Rang.

Guotai Theatre, Chongqing

The new Guotai Theatre derives its identity from the characteristic, formally aesthetic properties of nature, the clouds and the waterside landscapes of the Yangtze River.

The Guotai Theatre is not a building with the usual façade of traditionally proportioned wall and window areas. The light penetrating from the interior to the exterior, the reflection of the sun, clouds and water on the façades cause the structure to appear and shine in repeatedly new, mystic moods of light.

Vertical pilaster strips subdivide the circular elements and give the theatre its particular expressiveness. The pilaster strips alternate with open, glass façades so that a lively interaction is achieved between interior and exterior, transparency and closeness, looking in and looking out.

An expressive sculpture made of entwined regular cylinders that, seen from above or from the side, create the metaphoric representation of clouds.

The sculpture of the structure, despite the seemingly random expressivity and maritime analogies, strictly adheres to the functional requirements. A separate component is allocated to each function depending on its size and position within the building in the form of a cylinder.

The shell of these new high-rise components that form the theatre is developed in three stages: strict circular geometry of the individual functional sections, overlapping of the circular geometrical shapes and merging of the circles in analogy to the formations of rivers, islands and lakes.

The theatre stands on a base with curved flights of steps leading up to the level of the entrance to the foyer. A continuation of this is a bridge leading down to the banks of the Yangtze River.

The foyers are designed in elegant light shades throughout whereas the theatre auditorium itself shows quite a contrasting style. Here warm tones dominate. Warm cherrywood on the walls and ceilings and red velvet seats determine the character of the auditorium and make it appear warm and inviting. The geometry of the concert hall adheres to proven and traditional shapes and includes a circle.

Die Karte ist mit freundlicher Genehmigung dem GEO Special China entnommen, erhältlich im Zeitschriften- und Buchhandel 2003.

VOLKSREPUBLIK CHINA
ZHONGHUA RENMIN GONGHEGUO

Bauen in China, 1998–2005

Seit 1965 haben Meinhard von Gerkan, Volkwin Marg und ihre Partner in nahezu allen großen Städten der Bundesrepublik geplant und gebaut. Zu ihren bekanntesten Bauten gehören die Flughäfen in Berlin-Tegel, Hamburg und Stuttgart, die Neue Messe Leipzig und der Christus-Pavillon auf der Expo 2000 in Hannover.

Mit der Deutschen Schule Peking, für die gmp 1998 den ersten Preis im internationalen Wettbewerb gewann, begann die Bautätigkeit in China. Einer Gemeinschaftsausstellung in der Berliner Galerie Asian Fine Arts Factory Anfang 1999 folgte im gleichen Jahr anlässlich des XX. UIA-Weltkongresses in Peking eine Einzelausstellung mit dem Titel „Building for the Public" im Yan-Huang Art Museum. Im Herbst 2000 fand auf Anregung von Prof. von Gerkan ein deutsch-chinesischer Workshop als Kooperation der Tsinghua Universität Peking mit der Hochschule für bildende Künste Hamburg und der TU Braunschweig statt. Im Juli 2002 zeigte gmp im Rahmen des XXI. UIA-Weltkongresses in Berlin unter dem Titel „Building in China" eine Auswahl gebauter und geplanter chinesischer Projekte. 2003 fand im Museum für Kunst und Gewerbe in Hamburg eine umfassende gmp-Chinaausstellung statt.

Derweil wurde in den Büros fast kontinuierlich an chinesischen Wettbewerben gearbeitet und der Erfolg ließ nicht lange auf sich warten: Bereits 1999 gewann gmp den Wettbewerb zum Nanning International Convention & Exhibition Center, das 2005 fertiggestellt wurde. Es folgten weitere Wettbewerbe und etliche erste und zweite Preise kamen hinzu, darunter auch der erste Preis für die städtebauliche Masterplanung der 450.000-Einwohner-Stadt Lingang New City, deren erster Bauabschnitt bereits im Jahr 2006 abgeschlossen sein soll.

Heute befinden sich in China 13 Projekte in Bau, 30 Projekte in der Ausführungsplanung und sieben sind bereits fertiggestellt.

Dabei bleibt gmp seiner Philosophie des dialogischen Entwerfens mit den Grundpositionen Einfachheit, Einheit in der Vielfalt, Identität mit dem Ort und strukturelle Ordnung auch in Südostasien treu: „Wir bemühen uns, mit unserer Architektur in China gegen das verbreitete Klischee einer gefälligen Dekorationsarchitektur vorzugehen. Wir bekennen uns zu den klaren und einfachen Formen, die auch bei den großen Dimensionen vieler chinesischer Projekte gleichermaßen Berechtigung haben." Vielleicht erklärt gerade dieser Nonkonformismus den Erfolg von gmp in China.

Der Enthusiasmus, mit dem sich gmp und allen voran Meinhard von Gerkan neuen Entwürfen widmen, ist auch mit der ständig wachsenden Zahl von Projekten in China der gleiche geblieben: „Der größte Reiz an den chinesischen Projekten liegt in ihrer außergewöhnlichen Größe und Aufgabenstellung. Projekte dieser Dimension, sowohl inhaltlich als auch quantitativ, gibt es in Europa nur ganz selten, ebenso wie die Schnelligkeit, mit der viele der sehr großen Projekte in die Wirklichkeit umgesetzt werden."

Building in China, 1998–2005

Since 1965 Meinhard von Gerkan, Volkwin Marg and their partners have planned and realised buildings in almost all major German cities. The airports in Berlin-Tegel, Hamburg and Stuttgart, the New Leipzig Trade Fair and the Christ Pavilion at the Expo 2000 in Hanover are some of their best-known buildings.

The German School in Beijing, a winning concept in an international competition in 1998, initiated gmp's construction activities in China. A group exhibition in the Berlin Gallery Asian Fine Arts Factory in early 1999 was followed by a solo exhibition with the title "Building for the Public" in the Yan-Huang Art Museum on the occasion of the XX UIA World Congress in Beijing in the same year. On the initiative of Prof. von Gerkan a German-Chinese workshop took place in autumn 2000, a cooperation of the Tsinghua University Beijing, the University of Fine Arts Hamburg and the Institute of Technology Braunschweig. In July 2002 gmp presented a selection of built and planned Chinese projects at the XXI. UIA World Congress in Berlin. The exhibition was titled "Building in China". In 2003 a comprehensive exhibition in the Museum für Kunst und Gewerbe in Hamburg displayed numerous gmp-designs for China.

Simultaneously, the different offices worked continuously on Chinese competitions and the success was not a long time coming: Already in 1999 gmp won the competition for the Nanning International Convention & Exhibition Center, which is presently under construction. Further competitions and numerous first and second prizes followed, amongst them the first prize for the urban master planning of Lingang New City, a city for 450,000 inhabitants, with its first building phase due to be completed in 2006.

At present thirteen projects are under construction, thirty are in the planning stage and seven are already realized in China.

In East-Asia gmp also remains true to its philosophy of dialogical design with its basic principles of simplicity, unity in variety, identity with the location and structural order: "We endeavour to confront the widely prevailing cliché of a pleasing decorative architecture in China with our architectural approach. We declare ourselves for clear and simple forms, which are equally justified for the large dimensions of some of the Chinese projects." Maybe it is this non-conformism which explains gmp's success in China.

Despite the ever growing number of projects in China, the enthusiasm with which gmp and especially Meinhard von Gerkan dedicates himself to new projects, has been maintained: "The biggest attraction of Chinese projects is based on their extraordinary dimension and task. Projects of this scale regarding their content as well as the quantity are rare in Europe. The same is true for the speed with which many of the large projects are realised."

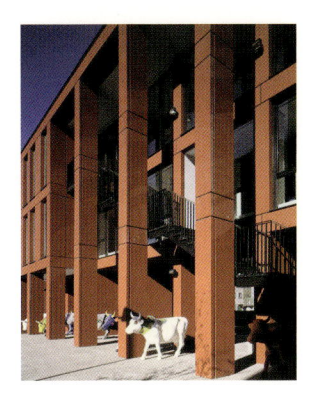

German School and Apartment House in Beijing
Competition: 1998 – 1st prize
Design: Meinhard von Gerkan with Michael Biwer
Partner: Klaus Staratzke
Project managers: Michael Biwer, Sibylle Kramer
Project team, design: Bettina Groß, Elke Hoffmeister
Project team, construction: Michèle Watenphul, Knut Maass, Ulrich Rösler, Diana Heinrich, Jörn Bohlmann, Rüdiger von Helmolt, Robert Wildegger
Structural engineers: Weber-Poll Ingenieure
Operating construction company: Philipp Holzmann
Client: Fed. Rep. of Germany
Gross floor area: School 9,658 m², Apartment House 9,657 m²
Construction period: 1999–2000

Nanning International Convention & Exhibition Center
Competition: 1999 – 1st prize
Design: Meinhard von Gerkan and Nikolaus Goetze
Project managers: Dirk Heller, Karen Schroeder
Project team, design: Oliver Christ, Jens Niemann, Andreas Gärtner, Mike Berrier, Antonio Caetita-Soeiro, Malte Wolf
Project team, construction: Christoph Berle, Wencke Eissing, Kai Siebke, Georg Traun, Friedhelm Chlosta, Meike Schmidt, Stefanie Schupp, Jochen Schwarz, Eckhard Send, Iris van Hülst, Thomas Eberhardt
Structural engineers, design: Schlaich Bergermann und Partner
Technical building equipment, design: HL-Technik
Landscape architects, design: Breimann, Bruun, Stief
Chinese partner practice: Guangxi Architectural Comprehensive Design & Research Institute
Client: Nanning International Convention & Exhibition Co., Ltd.
Gross floor area: 90,000 m²
Construction period: 1999–2003

Trade Fair, Shanghai-Pudong
Competition: 1998
Design: Volkwin Marg
Design team: Eun Young Yi, Gunter Köhnlein, Erik Recke, Wolfram Grothe, Marc Frohn, Mario Rojas Toledo, Thomas Behr
Gross floor area: 236,000 m²

G.W. Plaza, Beijing
Urban planning
Competition: 2000 – 1st prize
Design: Meinhard von Gerkan
Design team: Kristian Uthe-Spencker, Stephan Schütz, Tim Schmitt, Markus Pfisterer
Client: G.W. Group Ltd., Beijing

Exhibition Pavilion for Xinzhao Residential Area
2000
Design: Meinhard von Gerkan
Project manager: Dirk Heller
Project team: Christoph Berle, Astrid Lapp
Client: Beijing Xinzhao Real Development Co., Beijing Town-Country Houses Construction Development Co.
Gross floor area: 1,400 m²
Construction period: 2000–2001

Guangzhou International Convention & Exhibition Center
Competition: 2000 – 2nd prize
Design: Volkwin Marg with Marc Ziemons
Partner: Nikolaus Goetze
Design team: Thomas Schuster, Sven Greiser, Tom Eberhard, Gudrun von Schau, Kristina Milani, Martin Marschner, Moritz Hoffmann-Becking, Mario Rojas-Toledo
Client: Guangzhou Urban Planning Office
Gross floor area: 520,000 m²

Tourism Center, Hangzhou
Competition: 2000 – 1st prize
Design: Meinhard von Gerkan
Partner: Nikolaus Goetze
Project manager: Volkmar Sievers
Design team, phase 1: Walter Gebhardt, Christoph Berle, Andreas Gärtner, Astrid Lapp, Jochen Meyer
Design team, phase 2: Christoph Berle, Wu Wei, Justus Klement, Tanja Markovic, Kristina Milani, Andrea Moritz
Project team, phase 1: Heiner Gietmann, Dirk Hünerbein, Dominik Reh, Holger Schmücker
Project team, phase 2: Simone Nentwig, Jörn Bohlmann, Karen Heckel, Nicole Loeffler, Rouven Oberdiek, Thies Böke, Tobias Plinke, Andrea Moritz, Heike Kugele, Nils Dethlefs, Leif Henning
Chinese partner practice: ZADRI, Zhejiang Building Design & Research Institute, Hangzhou
Client: Hangzhou Canhigh Estate Co.
Gross floor area: 117,000 m²
Construction period: 2004–2006

Cultural Forum, Lang Fang near Beijing
Consultancy: since 2000
Design: Meinhard von Gerkan
Partner: Nikolaus Goetze
Design team: Jessica Weber, Heiko Thiess Annika Schröder, Sona Kazemi, Stephanie Heß, Richard Sprenger, Kristina Milani, Christoph Berle, Philipp Kamps, Justus Klement
Client: Lang Fang Urban Planning Bureau
Area: 44 ha

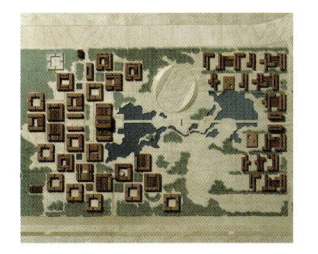

New Campus of the Shenyang Architectural and Civil Engineering Institute
Competition: 2000 – 2nd prize
Design: Meinhard von Gerkan and Joachim Zais
Design team: Astrid Lapp, Jochen Meyer, Sigrid Müller, Jörn Ortmann, Matias Otto, Monika van Vught, Claudia Weitemeier, Gabi Wysocki, Ioannis Zonitsas

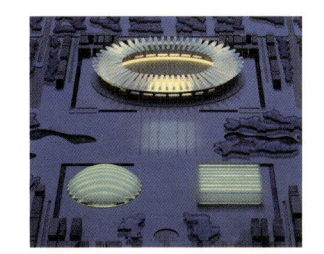

World Exhibition and Sports Center, Beijing
Competition: 2000 – commended
Design: Meinhard von Gerkan and Joachim Zais
Design team: Christoph Berle, Astrid Lapp, Jens Niemann, Matias Otto, Hajo Paap, Magdalene Weiß, Monika van Vught, Ioannis Zonitsas
Client: Beijing Planning Committee
Gross floor area: 3,410,000 m²

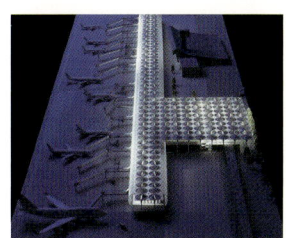

Qingdao Liuting Airport
Competition: 2000
Design: Meinhard von Gerkan with Walter Gebhardt
Design team: Stefanie Driessen, Andreas Gärtner, Jens Niemann, Rüdiger von Helmolt, Patrick Huhn, Thomas Pehlke
In cooperation with: Agiplan and Initec
Client: Qingdao Airport Construction Headquarters

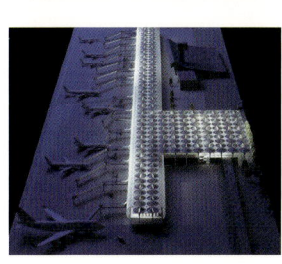

Shenzhen Convention & Exhibition Center
Competition: 2001 – 1st prize
Design: Volkwin Marg with Marc Ziemons
Partner: Nikolaus Goetze
Project managers: Marc Ziemons, Thomas Schuster
Design and project team: Karen Seekamp, Dirk Balser, Sven Greiser, Martin Marschner, Moritz Hoffmann-Becking, Wei Wu, Susanne Winter, Yingdi Wang, Robert Wildegger, Martina Klostermann, Iris van Hülst, Xiaolong Hu, Flori Wagner, Tina Stahnke, Marina Hoffmann, Heike Kugele, Magdalene Weiß, Birgit Föllmer, Otto Dorn, Katja Zoschke, Jeanny Rieger, Carsten Plog, Holger Schmücker, Gudrun von Schau, Jochen Köhn
Structural engineers, design: Schlaich Bergermann und Partner
Technical building equipment, design: HL-Technik
Landscape architects, design: Breimann, Bruun
Light planning: Schlotfeld Licht
Chinese partner practice: China Northeast Architectural Design Institute, Shenzhen
Client: Shenzhen Convention & Exhibition Center
Gross floor area: 256,000 m^2
Construction period: 2002–2006

Xinzhao Residential Area, Beijing
2000
Design: Meinhard von Gerkan and Nikolaus Goetze
Project managers: Dirk Heller, Karen Schroeder
Design and project team: Christoph Berle, Wencke Eissing, Iris van Hülst, Kai Siebke, Georg Traun, Friedhelm Chlosta, Meike Schmidt, Oliver Christ, Eckhard Send, Patrick Huhn, Patrick Klugesherz, Andreas Gärtner, Yingdi Wang, Holger Wermers
Chinese partner practice: Beijing Victory Star Architecture Design Co., Beijing Huazi Engineering Design Co.
Client: Beijing Xinzhao Real Development Co., Beijing Town-Country Houses Construction Development Co.
Gross floor area of 4 construction phases: 600,000 m^2 – 5,800 apartments
Gross floor area of 1st and 2nd phase: 235,000 m^2 – 2,163 apartments
Construction period of phases 1 and 2: 2001–2004

Oriental Art Center, Shanghai
Exhibition complex
Competition: 2001 – 1st prize
Design: Meinhard von Gerkan with Walter Gebhardt
Partner: Joachim Zais
Design team: Evelyn Pasdzierny, Jörn Bohlmann, Yingdi Wang, Tilo Günther, Barbara Henke, Rouven Oberdiek
Client: Pudong Municipal Culture Radio & TV Administration, Shanghai
Gross floor area: 44,000 m^2

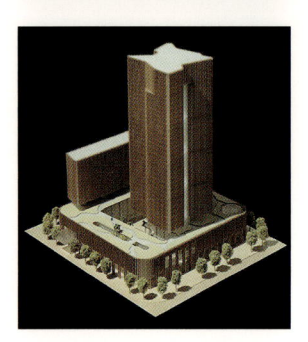

Mobile Communication Center, Guangzhou, Office building
Competition: 2001 – 2nd prize
Design: Meinhard von Gerkan
Partner: Nikolaus Goetze
Design team: Volkmar Sievers, Simone Nentwig, Tobias Plinke, Rouven Oberdiek
Client: Guangdong Mobile Communication Co.

Gross floor area: 16,640 m^2

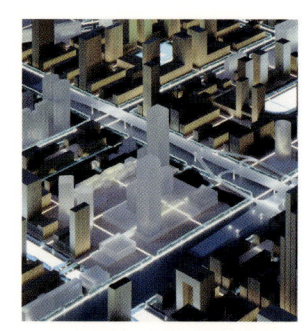

Central Business District, Beijing
Urban planning
Competition: 2001
Design: Meinhard von Gerkan and Nikolaus Goetze
Design team: Jessica Weber, Heiko Thiess, Martin Tamke, Michael Bucherer, Nico Rickert
Proprietor: Construction & Management Office of Beijing CBD
Area: 4 km^2

Fortune Plaza, Beijing
Urban planning
Competition: 2001 – 1st prize
Design: Meinhard von Gerkan with Stephan Schütz and Kristian Uthe-Spencker
Design team: Christian Dorndorf, Nicolas Pomränke, Sophie von Mansberg
Client: Beijing Xiangjiang Real Estate Development Co., Ltd.
Gross floor area: 700,000 m^2

Finance Street, Beijing
Urban planning
Competition: 2001 – 3rd prize
Design: Meinhhard von Gerkan and Klaus Staratzke
Design team: Michael Biwer, Hinrich Müller, Udo Meyer, Christoph Schulze-Kölln, Julia Strunk, Tobias Plinke, Melanie Klusmeier, Barbara Henke, Myriam Engels, Bettina Groß
Client: Beijing Finance Street Construction & Development Co., Ltd.

New City Jia Ding
Urban planning
Consultancy: 2001
Design: Meinhard von Gerkan
Design team: Hinrich Müller, Heiko Thiess, Jessica Weber, Svenia Oehmig, Julia Strunk, Holger Schmücker
Client: Jia Ding Urban Planning Administration
Gross floor area: 2,262,000 m^2

Shanghai South Railway Station
Competition: 2001
Design: Meinhard von Gerkan
Design team: Walter Gebhardt, Evelyn Pasdzierny, Simone Nentwig, Jörn Bohlmann, Lars Neininger, Christoph Thomsen
Client: Construction Command Post of Shanghai South Railway Station of Shanghai Railway Administration
Gross floor area: 60,000 m^2

Harbin International Convention, Exhibition and Sports Center
Competition: 2001
Design: Volkwin Marg
Project team: Marek Nowak, Stefan Nixdorf, Christoph Helbich, Stephan Menke, Sven Laurin, Johannes Klein, Burkhard Floors
Client: Harbin International Conference Exhibition Center Company Ltd.
Gross floor area: about 230,000 m^2

Shenyang Hunnan New District
Competition: 2001 – 2nd prize group
Design: Meinhard von Gerkan
Design team: Stephan Schütz, Kristian Uthe-Spencker, Christian Dorndorf, Michèle Rüegg, Katina Roloff

**Shih Chien University Gymnasium
Taipei, Taiwan**
2001
Design: Meinhard von Gerkan with
Monika van Vught
Partner: Joachim Zais
Design team: Udo Meyer, Claudia Schultz,
Friedhelm Chlosta
Client: Shih Chien University
Gross floor area: 20,000 m²
Planning period: 06/01–10/02

**Development Central Building,
Guangzhou, Office building**
Competition: 2001 – 1st prize
Design: Meinhard von Gerkan
Project manager: Volkmar Sievers
Design and project team:
Simone Nentwig, Jörn Bohlmann, Huan
Zhu, Robert Wildegger, Tilo Günther, Lars
Neininger, Andrea Moritz, Tobias Plinke,
Heike Kugele, Nils Dethlefs, Knut Maass
Structural engineers:
Ove Arup & Partners
Chinese partner practice:
GZDI, Guangzhou Design Institute
Client: Guangzhou Developing New City
Investment Co., Ltd.
Gross floor area: 75,000 m²
Construction period: 2002–2004

Lingang Main City
Competition: 2002 – 1st prize
Design: Meinhard von Gerkan
Partner: Nikolaus Goetze
Design team: Jessica Weber, Annika
Schröder, Beate Quaschning, Christoph
Böttinger, Wei Wu, Sigrid Müller, Eduard
Kaiser, Hung-Wei Hsu, Richard Sprenger,
Stephanie Heß, Christian Krüger, Hector
Labin, Markus Carlsen
Port planning: HPC Hamburg Port
Consulting
Landscape architects: Breimann, Bruun
Light planning: Schlotfeldt Licht
Client: Shanghai Urban Planning
Administration Bureau
Area: 65 km²
In planning stage

Yuelu Campus Town, Changsha
Competition: 2001 – 1st prize
Design: Meinhard von Gerkan
Partner: Joachim Zais
Design team: Dominik Reh, Jörn
Herrmann, Udo Meyer, Gabi Wysocki,
Xialong Hu, Huan Zhu
Client: Human Provincial Development
Planning Commission
Gross floor area: 2,872,500 m²

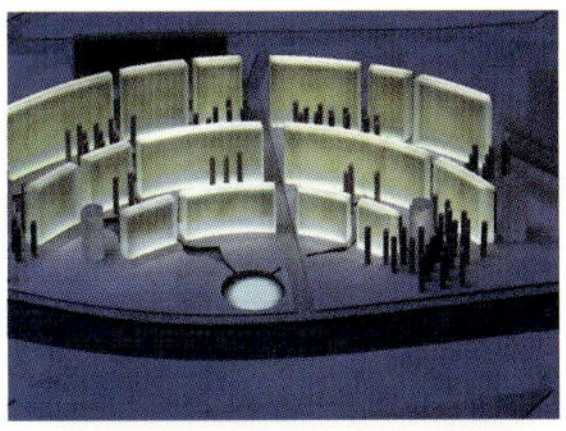

Pacific City, Beijing, Urban planning
Competition: 2001
Design: Meinhard von Gerkan
Partner: Nikolaus Goetze
Design team: Karen Schroeder, Dirk Heller,
Oliver Christ, Wencke Eissing, Svenia
Oehmig, Ole Seidel
Client: World Lexus Pacific Ltd. Beijing
Gross floor area: 450,000 m²

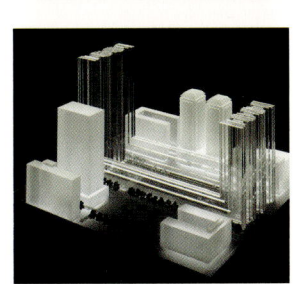

CATIC Zone, Shenzhen, Urban planning
Competition: 2001 – 1st prize
Design: Meinhard von Gerkan with Walter
Gebhardt
Project team: Evelyn Pasdzierny, Heiner
Gietmann, Mark Kelting, Rouven Oberdiek,
Barbara Henke, Matthias Meinheit
Client: Shenzhen Catic Real Estate Inc.
Gross floor area: 280,000 m²

**East China Normal University,
Jia Ding Campus**
Competition: 2001
Design: Meinhard von Gerkan with Walter
Gebhardt
Design team: Hinrich Müller, Sigrid Müller,
Heiko Thiess, Matias Otto, Gunnar Müller,
Matthias Meinheit, Sven Gaedt, Georg
Traun
Client: East China Normal University
Gross floor area: 200,000 m²

Mapo Villas, Beijing
Consultancy: 2001
Design: Meinhard von Gerkan and
Nikolaus Goetze
Design team: Oliver Christ,
Karen Seekamp, Dirk Balser,
Katja Zoschke, Iris van Hülst
Client: Beijing Town-Country Houses
Construction Development Co.
Gross floor area: 600,000 m²

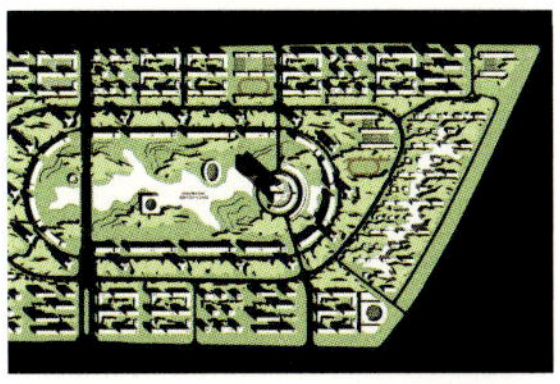

Ziwei Garden City, Xi'an
Competition: 2002
Design: Meinhard von Gerkan
Design team: Stephan Schütz,
Doris Schäffler, Giuseppina Orto, Gregor
Hoheisel
Client: XAGK Group
Area: 147 ha

Zongguancun Cultural Center, Beijing
Competition: 2002 – 1st prize
Design: Meinhard von Gerkan
Project managers: Doris Schäffler,
Stephan Schütz
Project team: Nicolas Pomränke, Gero
Heimann, Xia Lin, Giuseppina Orto, Jan
Pavuk
Structural engineers: Schlaich
Bergermann und Partner
Chinese partner practice: Sunlight
Architects & Engineers Co., Ltd.
Client: China Zongguancun Culture
Development Co., Ltd.
Gross floor area: 85,000 m²
Construction period: 2003–2005

Office- and Commercial Building, Ningbo
2002
Design: Meinhard von Gerkan with
Volkmar Sievers
Partner: Nikolaus Goetze
Design and project team: Simone
Nentwig, Huan Zhu, Jörn Bohlmann, Nicole
Loeffler, Tilo Günther
Client: Hangzhou Canhigh Estate Co.
Gross floor area: 215,000 m²
In planning stage

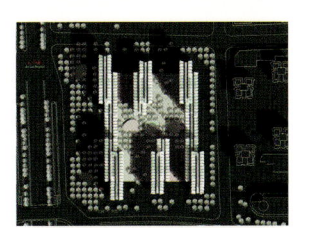

**Chaoyang Plaza, Beijing
Urban planning**
Competition: 2002
Design: Meinhard von Gerkan
Design team: Stephan Schütz, Nicolas
Pomränke
Client: Beijing Unionland Property
Development Co., Ltd.
Gross floor area: 400,000 m²

**CCTV Beijing
Office and Commercial Block
with TV Studios**
Competition: 2002
Design: Meinhard von Gerkan with Doris
Schäffler and Stephan Schütz
Design team: Giuseppina Orto, Nicolas
Pomränke, David Schenke, Gregor
Hoheisel, Patrick Pfleiderer
Client: CCTV Beijing
Gross floor area: 551,000 m²

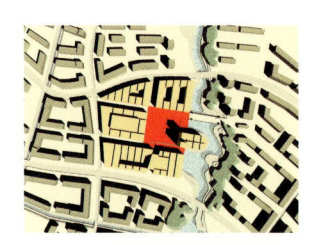

New Town Anting – Development of a German Town
Competition: 2002
Design: Meinhard von Gerkan with Stephan Schütz
Project managers: Stephan Schütz, Doris Schäffler
Project team: Giuseppina Orto, Gero Heimann
Structural engineers: The Ninth Design and Research Institute, Shanghai
Client: Shanghai International Automobile City Real Estate Co., Ltd.
Area: 100,000 m²

New Town Anting – Church
Project team: Giuseppina Orto, Gero Heimann
Gross floor area: 3,400 m²
Estimated construction period: 2005–2006

New Town Anting – Theatre and Boarding House
Project team: Giuseppina Orto, David Schenke, Chen Lan, Dong Chun Song
Gross floor area: 20,500 m²
Estimated construction period: 2005–2006

New Town Anting – Shopping Mall
Project team: David Schenke, Dong Chun Song, Zhou Jing Jun
Gross floor area: 41,100 m²
Estimated construction period: 2005–2006

Museum, Shanghai-Pudong
Competition: 2002 – 1st prize
Design: Meinhard von Gerkan
Partner: Nikolaus Goetze
Project managers: Dirk Heller, Karen Schroeder
Design and project team: Christoph Berle, Wencke Eissing, Georg Traun, Friedhelm Chlosta, Kai Siebke, Meike Schmidt, Wei Wu, Holger Wermers, Birgit Föllmer, Hinrich Müller, Udo Meyer, Thomas Eberhardt
Chinese partner practice: SIADR, Shanghai Institute of Architectural Design & Research Co., Ltd.
Client: City of Shanghai, New District Pudong
Gross floor area: 41,000 m²
Construction period: 2003–2005

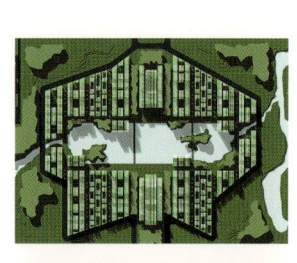

Songjiang University for Visual Arts, Shanghai
Competition: 2002
Design: Meinhard von Gerkan
Design team: Doris Schäffler, Giuseppina Orto, Stephan Schütz, Nicolas Pomränke
Client: Administration Bureau of Songjiang University
Gross floor area: 120,000 m²

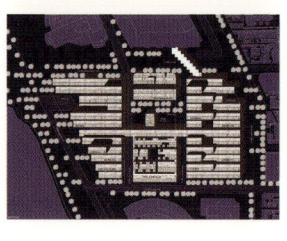

Hotel and Commercial Block, Hubin, Hangzhou
Competition: 2002
Design: Meinhard von Gerkan
Partner: Nikolaus Goetze
Design team: Volkmar Sievers, Andrea Moritz, Jörn Bohlmann, Simone Nentwig, Huan Zhu, Thies Böke, Nicole Loeffler, Tobias Plinke, Rouven Oberdiek
Gross floor area: 150,000 m²

Campus Town, Nanjing-Xianling
Competition: 2002
Design: Meinhard von Gerkan
Design team: Walter Gebhardt, Annika Schröder, Evelyn Pasdzierny, Eduard Kaiser, Hinrich Müller, Christian Krüger
Client: Urban City Planning Administration of Nanjing
Gross floor area: 1,400,000 m²

Wukesong Cultural and Sports Center, Beijing
Competition: 2002
Design: Meinhard von Gerkan
Partner: Jürgen Hillmer
Design team: Mike Berrier, Tanja Gutena, Hauke Petersen, Markus Carlsen, Heiko Thiess, Jörn Herrmann
Client: Beijing Municipal Planning Commisssion
Area: 50 ha

Century City, Beijing
Urban planning
Competition: 2002
Design: Meinhard von Gerkan with Stephan Schütz and Nicolas Pomränke
Design team: Doris Schäffler, Giuseppina Orto, David Schenke, Gero Heimann, Dong Chun Song
Client: Beijing Century City Real Estate Development Co., Ltd.
Gross floor area: 463,000 m²

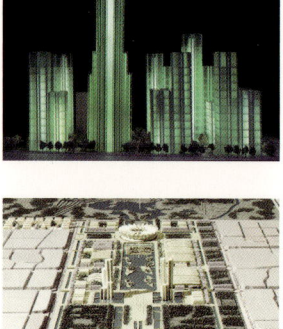

Beijing Olympic Green
Masterplan for the Olympic Games 2008
Competition: 2002
Design: Meinhard von Gerkan
Partner: Joachim Zais
Design team: Sigrid Müller, Dominik Reh, Julia Künzer, Friedhelm Chlosta, Hung-Wei Hsu
Client: City of Beijing
Gross floor area: 2,160,000 m²

Residential Area with Tennis Center, Shenzhen
Competition: 2002
Design: Meinhard von Gerkan with Walter Gebhardt
Design team: Evelyn Pasdzierny, Matthias Ismael, Enno Maass, Matthias Meinheit, Hans Münchhalfen, Jan Stecher
Client: Jin Di Group Co., Ltd. Golden Field Group Co., Ltd.
Gross floor area: 250,000 m²

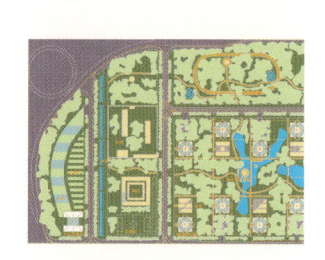

Chaoyang Park, Beijing
Urban planning
Competition: 2002
Design: Meinhard von Gerkan
Design team: Thomas Krautwald, Peter Glaser, Michael Bucherer, Peter Tröster, Tillmann Weiß, Birgit Wachhorst
Client: Beijing Gouxing Real Estate Development Co., Ltd.
Gross floor area: 500,000 m²

Anti-Ageing Clinic near Beijing
2002
Design: Meinhard von Gerkan
Design team: Doris Schäffler, Kristian Uthe-Spencker, Katina Roloff, Christiane Scheuermann
Gross floor area: 6,000 m²

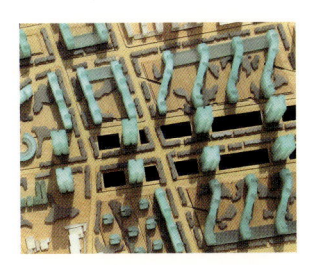

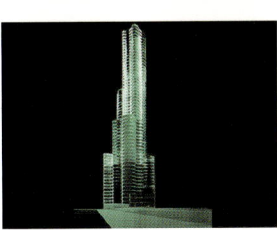

Jian Gou Dong, Shanghai
Urban planning
Design: Meinhard von Gerkan
Partner: Nikolaus Goetze
Design team: Udo Meyer, Niko Rickert, Beate Quaschning, Michèle Watenphul, Evagelia Segkis
Client: Shanghai COB Development Co., Ltd.
Gross floor area: 448,000 m²

Duftberg Villas, Beijing
Consultancy: 2002
Design: Meinhard von Gerkan with Klaus Lenz
Design team: Monika van Vught, Jörn Ortmann, Hauke Petersen
Gross floor area: 81,000 m²

Residential Area, Tianjin
2002
Design: Meinhard von Gerkan
Partner: Nikolaus Goetze
Design team: Dirk Heller, Karen Schroeder, Meike Schmidt, Friedhelm Chlosta, Christoph Berle, Wencke Eissing, Georg Traun, Kai Siebke, Holger Wermers
Client: Beijing Yin Xin Guang Hua Real Estate Development PTY Ltd.
Gross floor area: 730,000 m²

Tsinghua University, Academy of Arts and Design, Beijing
Competition: 2002 – one 1st prize
Design: Meinhard von Gerkan
Design team: Doris Schäffler, Stephan Schütz, Giuseppina Orto, Nicolas Pomränke, Gero Heimann
Client: Tsinghua University Beijing
Gross floor area: 80,000 m²

Jingan International District, Shanghai
Competition: 2002
Design: Meinhard von Gerkan
Partner: Nikolaus Goetze
Design team: Annika Schröder, Heiko Thiess, Jörn Herrmann, Hun-Wei Hsu, Stephanie Heß, Eduard Kaiser, Albrecht Bauer
Client: Urban Planning Administration of Jingan District, Shanghai; Fine Time Investments Co., Ltd., Hong Kong
Gross floor area: 862,400 m²

Yangshan New City
Competition: 2002
Design: Meinhard von Gerkan
Partner: Klaus Staratzke
Design team: Sigrid Müller, Annika Schröder, Hun-Wei Hsu, Eduard Kaiser, Stephanie Heß
Client: Urban Planning Society of China and Development and Environment Protection Bureau of Shengsi County
Gross floor area: 2,100,000 m²

CaiYuan Building, Beijing
Competition: 2002
Design: Meinhard von Gerkan
Design team: Evelyn Pasdzierny, Matthias Ismael, Matthias Meinheit, Niko Rickert, Barbara Henke, Rouven Oberdiek
Client: Beijing Jianji Tianrun Estate Co., Ltd.
Gross floor area: 180,000 m²

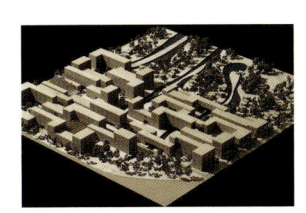

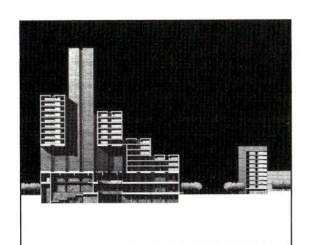

Office Building, Beijing
Competition: 2002
Design: Meinhard von Gerkan
Design team: Volkmar Sievers, Simone Nentwig, Huan Zhu, Nicole Loeffler, Tilo Günther, Rouven Oberdiek
Gross floor area: 90,000 m²

Chongqing Residential Area Sunshine 100
Consultancy: 2002
Design: Meinhard von Gerkan
Partner: Nikolaus Goetze
Design team: Dirk Heller, Karen Schroeder, Meike Schmidt, Friedhelm Chlosta, Christoph Berle, Wencke Eissing, Georg Traun, Kai Siebke, Holger Wermers
Client: Beijing Yin Xin Guang Hua Real Estate Development PTY Ltd.
Gross floor area: 800,000 m²

Chaofu Avenue, Beijing
Consultancy: 2002
Design: Meinhard von Gerkan
Design team: Hinrich Müller, Gregor Hoheisel, Udo Meyer, David Schenke, Gero Heimann, Zhou Jing Jun, Xu Yun Fang
Client: Beijing Municipal Planning Commission
Gross floor area: 1,876,000 m²

Opera House, Guangzhou
Competition: 2002
Design: Meinhard von Gerkan with Klaus Lenz
Design team: Dominik Reh, Jörn Herrmann, Svenia Oehmig, Hauke Petersen, Kai Ladebeck, Hung-Wei Hsu, Sandra Glass
Client: The Organizing Committee of Architectural Design Competition by International Invitation for Guangzhou Opera House
Gross floor area: 73,000 m²

University of Aeronautics and Astronautics, Beijing
Competition: 2003 – 1st prize
Design: Meinhard von Gerkan
Partner: Joachim Zais
Design team: Tanja Gutena, Sigrid Müller, Julia Künzer, Kai Ladebeck, Dominik Reh, Matias Otto, Mike Berrier, Jörn Herrmann, Hauke Petersen
Client: Beijing University of Aeronautics and Astronautics
Gross floor area: 620,000 m²

Electron Administrative Affair Center, Beijing
Competition: 2003
Design: Meinhard von Gerkan with Nicolas Hünerwadel
Partner: Nikolaus Goetze
Design team: Sigrid Müller, Annika Schröder, Markus Carlsen, Jörn Herrmann, Hung-Wei Hsu, Sona Kazemi, Stephanie Heß, Richard Sprenger
Client: Beijing Wanjing Real Estate Development Co., Ltd.
Gross floor area: 175,000 m²

Science Park of the University of Zhejiang, Urban planning
Competition: 2003 – 1st prize
Design: Meinhard von Gerkan with Walter Gebhardt
Project manager: Volkmar Sievers
Design team: Evelyn Pasdzierny, Matthias Ismael, Niko Rickert, Arne Kleinhans, Hinrich Müller, Hauke Petersen
Project team: Simone Nentwig, Christian

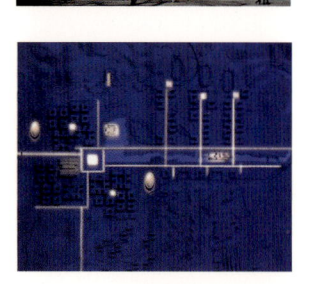

Krüger, Arne Kleinhans, Rouven Oberdiek
Chinese partner practice: ZUADR, Architectural Design and Research Institute of Zhejiang University
Client: Zhejiang University Science Park Construction Co., Ltd.
Gross floor area: 297,000 m²
In planning stage

Wanda Plaza, Beijing, Urban planning
Competition: 2002 – 1st prize
Design: Volkwin Marg with Alexander Buchhofer and Sylvia Schneider
Partner: Hubert Nienhoff
Design team: Christian Dorndorf, Martin Duplantier, Xia Lin, Nicolas Pomränke, Stephan Schütz
Client: Wanda Plaza Estate Co., Ltd.
Gross floor area: 135,000 m²
In planning stage

Renmin University of Zhuhai
Competition: 2002
Design: Meinhard von Gerkan
Partner: Nikolaus Goetze
Design team: Volkmar Sievers, Simone Nentwig, Jörn Bohlmann, Huan Zhu, Nicole Loeffler, Rouven Oberdiek, Leif Henning
Client: Renmin University
Gross floor area: 1,137,000 m²

Shunchi Plaza, Tianjin
Urban planning
Competition: 2002
Design: Meinhard von Gerkan with Stephan Rewolle, Kristian Uthe-Spencker and Stephan Schütz
Partner: Hubert Nienhoff
Design team: Michèle Rüegg, Patrick Pfleiderer, Uta Graff, Christian Dorndorf, Markus Pfisterer, Helga Reimund, Martin Duplantier
Client: Tianjin Shunchi Investment Co., Ltd.
Gross floor area: 110,000 m²

Wuxi Husian Live Science and Technology Park
Competition: 2003
Design: Meinhard von Gerkan with Magdalene Weiß
Design team: Michèle Watenphul, Kai Ladebeck, Jun Wen, Holger Schmücker, Evagelia Segkis
Client: Wuxi Live SCI & Tech. Development Co., Ltd.
Gross floor area: 10,000 m²

Shenzhen Central Plaza
Urban planning
Competition: 2003 – one 1st prize
Design: Meinhard von Gerkan with Doris Schäffler and Stephan Schütz
Design team: Giuseppina Orto, David Schenke
Client: Shenzhen Guanghai Investment Co., Ltd.
Gross floor area: 161,500 m²

Nanxiang Central Town
Urban Planning
Competition: 2003
Design: Meinhard von Gerkan
Partner: Joachim Zais
Design team: Sigrid Müller, Jörn Herrmann, Hector Labin, Monika van Vught
Gross floor area: 3,000,000 m²

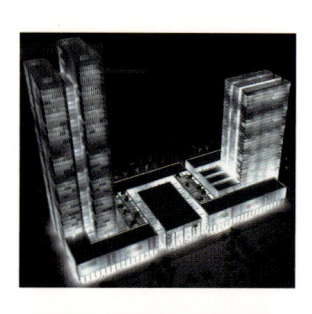

Dong Cheng International Center, Nanjing
Competition: 2003 – 1st prize
Design: Meinhard von Gerkan
Design team: Volkmar Sievers, Simone Nentwig, Huan Zhu, Nicole Loeffler, Tobias Plinke, Leif Henning, Christian Krüger, Wu Wei
Client: Jiangsu Rendi Property Development Company Ltd. Yurun Group
Gross floor area: 188,000 m²

Xinyuan Tower, Beijing
Residential building
2002
Design: Meinhard von Gerkan with Magdalene Weiß
Partner: Nikolaus Goetze
Project manager: Magdalene Weiß
Design and project team: Michèle Watenphul, Kai Ladebeck, Holger Schmücker, Xia Lin, Gregor Hoheisel, Stephanie Heß, Iris van Hülst, Sigrid Müller, Jörn Ortmann, Marcus Tanzen, Hito Ueda, Holger Wermers
Client: Beijing Shoulu-Huayuan Property Co., Ltd.
Gross floor area: 69,000 m²
Construction period: 2003–2005

Qinghe Jade Residences, Beijing
Survey: 2003
Design: Meinhard von Gerkan
Partner: Nikolaus Goetze
Design team: Stephanie Heß, Hinrich Müller, Mike Berrier, Hung-Wei Hsu, Richard Sprenger
Client: Beijing Qiangyou Real Estate Development Co.
Gross floor area: 1,000,000 m²

Dixingju Building, Beijing
Consultancy: 2003
Design: Meinhard von Gerkan with Doris Schäffler and Stephan Schütz
Design and project team: David Schenke, Chunsong Dong
Chinese partner practice: CABR, Building Design Institute – China Academy of Building Research
Client: Beijing Shoulu-Huayuan Property Co., Ltd.
Gross floor area: 33,000 m²
Construction period: 2004–2005

Suzhou Convention and Exhibition Center
Competition: 2003 – 3rd prize
Design: Volkwin Marg with Marc Ziemons
Partner: Nikolaus Goetze
Design team: Dirk Balser, Christiane Fickers, Hung-Wei Hsu, Udo Meyer
Client: Suzhou Industrial Park Housing & Development Co., Ltd.
Gross floor area: 300,000 m²

Qingdao Sailing Base for the Olympic Games 2008
Competition: 2003
Design: Meinhard von Gerkan with Walter Gebhardt
Design team: Matthias Ismael, Enno Maass, Hinrich Müller, Evelyn Pasdzierny, Christoph Thomsen
Client: Qingdao Development & Construction Group Corporation
Gross floor area: 730,000 m²

Orient Wenhua International Center, Beijing, Commercial block with concert hall and hotel
Competition: 2003
Design: Meinhard von Gerkan with Walter Gebhardt
Project manager: Stephan Schütz
Design team: Evelyn Pasdzierny, Matthias Ismael, Arne Kleinhans, Christoph Thomsen, Hinrich Müller, David Schenke, Chen Lan
Client: Beijing Oriental Continent Real Estate Development and Management Co., Ltd.
Gross floor area: 140,000 m²
In planning stage

Beijing National Stadium for the Olympic Games 2008
Competition: 2003
Design: Volkwin Marg with Hubert Nienhoff and Markus Pfisterer
Design team: Christian Dorndorf, Uta Graff, Jochen Köhn, Katina Roloff, Anke Rieber, Sylvia Schneider, Caspar Teichgräber, Helga Reimund, Holger Betz
Client: Beijing Municipal Government

Lanhai Hotel, Jinan
Competition: 2003 – 1st prize
Design: Meinhard von Gerkan with Stephan Schütz and Doris Schäffler
Design and project team: Chun Song Dong, Gero Heimann, Giuseppina Orto, Nicolas Pomränke, David Schenke
Client: Shan Dong Lanhai Stock Co., Ltd.
Gross floor area: 57,000 m²
In planning stage

Jinglun Hotel, Beijing
Facade study: 2003
Design: Meinhard von Gerkan
Design team: Stephan Schütz, Nicolas Pomränke

Science Center Guangdong, Guangzhou
Competition: 2003
Design: Meinhard von Gerkan
Partner: Nikolaus Goetze
Design team: Evelyn Pasdzierny, Tobias Jortzick, Arne Kleinhans, Jörn Herrmann, Christian Krüger, Rouven Oberdiek
Client: Guangdong Provincial Department of Science & Technology
Gross floor area: 115,000 m²

Nansha Business Center, Guangzhou
Competition: 2003
Design: Meinhard von Gerkan
Design team: Evelyn Pasdzierny, Matthias Ismael, Niko Rickert, Hinrich Müller, Matthias Meinheit, Elena Melnykova, Alexander Behn, Henry Rodatz
Client: Guangzhou Nansha Assets Operation Co., Ltd.
Gross floor area: 300,000 m²

Shooting Range for the Olympic Games 2008, Beijing
Competition: 2003
Design: Volkwin Marg with Marc Ziemons
Partner: Nikolaus Goetze
Design team: Dirk Balser, Christiane Fickers, Hung-Wei Hsu, David Schenke, Meike Schmidt, Flori Wagner
Client: State General Administration of Sports of P.R. China
Gross floor area: 40,000 m²

Zongguancun International City, Beijing, Office and commercial building with hotel
Competition: 2003
Design: Meinhard von Gerkan
Design team: Doris Schäffler, Stephan Schütz, Giuseppina Orto, Nicolas Pomränke
Client: Gulf Group Gulf Land Development Co., Ltd.
Gross floor area: 79,500 m²

Olympic Village & National Gymnasium, Beijing
Competition: 2003
Design: Meinhard von Gerkan and Nikolaus Goetze with Walter Gebhardt
Design team: Hinrich Müller, Enno Maass
Client: Beijing Beichen Real Estate Co., Ltd.

Human Resource Center, Shenzhen
Consultancy: 2003
Design: Meinhard von Gerkan with Walter Gebhardt
Partner: Nikolaus Goetze
Design team: Jan Stecher, Matthias Meinheit
Client: SZRC
Gross floor area: 43,000 m²

China Telecom Information Park, Shanghai
Competition: 2003 – open
Design: Meinhard von Gerkan
Partner: Nikolaus Goetze
Design team: Evelyn Pasdzierny, Matthias Meinheit
Client: China Telecom Group Co., Ltd.
Gross floor area: 550,000 m²

Dalian Airport City, Dalian
Competition: 2003 – 1st prize
Design: Meinhard von Gerkan with Walter Gebhardt
Design team: Alexander Behn, Niko Rickert, Henry Rodatz, Jan Stecher
Client: Urban Planning Bureau of Gangjingzi District, City of Dalian
Gross floor area: 7,683,000 m²

National Library of China, Beijing
Competition: 2003
Design: Meinhard von Gerkan
Partner: Nikolaus Goetze
Design team: Karen Schroeder, Dirk Heller, Christoph Berle, Georg Traun, Friedhelm Chlosta, Meike Schmidt, Kai Siebke, Wencke Eissing, Rouven Oberdiek
Client: Preparatory Office for National Library of China
Gross floor area: 77,000 m²

CYTS Tower, Beijing
Office building
2003
Design: Meinhard von Gerkan with Doris Schäffler and Stephan Schütz
Design team: Giuseppina Orto, Nicolas Pomränke
Client: China CYTS Tours Holding Co., Ltd.
Gross floor area: 65,000 m²
Construction period: 2004–2005

Office and Residential Complex, Huanglong-Hangzhou
2003
Design: Meinhard von Gerkan
Partner: Nikolaus Goetze
Project manager: Volkmar Sievers
Design and project team: Simone Nentwig, Huan Zhu, Jörn Bohlmann,

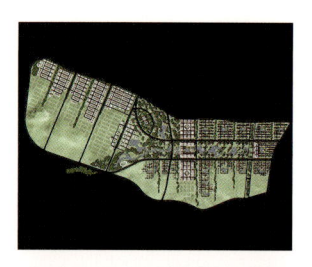

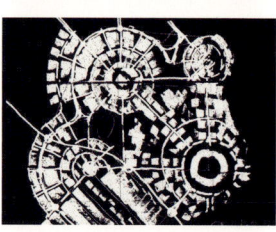

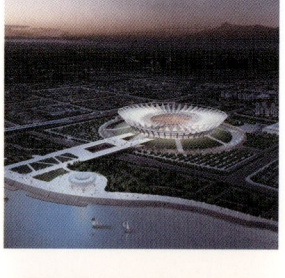

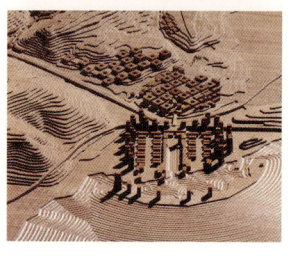

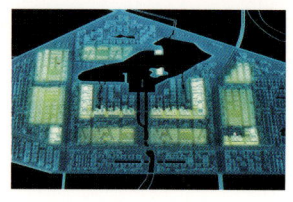

Andrea Moritz, Knut Maass, Rouven Oberdiek, Tobias Plinke, Nicole Loeffler, Wiebke Dorn
Client: Narada Real Estate
Gross floor area: 123,000 m²
Construction period: 2003–2005

Agricultural Bank of China, Shanghai Computing Center
Competition: 2003
Design: Meinhard von Gerkan with Walter Gebhardt
Partners: Joachim Zais, Jürgen Hillmer
Design team: Jan Stecher, Richard Sprenger, Markus Carlsen, Alexander Behn
Client: Agricultural Bank of China (ABC)
Gross floor area: 90,000 m²

Lingang Development District Urban extension of Luchao
Competition: 2003
Design: Meinhard von Gerkan
Design team: Heiko Thiess, Sigrid Müller, Julia Künzer, Matthias Ismael
Client: Shanghai International Tendering Co., Ltd.
Area: 293 km²

Beijing New Vision International Exhibition Center
Competition: 2003 – 2nd prize
Design: Volkwin Marg with Marc Ziemons
Partner: Nikolaus Goetze
Design team: Udo Meyer, Hung-Wei Hsu, Dirk Balser, Alexander Behn
Client: Beijing New Vision International Exhibition Center Co., Ltd.
Gross floor area: 150,000 m²

Sports Park with Stadium and Swimming Arena, Foshan
Competition: 2003
Design: Volkwin Marg with Marek Nowak
Design and project team: Christian Hoffmann, Christoph Helbich, Mario Rojas Toledo, Michael König, Sven Greiser, Sebastian Hilke, Mark Jackschat, Michael Haase, Stephan Menke, Franz Lensing, Björn Füchtenkord, Silke Flaßnöcker, Ebi Tang, Jennifer Kielas
Client: Foshan Construction Bureau, Foshan Sports Bureau
Construction Period: 2004 - 2006

Dalian Software Park
Competition: 2003
Design: Meinhard von Gerkan with Walter Gebhardt
Design team: Elena Melnikova, Jan Stecher, Tobias Jortzick, Christian Dahle, Julia Gronbach, Janis Guida
Client: China International Engineering Consulting Corporation
Gross floor area: 4,000,000 m²

Gold Tak Center, Guangzhou
Competition: 2003
Design: Meinhard von Gerkan
Design team: Enno Maass, Richard Sprenger, Hungwei Hsu, Julia Künzer, Markus Carlsen, Thomas Esper, Caroline Kolb, Jan Blasko
Client: Gold Sun Group, Guangzhou

Xuzhou New Central Area
Competition: 2003
Design: Meinhard von Gerkan
Design team: Enno Maass, Richard Sprenger, Hungwei Hsu, Matthias Meinheit
Client: City of Xuzhou
Gross floor area: 8,33 km²

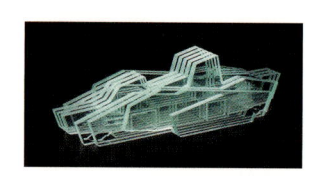

International Medical Garden, Shanghai
Competition: 2003
Design: Meinhard von Gerkan and Joachim Zais
Design team: Heiko Thiess, Richard Sprenger, Robert Friedrichs, Monika van Vught, Matthias Ismael, Matias Otto, Xuelai Xu
Client: International Medicine Garden Co. Ltd.
Gross floor area: 1,15 ha

Chongqing Grand Theatre
Competition: 2003 – 1st prize
Design: Meinhard von Gerkan
Partner: Nikolaus Goetze
Project manager: Klaus Lenz
Design and project team: Knut Maass, Kerstin Steinfatt, Jan Stolte, Nils Dethlefs, Heiko Thiess, Monika van Vught, Robert Friedrichs, Matthias Ismael, Tobias Jortzick, Dominik Reh, Christian Dahle, Julia Gronbach
Client: Chongqing Urban Construction Investment
Gross floor area: 70,000 m²
Construction period: 2004–2007

Phoenix TV, Shenzhen
2003
Design: Volwin Marg
Partner: Nikolaus Goetze
Design team: Marc Ziemons, Christiane Fickers, Flori Wagner, Dirk Balser, Hungwei Hsu, Janis Guida
Client: Phoenix Satellite TV Ltd., Hongkong
Gross floor area: 107,264 m²

Dalian Twin Towers and CBD Xinghai Bay
Competition: 2003 – 1st prize
Design: Meinhard von Gerkan
Partner: Nikolaus Goetze
Project managers: Karen Schroeder, Dirk Heller
Design and project team: Christoph Berle, Friedhelm Chlosta, Georg Traun, Kai Siebke, Udo Meyer, Meike Schmidt, Eduard Kaiser, Christian Dahle, Wencke Eissing-Poggenberg
Client: Dalian Commodity Exchange
Gross floor area: 353,000 m²
Construction period: 2004–2007

China Petroleum, Beijing
Competition: 2003
Design: Meinhard von Gerkan with Stephan Schütz
Design team: Nicolas Pomränke, Giuseppina Orto, Gero Heimann, Dong Chunsong

Xi Han Grand Building, Beijing
Competition: 2003
Design: Meinhard von Gerkan with Stephan Schütz and Doris Schäffler
Design team: Wang Yi, Wang Yingzhe, Ralf Sieber
Gross floor area: 100,000 m²

Art Box, Beijing
Competition: 2003
Design: Meinhard von Gerkan with Stephan Schütz
Design team: David Schenke, Katrin Kanus
Client: Stiftung für Kunst und Kultur
Gross floor area: 58,923 m²

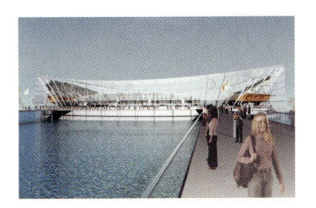

International Sailing Marina for the 29th Olympic Games, Qingdao
Competition: 2004
Design: Meinhard von Gerkan with Walter Gebhard
Design team: Holger Henningsen, Christian Scheelk, Gordon Schittek, Britta Schröder, Felix Wiesner
Client: Qingdao Urban Planning Bureau
Gross floor area: 77,000 m²

Huaneng Building, Beijing
Competition: 2004 – one 1st prize
Design: Meinhard von Gerkan with Stephan Schütz
Design team: Stephan Rewolle, Chunsong Dong, Katrin Kanus, Ralf Sieber, Peng Du
Client: China Huaneng Group
Gross floor area: 130,000 m²

Shanghai New Maritime University
Competition: 2004 – one 1st prize
Design: Meinhard von Gerkan
Design team: Heiko Thiess, Claudia Schultze, Marcus Carlsen, Eduard Kaiser
Client: New Maritime University, Shanghai
Gross floor area: 1,333,000 m²

Cloud Tower, Lingang Main City
Study: 2004
Design: Meinhard von Gerkan with Richard Sprenger
Design team: Heiko Thiess, Eduard Kaiser, Enno Maass
Client: Shanghai Urban Planning Administration Bureau, Mr. Bao Tieming
Height: 300 m

New Railway Station, Guangzhou
Competition: 2004 – 1st phase 2nd prize
Design: Meinhard von Gerkan
Partner: Jürgen Hillmer
Design team: Volkmar Sievers, Sigrid Müller, Christian Dahle, Tilo Günther, Matthias Meinheit, Simone Nentwig, Rouven Oberdiek, Nicole Loeffler, Susi Winter, Huan Zhu
Client: Guangzhou Railway (Group) Corporation
Gross floor area: 342,000 m²

New China International Exhibition Center, Beijing
Competition: 2004
Design: Volkwin Marg
Partner: Nikolaus Goetze
Design team: Christiane Fickers, Flori Wagner, Dirk Balser, Hinrich Müller, Matthias Ismael
Client: China International Exhibition Center Investment & Development Co., Ltd.
Gross floor area: 340,000 m²

Hotel Oriental Art Center, Shanghai
Competition: 2004
Design: Meinhard von Gerkan
Partner: Nikolaus Goetze
Design team: Volkmar Sievers, Huan Zhu, Matthias Meinheit, Simone Nentwig, Nicole Loeffler, Andrea Moritz
Client: Shanghai Pudong Land Development (Holding) Corp.
Gross floor area: 27,000 m²

National Tennis-Center and Hockey-Stadium, Beijing
2004
Design: Volkwin Marg
Partner: Nikolaus Goetze
Design team: Marc Ziemons, Dirk Balser, Christiane Fickers, Flori Wagner, Katja Zoschke, Carsten Plog, Janis Guida

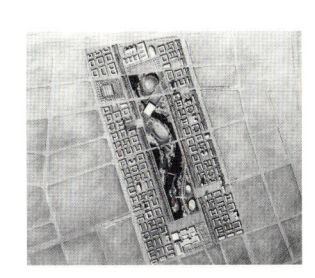

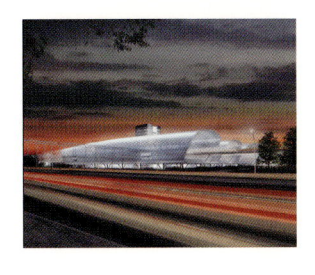

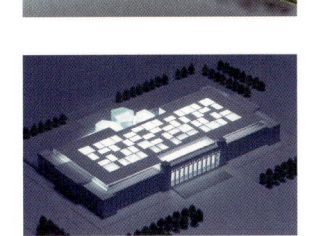

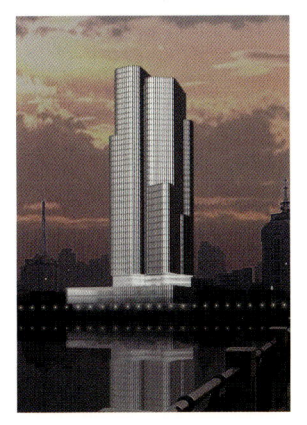

Organizer: Beijing Municipal Planning Commission
Gross floor area: 67,208 m²

Loudun-Shahe, Education Center, Beijing
Study: 2004
Design: Meinhard von Gerkan
Partner: Stephan Schütz
Design team: Sophie Baumann, Kristian Uthe-Spencker

Sheshan Erzhan Station of Shanghai No 9, Shanghai
Competition: 2004
Design: Meinhard von Gerkan
Partner: Nikolaus Goetze
Design team: Magdalene Weiss, Christian Dahle, Enno Maass, Elena Melnikova, Hinrich Müller, Jan Stecher, Stephanie Heß
Client: CITIC
Gross floor area: 90,000 m²

Ningbo Science Park
Competition: 2004
Design: Meinhard von Gerkan
Partner: Nikolaus Goetze
Design team: Volkmar Sievers, Simone Nentwig, Rouven Oberdiek, Nicole Loeffler, Kay-Peter Kolbe, Uli Rösler
Client: GREENTOWN, Hangzhou
Gross floor area: 140,000 m²

Changsha Riverfront Cultural Park
Competition: 2004
Design: Meinhard von Gerkan
Design team: Hinrich Müller, Evelyn Pasdzierny, Elena Melnikova, Eduard Kaiser, Rouven Oberdiek, Tilo Günther, Markus Carlsen
Gross floor area: 175,000 m²

National Museum of China, Beijing
Competition: 2004 - 1st prize
Design: Meinhard von Gerkan with Stephan Schütz
Design and project team: Stephan Rewolle, Doris Schäffler, Gregor Hoheisel, Katrin Kanus, Ralf Sieber, Du Peng, Chunsong Dong
Client: The National Museum of China
Gross floor area: 170,000 m²
Construction period: 2005–2007

Christian Church, Beijing
Competition: 2004 - 1st prize
Design: Meinhard von Gerkan with Stephan Schütz
Design team: Stephan Rewolle, Gero Heimann, Katrin Kanus, Ralf Sieber, Xia Lin, Gregor Hoheisel
Client: China Zhongguancun Culture Development Co., Ltd.
Gross floor area: 4,000 m²
Construction period: 2005–2006

Marriott Hotel, Binjiang Plaza, Ningbo
Competition: 2004 - 1st prize
Design: Meinhard von Gerkan
Partner: Nikolaus Goetze
Project manager: Volkmar Sievers
Design and project team: Evelyn Pasdzierny, Nils Dehtlefs, Simone Nentwig, Matthias Meinheit, Tilo Günther, Rouven Oberdiek, Nicole Loeffler
Client: Ningbo HaiCheng Investment Development Co., Ltd.
Gross floor area: 60,000 m²
Construction period: 2005–2006

Beijing Automobile Electronic Industry Park
Competition: 2004 – 1st prize
Design: Meinhard von Gerkan
Partner: Stephan Schütz
Design team: Giuseppina Orto, Nicolas Pomränke, Christian Dorndorf, Bin Bin Du, Sophie Baumann
Client: Majuqiao Town Government of Tongzhou District, Beijing
Gross floor area: 2,895,663 m²

Wuhan Railway Station
Competition: 2004
Design: Meinhard von Gerkan
Partner: Jürgen Hillmer
Design team: Sigrid Müller, Christiane Fickers, Dirk Balser, Diana Spanier, Janis Guida
Client: Zhengzhou Railway Administration
Gross floor area: 94,000 m²

Tianjin West Railway Station
Competition: 2004 – 1st phase 1st prize
Design: Meinhard von Gerkan with Stephan Schütz and Stephan Rewolle
Design team: Iris Belle, Shi Liang, Du Peng, Chunsong Dong
Client: Beijing Railway Administration

Management and Service Center of Lingang City
Competition: 2004
Design: Meinhard von Gerkan
Partners: Nikolaus Goetze, Wei Wu
Design team: Magdalene Weiss, Jan Stecher, Joern Ortmann, Xiangge Peng, Yang Li, Mo Sung, Enno Maass
Client: Shanghai Lingang Economic Development Group Co., Ltd.
Gross floor area: 45,000 m²

Guangzhou Twin Towers
Competition: 2004
Design: Meinhard von Gerkan
Partner: Nikolaus Goetze
Design team: Volkmar Sievers, Evelyn Pasdzierny, Rouven Oberdiek, Alexandra Kühne, Matthias Meinheit, Nicole Loeffler
Client: Guangzou Municipal Land Development Center
Gross floor area: 372,000 m²

Ningbo New Town
2004
Design: Meinhard von Gerkan
Partners: Nikolaus Goetze, Wei Wu
Design team: Magdalene Weiss, Jan Stecher, Wang Yi
Client: Ningbo Planning Bureau
Gross floor area: 620,000 m²

Ningbo NBCT
Competition: 2004
Design: Meinhard von Gerkan
Partner: Wei Wu
Design team: Magdalene Weiss, Hungwei Hsu, Wang Yi, Wang Yingzhe
Client: NBCT
Gross floor area: 400 m²

East China Power Central Building, Shanghai
Competition: 2004
Design: Meinhard von Gerkan
Partner: Nikolaus Goetze
Design team: Karen Schroeder, Dirk Heller, Christoph Berle, Meike Schmidt, Friedhelm Chlosta, Kai Siebke, Georg Traun, Hungwei Hsu, Matthias Meinheit, Holger Schmücker, Matthias Ismael, Nina Lhotzki, Xu Xuelai
Client: East China Power Dispatch Central Building
Gross floor area: 50,000 m²

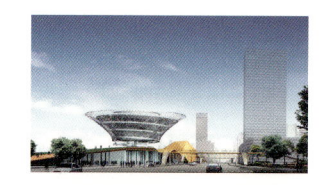

Shi Liu Pu, Shanghai
Competition: 2004 – 1st prize
Design: Meinhard von Gerkan with Stephan Schütz
Design team: Stephan Rewolle, Du Peng, Katrin Kanus, Ralf Sieber,
Client: Huangpu River Group

China Telecom B1, Shanghai
Competition: 2004
Design: Meinhard von Gerkan
Partner: Nikolaus Goetze
Design team: Dirk Heller, Karen Schroeder, Meike Schmidt, Kai Siebke, Friedhelm Chlosta, Christoph Berle, Georg Traun, Holger Schmücker, Nina Lhotzky, Hungwei Hsu
Client: China Telecom Shanghai
Gross floor area: 37,183 m²

CSSC Shanghai Shipyard Pudong
Competition: 2004
Design: Meinhard von Gerkan
Partners: Nikolaus Goetze, Wei Wu
Design team: Magdalene Weiss, Wang Yinzhe, Wang Yi, Hungwei Hsu, Annika Schröder, Yang Li

China Telecom B12 and B13, Shanghai
Competition: 2004 – 1st Prize
Design: Meinhard von Gerkan
Partner: Nikolaus Goetze
Design team: Dirk Heller, Karen Schoeder, Meike Schmidt, Christoph Berle, Georg Traun, Holger Schmücker, Nina Lhotzky, Hungwei Hsu
Client: China Telecom Shanghai
Gross floor area: 51,000 m²
Construction period: 2005–2007

Qingdao Grand Theater
Competition: 2004 – 1st prize
Design: Meinhard von Gerkan with Stephan Schütz
Design team: Nicolas Pomränke, Clemens Kampermann, Sophie v. Mansberg, Xia Lin, Li Ling, Stephan Rewolle, Ralf Sieber, Giuseppina Orto
Client: Qingdao Conson Industrial Corporation
Gross floor area: 60,000 m²
Construction period: 2005–2007

MOC Office Building, Beijing
Competition: 2004
Design: Meinhard von Gerkan
Partner: Stephan Schütz
Design team: Stephan Rewolle, Du Peng, Kathrin Kanus, Ralf Sieber

Xiamen Convention and Exhibition Center
Competition: 2004
Design: Volkwin Marg
Partner: Nikolaus Goetze
Design team: Hinrich Müller, Heiko Thiess, Richard Sprenger, Diana Spanier, Elena Melnikova, Ben Grope, Markus Carlsen
Client: Jianfa Group Real Estate
Gross floor area: 54,466 m²

Guotai Theater, Chongqing
Competition: 2004
Design: Meinhard von Gerkan with Volkmar Sievers
Partner: Nikolaus Goetze
Design team: Andrea Moritz, Sabrina Fienemann, Tilo Günther, Rouven Oberdiek
Client: Chongqing Real Estate Group
Gross floor area: 44,000 m^2

Lingang New City, Maritime Museum
Consultancy: 2004
Design: Meinhard von Gerkan
Partner: Nikolaus Goetze
Project manager: Klaus Lenz
Design team: Richard Sprenger, Elena Melnikova, Ben Grope, Markus Carlsen
Client: Shanghai Harbour City Investment Co.
Gross floor area: 72,400 m^2
Construction period: 2005–2007

Lingang New City, Western Island
Consultancy: 2004
Design: Meinhard von Gerkan
Partner: Nikolaus Goetze
Design team: Evelyn Pasdzierny, Alexandra Kühne, Markus Carlsen
Client: Shanghai Harbour City Investment Co.
Gross floor area: 135,000 m^2

Lingang New City, First Ring
Consultancy: 2004
Design: Meinhard von Gerkan
Partner: Nikolaus Goetze
Project manager: Annika Schröder
Design team: Barbara Henke, Diana Spanier, Christian Dahle, Eduard Kaiser, Nina Lhotzky, Markus Carlsen, Ben Grope
Client: Shanghai Harbour City Investment Co.
Gross floor area: 320,000 m^2

Jinling Library, Nanjing
Competition: 2004
Design: Meinhard von Gerkan
Partner: Nikolaus Goetze
Design team: Evelyn Pasdzierny, Alexandra Kühne, Barbara Henke, Wang Yinzhe, Wang Yi, Jörn Ortmann
Client: Nanjing National Assets Cultural Industry Co., Ltd.
Gross floor area: 25,000 m^2

Shanghai Yuexing Global Home Furnishing Expo Center
Competition: 2005
Design: Meinhard von Gerkan
Design team: Magdalene Weiss, Enno Maass, Song Mo, Lin Yi
Client: Yuexing Group
Gross floor area: 36,000,000 m^2

Research and Development Center, Beijing
Consultancy: 2005
Design: Meinhard von Gerkan
Partner: Stephan Schütz
Design team: Giuseppina Orto, Patrick Pfleiderer, Tobias Keyl, Nicolas Pomränke, Ji Xu
Gross floor area: 137,907 m^2

Shanghai Industrial Health Park
Competition: 2005
Design: Meinhard von Gerkan with Walter Gebhardt
Partner: Nikolaus Goetze
Design team: Holger Henningsen, Gordon Schittek, Nicole Döhr, Michael Sue, Simon Braun, Monika Sorokowska
Client: Tianshi Yihai Co., Ltd. 
Gross floor area: 600,000 m^2

Shanghai Nanhui District Administration Office Center, Lingang New City
Competition: 2005 – 1st prize
Design: Meinhard von Gerkan with Walter Gebhardt
Partner: Nikolaus Goetze
Design team: Evelyn Pasdzierny, Alexandra Kühne, Barbara Henke
Client: Shanghai Planning Administration
Gross floor area: 80,000 m^2

Business Center Hou Ren Road, Hangzhou
Competition: 2005
Design: Meinhard von Gerkan
Partner: Nikolaus Goetze
Design team: Volkmar Sievers, Simone Nentwig, Jan Stolte, Wiebke Meyenburg
Client: Hangzhou Canhigh Estate Co.
Gross floor area: 130,000 m^2

Shenyang International Convention and Exhibition Center
Competition: 2005
Design: Volkwin Marg
Partner: Nikolaus Goetze
Design team: Marc Ziemons, Hinrich Müller, Flori Wagner, Katrin Löser, Henning Fritsch, Kristina Milani
Client: Shenyang Zhi Cheng Tendering Co., Ltd
Gross floor area: 456,062 m^2

Hualian Qianjiang Times Square, Hangzhou
Competition: 2005
Design: Meinhard von Gerkan
Partner: Nikolaus Goetze
Design team: Volkmar Sievers, Simone Nentwig, Alexandra Kühne, Wiebke Meyenburg, Barbara Henke
Client: Hangzhou Hualian Economic Development Co., Ltd.

Hainan Sanya National Hotel
Competition: 2005 - 3rd prize
Design: Meinhard von Gerkan
Partner: Wu Wei
Design team: Magdalene Weiss, Annika Schröder, Hungwei Shu, Wang Yi, Wang Yinzhe
Client: Hainan State Estate
Gross floor area: 72,000 m^2

Jinsha Museum, Chengdu
Competition: 2005
Design: Meinhard von Gerkan with Stephan Schuetz, Stephan Rewolle and Ralf Sieber
Design team: Iris Belle, Zhou Bin, Wang Lei, Katrin Kanus, David Schenke
Gross floor area: 28,500 m^2

City Gates, Lingang Main City
2005
Design: Meinhard von Gerkan
Partner: Nikolaus Goetze
Co-worker: Richard Sprenger
Client: Shanghai Harbour City Investment Co.

Bildnachweis
Photo credits

Trotz intensiver Bemühungen konnten bis Produktionsschluss nicht alle Inhaber von Abbildungsrechten ausfindig gemacht werden. Personen und Institutionen, die möglicherweise nicht erreicht wurden und Rechte an verwendeten Abbildungen beanspruchen, werden gebeten, sich nachträglich mit dem Verlag in Verbindung zu setzen.

Meinhard von Gerkan im Gespräch mit Xu Xiaofei von der Tsinghua Universität Peking
Meinhard von Gerkan in Conversation with Xu Xiaofei of Tsinghua University Beijing
Abbildungen **Images**: gmp Archiv

Stadt und Architektur in China im Wandel zwischen gestern und heute
Chinese City and Architecture in Transformation between Yesterday and Tomorrow
Abbildungen **Images**: Prof. Zheng Shiling

Die europäische Stadt
The European City
Abbildungen **Images**:
01 Schedel, Hartmann, Liber chronicarum, 1971
Bayerische Staatsbibliothek, München
02 Braun, Georg, Civitas orbis terrarum, 1572 – 1618
Bayerische Staatsbibliothek, München
03 Ledoux, Claude Nicolas
L´architecture considerée sous le rapport de l'art, des moers et de la legislation, 1804
Bayerische Staatsbibliothek, München

Die Idealstadt im Spiegel der Zeit
The Ideal City as Reflected through the Ages
Abbildungen **Images**:
1, 5, 8 Eaton, Ruth, Die Ideale Stadt von der Antike bis zur Gegenwart, 2001
2, 3 Schaber, Tilo, Stadtarchitektur – Spiegel der Welt, 1990
4 Fischer von Erlach, Johann Bernhard, Entwurf Kaiserpalast Peking, 1725
Architekturmuseum der TU München
6 Scamozzi, Vincenzo, L´idea delle architettura universale, 1678
Bayerische Staatsbibliothek, München
7 Fritsch, Theodor, Die Stadt der Zukunft, 1912
Universitätsbibliothek, München
9 Howard, Ebenezer, Garden cities of tomorrow, 1970
Bayerische Staatsbibliothek, München
10, 11, 12, 13 Fritsch, Theodor, Die Stadt der Zukunft, 1895
14, 15 Associazione culturale Novecento
16, 17, 21 Niemeyer, Oskar, Eine Legende der Moderne, 2003
18 Plain de la ville de trois millions d`habitants, 1922
Le Corbusier, Gesamtwerk/1. Von 1910 bis 1930
Architekturmuseum der TU München
FLC/VG Bild/Kunst, Bonn 2005
22 Fischer, Friedhelm, Canberra, myths and models, 1984
Bayerische Staatsbibliothek, München

Lingang New City – Ideale Stadt – Reale Projekte
Lingang New City – Ideal City – Real Projects
Abbildungen **Images**: gmp Archiv

Chinakarte **Map of China**
Abbildungen **Images**: GEO, Hamburg

Verzeichnis der chinesischen Projekte, 1998–2005
Index of Chinese Projects, 1998–2005
Abbildungen **Images**: gmp Archiv

www.gmp-architekten.de